Maria Mies is Professor of Sociology at the Fachhochschule, Cologne. She has published widely on women in development and other feminist, ecological and international issues, and one of her main concerns is the development of an alternative approach in methodology and in economics. Having retired from teaching in 1993, she continues to be active in the women's and other social movements. She has just published a book on the Multilateral Agreement on Investment.

Veronika Bennholdt-Thomsen is Director of the Institute of the Theory and Praxis of Subsistence (ITPS) at Bielefeld, Germany. She holds a Visiting Professorship at the University for Soil Culture in Vienna. She has done research in Mexico and Germany and has published widely on Women's Studies, Peasant Studies and Social Anthropology. She is the editor of a much-read book on the matriarchal community of Juchitán (Mexico) and has recently published a book on subsistence alternatives in Europe and the Third World.

NEW ECONOMIC WORK

LISTENED TO "MORE PERFECT" ERA
+ HIDDEN BRAIN HOUSEWIFE
→ ECON abt consumption
as voting

NON ECONOMIC WORK HAS BEEN
DEFINED AS SUCH BECAUSE OF THE
REIFICATION OF MONETARY - PROFIT
& FREE MKT PRODUCTION. NON ECONOMIC
WORK HAS BEEN DEFINED AS THE
WORK FOR SUBSISTENCE - WHICH
HAS HISTORICALLY BEEN DONE BY ♀.
SEWING BEGAN AS CARING CRAFT -
EVERYONE NEEDED - SUSTAINED BY ♀
DYES & MECHANICS ♀ WENT TO ♂ INDUSTRIALIZATION
CHEAP CLOTHING CXON W/ MARGINALIZED +

LIKE A GROUNDHOG AT THE
END OF WINTER
TENDED TO HOME
I SEE THE NATURE OF
THIS FULLNESS IN MY MCEARTH
~~DREAMS ENFOLD~~
ONE MUSE TIDES LEFT
ME STRANDED AND DRY
— AT FIRST LOST AND
CRACKING, A MARSH IN
DROUGHT, I
GREENER GRASSES MADE
THEIR WAY FROM MARROW
TO CENTER
NOW FULL OF NEW GROWTH
WITHERED SEASONS PAST
AND ~~THE~~ BLOSSOMS BEARING
FRINGED WITH
THE PROMISE OF FUTURE
HARVESTS
THAT BRACKISH WATER
HAS FILLED ME
FERTILE SOIL ABSORBS
WATER BEST
WHERE I STAND, MAP
ROOTED AND SPRAWLING
I FEEL YOUR PRESENCE
BUDS STUFFED FULL
WITH PETALS
READY TO BURST OPEN IN THIS WINTER SUNLIGHT

The Subsistence Perspective
Beyond the Globalised Economy

Maria Mies
and
Veronika Bennholdt-Thomsen

Translated by
Patrick Camiller, Maria Mies and Gerd Weih

Zed Books
London and New York

Spinifex Press
Australia

The Subsistence Perspective: Beyond the Globalised Economy was first published in 1999 by
Zed Books Ltd, 7 Cynthia Street, London N1 9JF, UK,
and Room 400, 175 Fifth Avenue, New York, NY 10010, USA
zedbooks@zedbooks.demon.co.uk
http://www.zedbooks.demon.co.uk

Distributed in the USA exclusively by St Martin's Press,
Room 400, 175 Fifth Avenue, New York, NY 10010, USA

Published in Australia and New Zealand by Spinifex Press,
504 Queensberry Street, North Melbourne, Victoria, 3051, Australia
women@spinifexpress.com.au
http://spinifexpress.com.au

Original German edition, *Eine Kuh für Hillary: Die Subsistenzperspektive*, published 1997,
copyright © Verlag Frauenoffensive

Cover designed by Andrew Corbett.
Set in 10/12 pt Adobe Garamond, by Long House, Cumbria, UK.
Printed and bound in the United Kingdom
by Biddles Ltd, Guildford and King's Lynn.

A catalogue record for this book
is available from the British Library.

Zed Books ISBN 1-85649-775-5 hb
ISBN 1-85649-776-3 pb

Spinifex Press ISBN 1-875559-93-0 pb

National Library of Australia Cataloguing-in-Publication Data
Mies, Maria.

Subsistence perspective: beyond the globalised economy.
Bibliography.
Includes index.
ISBN 1 875559 93 0.

1. Competition, International. 2. Women - Social conditions - 20th century.
3. Subsistence economy. I. Bennholdt-Thomsen, Veronika. II. Title.
305.42'

Contents

Acknowledgements

Many persons helped us while we were writing this book: they told us stories, gave us valuable information, gave us hints about literature, discussed with us, criticised us, inspired us and gave us practical and emotional support. It is not possible to mention all these persons and groups by name, but we want to thank all of them.

In particular we want to thank Agnes Simon and Lisbeth Reuland who generously shared their life histories with us. We are grateful to our friend Farida Akther from Dhaka, Bangladesh, who allowed us to report two of her wonderful subsistence stories in this book. We also want to thank all those whose work inspired us for several of our subsistence stories: Terisa Turner, Zohl dé Ishtar, Rachel L. Bagby, Christa Müller, Corinna Milborn, Brigitte Holzer and Nicholas Faraclas.

We are particularly grateful to Hermine Karas (Cologne) and Eva May-Igelmund (Auel), who typed the manuscript, and to those who translated and edited part of the text: to Gerd Weih and Theresa Wolfwood of the Barnard Booker Centre Foundation (Canada), and to Patrick Camiller (UK). The Schweisfurth-Stiftung in Germany covered part of the translation costs. A special word of thanks goes to them.

Foreword to the English Edition

When this book was first published in German, it had the somewhat humorous title *Eine Kuh für Hillary: Die Subsistenzperspektive* (A Cow for Hillary: The Subsistence Perspective), based on the 'subsistence story' contained in the Introduction. We could not have dreamed then of the rapid changes that would take place in the fields of politics and economics in the following year, 1998. Not only was the stability of the world finance system threatened by turbulence in Asia, Japan, Russia and even the USA, but experts feared that these financial crises might develop into a fully fledged world recession, worse than that of 1929. When in Asia, particularly in Thailand and Indonesia, currency markets began to plunge in the middle of 1997, followed by sudden and massive unemployment, finance experts in the USA and the European Union could still say that this 'Asian flu' would not infect Western economies. This mood changed on 31 August 1998, when the Dow Jones index plunged by 554 points, 'its second largest decline in the history of the New York Stock exchange' (Chossudovsky 1998). This fall was followed by a freefall of the rouble in Russia which led to a meltdown of stock markets everywhere in the world. All of a sudden, faith in the everlasting stability and resilience of the neoliberal globalised 'market economy' was shaken. Rational analysis of economic processes gave way to panic, and the credo of neoliberalism was upheld with religious dogmatism. An example of this attitude is the way the 'global players' tried to push the Multilateral Agreement on Investment (MAI) in the Organisation for Economic Cooperation and Development (OECD).

Before the publication of our book we had not even heard of the MAI – an effort by the big transnational corporations to put the neoliberal dogmas of globalisation, liberalisation and privatisation on unshakeable legal ground worldwide. Meanwhile the MAI negotiations have been abandoned at the OECD – partly as a result of strong international opposition to supreme political rule by the transnational corporations (TNCs).

These changes were accompanied by political and military events which reveal both the weakness and the strength of the dominant powers: they included both a sexual affair with a young woman that came to threaten the position of Bill Clinton, president of the USA, and Clinton's renewed bombing of Baghdad in December 1998, a feat which not only his enemies interpreted as an effort to draw public attention away from his private problems and to 'regain his manhood'. With this we are back to the age-old and modern pattern of capitalist patriarchy: war is not only the last resort of patriarchal men when they want to prove their potency, it is also the last resort of the capitalist economy when it is shaken by crisis after crisis.

Due to these unexpected changes in 1998, we cannot present a simple translation of our book to an English-speaking readership. Where necessary we have had to update or to revise the text in the light of recent events. In spite of the fact that the discussion of the subsistence perspective transcends national boundaries, the German edition of the book, naturally, often refers to the German situation which may not be known to a wider public. We have tried to broaden this horizon in the English edition where possible. But even where this was not possible the German events discussed are not just German in a narrow sense. They may be seen as examples of general patterns typical of modern capitalist, industrialised societies.

But our general analysis of capitalist patriarchy and our development of an alternative perspective have not been undermined by the events of 1998. On the contrary. They have corroborated our arguments. We were able to observe that not only in the South but also in the North, not only in Germany but in all other countries also, the managers of globalised capitalism have no new ideas and methods for dealing with deepening economic crises, only the ones we criticised twenty years ago, namely the progressive exploitation of non-wage labour, exemplified in the work of housewives.

In 1998 it was not only the promoters of global neoliberalism who were shaken out of their complacency; what also became more visible was the extent of people's resistance to the ravages of this system. Both in the South and the North large grassroots movements stood up against unemployment, poverty and political disempowerment. They included not only movements of indigenous peoples, such as in Chiapas, Mexico, or in other countries, who fight for their autonomy, but also the Association of the Poor in Thailand, the Movement of the Landless (MST) in Brazil, and the movements of Indian and Bangladeshi farmers who resist neoliberalism. And in the North, particularly in France, the unemployed have started strong protest movements against the dominant economic policies. These protest movements are first of all directed against the politics of their respective governments. They are manifestations of anger and frustration. But they have not yet produced a vision of an alternative economy. This is particularly true of the movements in the North.

Whereas movements in the South counter neoliberal globalism with demands for local, regional and national self-reliance, the movements in Europe and the USA are confused when it comes to the question of an alternative perspective. Many of them look for some sort of neo-Keynesianism on a global level.

We hope that the English version of our book on the subsistence perspective will help to produce more clarity regarding this question and that it will broaden the discussion on a new vision of economy and society which will go beyond the models known so far.

Maria Mies and Veronika Bennholdt-Thomsen
Cologne/Bielefeld
January 1999

 # Introduction

In July 1996 Farida Akhter from Bangladesh told the following story to the women who had gathered at the conference on 'Women Power Worldwide' organised by the Summer Academy of Women's Studies in Munich.

In April 1995, some months before the beginning of the UN World Women's Conference in Beijing, Hillary Clinton, the First Lady of the USA, visited Bangladesh. She had come to find out for herself what was true of the success stories of the Grameen Bank projects in Bangladeshi villages, of which she had heard so much. The microcredits of the Grameen Bank were said to have improved the situation of rural women in Bangladesh remarkably. Ms Clinton wanted to find out whether the women had really been empowered by these microcredits. For the Grameen Bank and development agencies, 'empowerment for women' means that a woman has an income of her own and that she has some assets.

Hillary Clinton visited the women of Maishahati village and interviewed them about their situation. The women answered: Yes, they now had an income of their own. They also had some 'assets': some cows, chicken, ducks. Their children went to schools. Ms Clinton was satisfied. The women of Maishahati were obviously empowered. But she was not prepared for the next round of the interview, when the village women turned round and asked her the same questions. Farida Akhter reported the following exchange of questions and answers between the women of Maishahati and Hillary Clinton:

'*Apa* [elder sister], do you have cows?'

'No, I have no cows.'

'*Apa*, do you have your own income?'

'Well, formerly I used to have my own income. But since my husband

1

became president and moved to the White House I have stopped earning my own money.'

'How many children do you have?'

'One daughter.'

'Would you like to have more children?'

'Yes, I would like to have one or two more children, but we are quite happy with our daughter Chelsea.'

The women from Maishahati looked at each other and murmured, 'Poor Hillary! She has no cow, no income of her own, she has only one daughter.' In the eyes of the Maishahati women Hillary Clinton was not empowered. They felt sorry for her.

Our readers may ask why we tell this story at the beginning of our book on the subsistence perspective. What has the First Lady of the USA, the most powerful state in the world, to do with subsistence? What is the connection between her and the village women of Maishahati who feel empowered because they have a cow, chicken, children? Why do these 'poor' women pity Hillary Clinton? Hasn't she got everything she wanted? Are these women just naïve or ignorant?

We do not think so. They know well that Ms Clinton comes from a 'rich' country and that she must have heaps of money. But that is not what they would call empowerment. We report this story because it demonstrates in a nutshell the difference in perspective between Hillary Clinton and the village women of Maishahati. In their interview they show that they look at the world from a different point of view than does the First Lady of the USA. Theirs is a 'perspective from below', from what is necessary; theirs is a subsistence perspective. If one looks at the world from this perspective, all things and relations appear in a different light. Particularly the concept of what constitutes a good life is different from that of Ms Clinton and most of her rich sisters in the North who think that a good life requires a lot of money, a lot of goods, and a lot of luxuries, and that the rich countries of the North and the rich classes everywhere are the places where this so-called good life can be found. All others they consider as poor.

Most probably the meeting in Maishahati was a kind of culture shock for Ms Clinton. Most probably she had expected that the village women would humbly ask for some money for some projects and that they would look up to her, the wife of the most powerful man in the world, coming from the richest country in the world. But nothing of the sort happened. The women did not adopt Hillary's 'from above' perspective. In their interview they show that they have a different concept of wealth and poverty. They do not need a supermarket full of imported commodities. They demonstrate how absurd our concepts of poverty, wealth and good life are.

Perhaps Ms Clinton even realised, possibly for the first time, that something was lacking in her life. That in spite of all the wealth accumulated in her country she was missing something essential. Something the Maishahati women obviously still had. Was it their pride, their dignity, their self-assertion, their capacity to live by their own strength? Whatever we may call this something, we know that it comes from a subsistence perspective which enables people to produce and reproduce their own life, to stand on their own feet and to speak in their own voice.

In this book we adopt the subsistence perspective, too. We, like Hillary Clinton, live in a rich country. But we do not accept this model of wealth any more. We do not accept it not only because it cannot be generalised for the rest of the world, but more because of the destruction the pursuance of the concept of 'the good life' leaves behind: destruction of nature, of foreign peoples, of people's self-reliance and dignity, of children's future, of anything we call humanity. We know that the perspective 'from above', aiming at permanent growth of goods, services and money, cannot lead us out of the impasses this system has created. A radical break with the dominant paradigm and the search for a new perspective, a new vision, are necessary.

In our effort to draw the contours of the subsistence perspective the women from Maishahati and many other such women will be our teachers. Their interview with Hillary Clinton clearly shows what they consider important for a good life, not only for themselves in their villages but everywhere, for us, and for all the Hillaries and Bills. What is important is what secures an independent subsistence. What follows are the five main lessons we learned from the Bangladeshi women.

The first lesson is the view from below. This means that when we look at reality, when we want to gain clarity about where to go and what to do, we start with the perspective of women, particularly rural women and poor urban women in the South. Further, we start with everyday life and its politics, the strategies of women to keep life going. This view from below enables us to demystify the delusions created by those 'on top' that their life and lifestyle are not only the best possible ones but also the image of the future for everybody on this planet. This demystification helps us to see that this so-called good life is possible only for a minority and, moreover, that it is at the expense of others: of nature, of other people, of women and children.

Second, the Bangladeshi women teach us that the realisation of the subsistence perspective depends primarily not on money, education, status and prestige but on control over means of subsistence: a cow, some chicken, children, land, also some independent money income. This means that what is necessary is the capacity of communities to produce their life without being dependent on outside forces and agents.

Third, this awareness of their own capacity to subsist independently gives the Maishahati women the pride, the dignity, the courage and the sense of equality to address the First Lady of the USA as 'elder sister'. They are not beggars, they are not subservient, they can stand on their own feet.

The fourth lesson we learned is that the mindset behind the women's interview reveals that they do not believe in the sentence Frederick Engels formulated at the end of *The Origin of the Family, Private Property and the State*, namely: 'What is good for the ruling class should be good for the whole of the society with which the ruling class identifies itself' (Engels 1976 p. 333). Instead, the questions of the women of Maishahati suggest the opposite: 'what is good for the village women of Bangladesh should be good for the whole society'. This means concretely: The utopia of a socialist, non-sexist, non-colonial, ecological, just, good society cannot be modelled on the lifestyle of the ruling classes – a villa and a Cadillac for everybody, for instance: rather, it must be based on subsistence security for everybody. Meanwhile we know that the historic project to realise Engels's utopia in the actually existing socialist countries has ended in the collapse of this model.

Fifth, in this book we shall abandon the schizophrenia that divides the world up into a 'first' and 'third' part. The Bangladeshi women know, of course, that this division exists. They are aware of the gap that separates them from the First Lady of the USA. But they do not accept this division and the differential valuation that goes along with it as something natural. For them Hillary Clinton is first and foremost an 'elder sister' and a woman, who basically has the same needs and desires as they themselves have, namely to have subsistence security ('a cow'), some independent income – independent from a husband – and children. They consider this subsistence orientation good not only for themselves but also for Hillary Clinton.

We are of the same opinion as the village women of Bangladesh. A subsistence perspective is not only good for so-called developing countries and classes. It can only be a *new* perspective if it is equally valid for the so-called developed countries and classes – two dualistically and hierarchically divided and ordered economies are no longer acceptable.

Such a statement, of course, challenges our common understanding of what 'economy' means. If an 'economy' is defined as a system aimed at constant expansion of industry, of production and consumption of commodities and of capital accumulation, then such an 'economy' is incompatible with a subsistence perspective. Since the fall of the Berlin Wall this system has been promoted as the only possible and viable model to organise an economy. There Is No Alternative (TINA), one often hears. Instead of getting infected by this TINA syndrome ourselves, we want to demonstrate in this book that there exists a different conception of 'economy', which is both older and younger than the capitalist patriarchal one which is based on the ongoing colonisation of women, of other peoples and nature. This 'other' economy puts life and everything necessary to produce and maintain life on this planet at the centre of economic and social activity and not the never-ending accumulation of dead money.

The concept 'subsistence' is usually associated with poverty and backwardness. In this book, however, we want to show that subsistence not only means hard labour and living at the margins of existence but also joy in life, happiness and abundance. Such an understanding of subsistence requires that people, particularly women, stop devaluing their own – their own work, their own culture, their own power – and stop expecting the good life to be handed down to them by those 'on top'. This devaluation of one's own is, of course, a consequence of forced colonisation and degradation. But it has been internalised by all colonised people, including women. This devaluation is further maintained by the delusion of what we call 'catch-up development' and 'catch-up consumerism'. It is upheld by the promise that eventually all the colonised people at the bottom of the social pyramid will reach the level of those on the top. In this book we want to show that more and more people are rejecting this model of a 'catching-up' economy – not only the women of Maishahati. Our last subsistence story (see pages 223–6) provides evidence that farmers in Bangladesh also are rejecting this development model. For them catch-up development is not a desirable goal.

The view from below of the globalised, expanding, patriarchal–capitalist economy does not lead to despair, as some might fear, but helps us to reflect again on what we really mean when we look for the good life, and where the true sources of empowerment are to be found. Farida Akhter told the story of the women of Maishahati to demonstrate that the discourse on 'empowerment' for 'poor' women misses the point. Rural women in Bangladesh and in other countries of the South do not need any empowerment from the White House or from other sections of the rich world. They are strong women. What they really need is that various kinds of oppressors get off their backs: patriarchal men in their own country, transnational corporations (TNCs), the World Bank and the International Monetary Fund (IMF) with their structural adjustment programmes, national bureaucracies who follow the orders of these guardians of international capital. Empowerment can only be found in ourselves and in our cooperation with nature within us and around us. This power does not come from dead money. It lies in mutuality and not in competition, in doing things ourselves and not in only passively consuming. It lies in generosity and the joy of working together and not in individualistic self-interest and jealousy. This power also lies in our recognition that all creatures on earth are our relatives.

In this book we want to remind our readers and ourselves that the present, dominant economic system is not the outcome of some immutable natural law, but that it was constructed by men some centuries ago and can be changed. It is not without an alternative as people suffering from the TINA syndrome try to make us believe. We believe that *Subsistence Is The Alternative (SITA)*. Moreover, it is important to understand that what is called globalisation of the economy today is not a totally new and extraordinary feature but that it constitutes the necessary, continuing colonisation and 'primitive accumulation' that has been part and parcel of capitalist patriarchy right from its beginning. Today, however, this ongoing colonisation and its consequences are also felt in the industrialised countries of the North, where the Third World is returning to the First. This is clearly manifested not only in the growing gap between rich and poor in the North but also in the financial and economic crises that are now also hitting the industrialised world.

All of a sudden people in the North are forced to realise that they are not so far away from the village women in Bangladesh. True, there is still a large quantitative gap, but structurally the situations of poor people in the North and of poor people in the South are no longer different. When this insight dawns on people in the North most of them react either with denial or with panic. Economists and politicians have always told them that there is no alternative to capitalism, that this economic system is the only way to achieve 'sustainable' wealth, not only in the North and for the rich, but eventually also, through a process of catch-up development, also for the South and the poor. People have never learned that this catch-up development is a myth, that there is a link between the wealth and the progress of one pole and the poverty and regression of the other pole, and that the gap between the two is getting wider and wider.

The present crisis situation forces people to understand, however, that all these affirmations of the stability of the dominant economic system are so much hot air. They are forced to see that the accumulation of wealth in the hands of ever fewer people is accompanied by growing poverty and joblessness of ever more people, even in the North. The financial and economic crises in Asia and Russia force them to see that money and capital are not a solid base upon which to build one's hope for security. From one day to the next this base can collapse and throw even bankers into abject poverty, as recently happened in Thailand. In this situation the majority of people in the urban centres of the world, people dependent for their livelihoods on money income, see nothing but big black holes in front of them. For them the collapse of the economy signals the end of the world, the end of their material security. Unlike the women from Maishahati they do not even have a cow from which they could get food.

But if one looks at the world from the perspective of the village women of

Bangladesh – and they represent the majority of people in the world – then one is immune to this mood of apocalyptic despair. One realises that such despair is the luxury of a pampered minority in the North. It hinders people from arriving at a realistic assessment of the present situation and acting accordingly. It hinders them in particular from understanding that their privileges are based on loot and that a good life for all – that is what we call subsistence – does not need such privileges. People who share a subsistence orientation also do not expect big social changes from agencies from outside and above them. They are aware of their own power and can act as individuals and in a community.

In this book we want to show not only that a look at the world from a subsistence perspective is necessary – necessary from an ecological, economic, feminist, anti-colonial point of view – but also that such a new orientation has already begun in manifold ways in different parts of the world. We want further to make clear that such a new perspective will eventually lead to a change of *all* basic social relations: those between women and men, between generations, between rural and urban areas, between different classes, between different peoples, and, above all, between humans and nature. If the central concern of all economic and social activity is not the accumulation of dead money but the creation and maintenance of life on this planet, nothing can remain as it is now.

The subsistence perspective is not an abstract theoretical model. To demonstrate this we introduce each chapter with a short or long 'true life' subsistence story. These stories provide evidence that the subsistence perspective already exists in diverse forms, that it is necessary, desirable and possible. More than statistics and theoretical elaborations they show the depth and richness of the concept. Those who are ready to look at the world from this perspective will themselves discover many such subsistence stories, old and new. Because the subsistence perspective is a *perspective*, a conversion of our view. It is not a new economic model.

1

The History of the Subsistence Approach

My mother and the sow. Life has to go on.

For me, Maria Mies, the history of 'The Subsistence Perspective' started with my mother. The quest for the history of subsistence leads unavoidably to the recognition of the interconnectedness of one's own life history with the history of time. When I asked myself where to begin with this retrospective, I remembered my mother and her sow. In honour of my mother, I would like to recount this story.

It was in February or March of the year 1945. The end of the war was approaching. My parents were peasants. Our village was close to the Western front in the Eifel. Five of my brothers were soldiers, somewhere in the East. Around this time the ragged and lice-ridden soldiers of the beaten German army returned from the West and were searching for a bit of warmth and something to eat from the peasants. Every evening, mother cooked a pot of milk soup and boiled a pot of potatoes in their jackets. Every night, soldiers sat around the table with us. People had given up hope. Most of the peasants butchered their cows and pigs; they did not bother to plough or to sow. Everybody was waiting for the end of the war without a thought beyond that end. At that time, my mother took the sow to the boar in the neighbouring village – pigs and the raising of piglets was women's work. It also was a source of revenue for them. The neighbours laughed at her and said she should slaughter the pig instead; did she not see that everything was coming to an end. My mother replied, 'Life goes on.' Perhaps she even said, 'Life has to go on!'

She took the sow to the boar. And at the end of May, after the war had ended, the sow had twelve piglets. Nobody had young pigs, calves, or foals. Since money had lost its value, mother traded her piglets for shoes, trousers, shirts and jackets for her five sons, who one after the other returned from the war. Life went on. But did it go on by itself? My mother didn't just sit down and say, 'Life will go on,' or, as a Christian peasant woman, 'The Lord will provide.' She knew that she had to act, that she had to cooperate with nature – so that life could continue. That is what she always said: life has to go on. That was her wish, her passion, which constituted her joy and her will for life.

My mother was not a feminist and she didn't know the word ecology, but she had recognised something which is today as urgently needed as daily bread, namely that we have to assume responsibility for life if we want it to continue. The increasing ecological catastrophies teach us that modern industrial society destroys, with its relentless pursuit of continuous growth of goods and money, the ability of nature to regenerate herself, until she is totally exhausted. This applies to human life, particularly that of women and children, as well as to non-human nature. Women, women like my mother, have so far shouldered the responsibility in everyday life, particularly after wars and other catastrophies, that life should go on for their daughters, sons, husbands, and nature. They clean up after the wars that the men wage against nature and foreign peoples. The subsistence perspective, however, means for us feminists that we are concerned not only that life will continue after patriarchal wars, but that such wars should no longer occur.

How did we come to the subsistence perspective?

We, Veronika Bennholdt-Thomsen, Maria Mies and Claudia von Werlhof, became involved at the beginning of the seventies in the new women's movement. In our case, this happened against the background of many years' experience we had obtained in different countries of the South: in India, Costa Rica, San Salvador, Venezuela and Mexico. Thus from the very beginning we connected the 'women's question' with the 'Third World question'. In the process, we rediscovered Rosa Luxemburg's work on imperialism, and found there a plausible explanation of why capitalism requires, contrary to Marx's opinion, 'non-capitalistic classes', societies and milieux in order to start and maintain the 'extended reproduction of capital', that is to say, the accumulation of capital – the essence of capitalism (Luxemburg 1923: 15).

This simultaneous forceful conquering, acquisition and destruction of 'non-capitalistic economies' – the traditional subsistence economies – is not only the bloody prehistory of capitalism, of the 'original accumulation', as Marx supposed, but is still today the basic precondition for the ongoing accumulation of capital, what generally is called 'economic growth'. Rosa Luxemburg considered only the peasant–artisan and the natural or subsistence economies in the colonies as preconditions for capitalism. We, however, included in our analysis housework in the industrial core countries and the labour of peasants in the South and of marginalised people in the so-called informal sector – in the North as well as in the South (von Werlhof 1978).

The commonalities in such at first sight heterogeneous relations of production as the work of a middle-class housewife and mother in Germany and the work of a subsistence peasant woman in the Himalayas, or the work of a smallholder in Mexico, are as follows:

1. These producers are directly concerned with producing and maintaining food and life, and not with the acquisition of money in order to buy food to live.

2. These subsistence producers (men and women) do not live in a pre-capitalistic or non-capitalistic world – as Rosa Luxemburg still assumed; their work is exploited by capital not through wages but through their product, which is taken from them free of cost or very poorly paid for. Bennholdt-Thomsen calls this the subsumption of the market under capital (Bennholdt-Thomsen 1979). Many products of the Third World which today are displayed in the supermarkets of the North – such as orchids from Thailand, handicraft items from Mexico and India – stem from this kind of work. This means, in effect, that capitalism exploits more work and production relations than just wage labour relations. Capitalism is qualitatively different from what has so far been understood by Marxists as well as by liberals.

By including subsistence in the analysis of capitalism, it became possible to explain why in the highly developed industrial countries women's work is still of less value than that of men and why the hope of the Third World for 'catch-up development' is as little able to be fulfilled as the hope of women for equality.

During 1978 and 1979, we conducted empirical action research projects in order to find out if these early hypotheses would stand up to empirical tests. We did these on the peasant economy in Mexico (Bennholdt-Thomsen), among peasant women in India (Mies), and in Venezuela (von Werlhof). This research not only reinforced our assumption that women's subsistence work was the essential basis for the integration of these economies into the capitalist world market: we also discovered further dimensions of these relationships. Maria Mies discovered during her investigation of women in a home-based industry in India the process of *Hausfrauisierung* (housewifeisation), by which women's work under capitalism is universally made invisible and can for that reason be exploited limitlessly. This applies not only to 'housewives' in the narrow sense in the industrial countries but also to the work of the women who do home work, to farm labourers, peasants, small traders, and factory workers in the South (Mies 1982).

Several conferences on subsistence reproduction were held during the years 1978 and 1979 at the Centre for Development Studies at the University of Bielefeld. The conceptual framework for these conferences was largely provided by Veronika Bennholdt-Thomsen and Claudia von Werlhof. The approach, developed out of women's and Third World research, was now explicitly called 'the subsistence approach'. The theme of the conferences was subsistence reproduction in developing countries.

It became clear to us early on, after the analysis of peasant work in the Third World, that the exploitation of subsistence work, due to the latter's life-creating and life-maintaining character, is qualitatively different from that of wage labour. From this point of view the work of women and that of small peasants is conditioned by a similar logic. Their exploitation follows the example of the exploitation of nature as a resource which is allegedly free and inexhaustible. The means for the creation and maintenance of such an exploitative relationship is not the labour contract, as is the case with the wage labourer, but violence, physical and structural violence. Natural resources are considered 'free goods' and are exploited and appropriated by the industrial system in the same way as life, created by women. This analysis was the key which opened up a new way of looking at not only the man–woman relationship but also the relations between humans and nature in the industrial system. There is not only a structural analogy between these two relationships but also a causal connection, the basis of which is the modern people–nature relationship. The division of labour by gender and between wage labour and house-work, public and private work, production and reproduction, was only possible through the *naturalisation* of one pole of this division of labour, namely of women. For that reason we have called nature, women, and the exploited countries of the Third World 'the colonies of the White Man'. Colonies are not subjected and exploited through agreement but by force. With this approach we linked the women's problem with the Third World problem as well as with the ecological movement, which had gained in significance during the seventies (Mies, Bennholdt-Thomsen and von Werlhof 1988).

At that time, the connection between the exploitation of women and the exploitation of nature became obvious to many women who were active in the anti-nuclear movement. It became impossible to ignore, particularly after Chernobyl (1986), not only that the total project of the modern industrial system – both in its capitalistic ans well as in its socialistic form – was based on the colonisation of nature, women, and de-developed peoples, but also that in this process nature herself – the basis of all life – was being destroyed (Gambaroff *et al.* 1986). The thesis of Rosa Luxemburg that the accumulation of capital not only exploits subsistence production but also destroys it, was again confirmed. In particular, the increasing concern with the ecological issue made it clear that the strategy of catch-up development is a dead-end street.

According to this strategy, all societies would reproduce the economic path of the capitalist industrial countries, in order finally to achieve the production and consumption level that predominates in the rich countries. In the meantime it has become evident that such catch-up development is an economic and ecological impossibility for all people. This model cannot be generalised (Mies and Shiva 1993).

But this meant that the hope that further industrialisation could eliminate misery, hunger, social injustices, and also the exploitation of women, was definitely destroyed. Therefore it was necessary to search for a perspective of the liberation of nature, women, and the South that did not rest upon the continuation of the exploitative, colonising, industrial system and was not based on the strategy of 'catch-up development.'

In the early eighties it became evident that the industrial system continued to expand at the expense not only of the environment and the Third World; this particular expansion was driven by – among other factors – the new technology of microelectronics and the fundamental changes this brought about in the field of work which were leading to increasing unemployment. Unemployment particularly hit women. Because of that, in 1983 we organised a women's conference in Bielefeld with the theme 'The Future of Women's Work'. This conference was a reaction to a similarly titled congress held in Bielefeld the previous year, 'On the Future of Work', at which unpaid and poorly paid work performed by women was not even mentioned. Our subsistence approach was publicly presented for the first time during the 1983 conference, not only as a criticism of the dominant analyses of capitalism, but also as a necessary and possible perspective for women in the First as well as in the Third World and for all colonised peoples. Already we were predicting that the expanding 'housewifeisation' of work would also affect the men of the North.

Reception and criticism

An indignant outcry arose when we emphasised that the subsistence perspective was, particularly for us in the industrialised countries and especially for us women, a perspective for the future, in contradistinction to the strategy of catch-up development. At the congress on 'Women and Ecology' held in Cologne in 1986 – which had been organised by Green women – it suddenly became evident that women in the industrialised countries and middle-class women in the South are not only victims but also beneficiaries of the international exploitative system. It became clear that we have to relinquish this complicity if we want to dissociate ourselves from this system. We explained that we have to learn from the women and men in the Third World what a good life can be and that it is not totally dependent on international trade.

Several feminists rejected the suggestion not only that as well as recognising the connection between the exploitation of women, nature and the Third World and our consumer attitude in the First World, we should fight it through political action with the shopping bag, that is, with a movement against consumerism (Böttger 1987; Lenz 1988; Wichterich 1992). Later, when German feminists did occupy themselves at length with the subsistence approach and with ecofeminism, other criticisms came up. For some this approach was not sufficiently orthodox Marxist; for others, it contained too much of Marx, particularly in its concepts. Some so-called realists found it utopian, romanticising, ignorant of the ways of the world. Several dissertations were written, which reflect the split in the German women's movement between approval and rejection of industrial society as such, and therefore either lauded or tore apart the Bielefeld Approach, as it came to be called.

The following are some of the most commonly raised criticisms:

- The subsistence approach is not woman-friendly, because we women are again the first to be asked to forgo things. Women already have hardly any money (politicisation of consumption). (among others, Böttger 1987; Pinl 1993).
- You want us women to be the perpetual 'rubble women' (Trümmerfrauen)[1] of society (among others, Wichterich 1992).
- Your approach is moralistic. We are tired of such moralistic appeals. Morality has no place in the economy. At issue are interests. (Becker 1988; Klinger 1988; Schultz 1994; Wichterich 1992)
- What you say may be good for the Third World but not for us. We are used to a different standard of living. Why must women feel responsible for the whole world? (Klinger 1988)
- The subsistence approach reinforces the traditional female role, glorifies motherhood and childbearing. (Becker 1988; Pinl 1993).
- Your subsistence approach may be good for rich, middle-class women who can afford to buy organic food. What about the poor woman, the woman on social welfare or a student?
- We don't all want to go back to the farm in order to grow our own potatoes.
- Yours is almost 'blood and soil' ideology. (Ökolinx)[2]
- Your approach means regression (to the Stone Age, to the Middle Ages) but history does not go backwards.
- You are women Luddites!
- Something like that could be quite interesting for individuals and small groups, but it does not bother the capitalists. It does not lead to an overall change of the system. Your talk about limitation of consumption, for instance, remains a call to individuals and so far has remained powerless. (Pinl 1993, Wichterich 1992).

- And finally, this is not political. Subsistence has to be first politicised. A patchwork quilt of a thousand subsistence communes or eco-villages is not enough. Everybody would be totally occupied with securing their daily existence. (Spehr 1996)

We have the impression that many of our critics are scared by the fact that we do proceed logically from our criticism of capitalist patriarchy to an alternative perspective. On the contrary they passively expect that our problems will be solved through more regulation and equality politics within the framework of the existing welfare state, for instance through a guaranteed minimum income for all. They don't want to be continually reminded that others (nature, foreign women and men) will have to bear the costs for such a model. Most expect a solution of the ecological problems through an eco-tax. We will endeavour to find a reply to some of these questions in the following chapters.

Methodologically, we will adhere to the principles we had already formulated by the end of the seventies (Mies 1978; Bennhold-Thomsen 1979). That is to say, during the presentation of the subsistence perspective we will adhere to the 'view from below'. This is the only way that a subsistence perspective makes sense.

In the course of time this approach became well known in Germany among people who are beginning to search for a way out of the dead end of the industrial system. These are women and men of commune projects and the eco-village movement, anarchists, women who so far have not considered themselves as feminists, but who are concerned about the future of life on earth and future generations, feminist theologians, people who are looking for a 'third way' between capitalism and socialism, eco-organisations in eastern Germany like the 'Grüne Liga', eco-educational institutions, community colleges, organic farmers, consumer–producer organisations, women and men in church organisations, the Third World movement, environmental, anti-genetic engineering and anti-nuclear movements. In short, the subsistence approach which originated in the women's movement has by now gone far beyond these circles and is being discussed under different headings by many people.

The worldwide crises that began in the early nineties and involved also the rich countries of the North, and Germany where they caused a real panic, particularly after the euphoria over the collapse of socialism in Eastern Europe, certainly contributed to the broader and more positive reception of this approach. Suddenly it became clear to many people that the ground under the model called market economy is fragile and may crack at any time like a thin sheet of ice. Many say, 'It can't go on like this much longer'. Many are suddenly beginning to look for alternative ways, particularly in the face of the fact that our predictions of the early eighties are now confirmed and visible for all: namely that the time of full and protected employment is over, even in industrialised countries. We arrived at that conclusion from our study of the exploitation of women's work, of peasants, and of the Third World through capitalism. Today 'housewifeisation', that is, the flexibilisation of labour, has become reality for men also. More and more people are slowly realising that the old leftist union strategy, based upon the male 'normal wage labour relationship', no longer has a future when faced with global exploitation of 'housewifeised' flexibilised labour relations and the unimpeded advancing destruction of our natural basis for survival through the delusion of growth. But where is the alternative to this strategy? Where is a different vision?

The subsistence approach also had a broad impact in other countries. Some of our writings were first published in English. Several books were translated into English, Spanish, Japanese, Korean, Portuguese and French.

The subsistence perspective – a path into the open

In March 1987 Claudia von Werlhof, Irmgard Ehlers and Maria Mies organised a conference with the theme 'The Subsistence Perspective: A Path into the Open?' We invited to this conference women and men activists of the women's, peasants', Third World, and ecology movements in Germany, Asia and Latin America – people who agreed, in spite of all differences, that the current trend in development policy was a dead end, people who were looking for a way out, who fought against being 'developed' away from their subsistence basis into the 'modern age', like those presented by Helena Norberg-Hodge in the Ladakh project (Norberg-Hodge1991).

Vandana Shiva spoke about the Chipko movement in the Himalayas where women in particular prevented so-called 'modern development' (in this case the cutting of their forests for among other things the production of sports equipment) by embracing the trees. Activists from Venezuela reported on their peasant movement and its struggle to reestablish subsistence farming. From Germany, women and men activists attended from the Socialist Self-Help Organisation in Cologne (SSK), an initiative that has existed since the student movement. This group has lived for years on the garbage of the rich society, and refuses to accept social handouts. Most of its members are people who haven't found a place in our society: escapees from psychiatric clinics, homeless youth, old people. Some members of the SSK suddenly realised during the conference that they had the same perspective as the people of the Ladakh project, the women in the Chipko movement and the peasants in Venezuela. This commonality was the concept of subsistence. One group of people did not want to be 'developed' into the modern industrial society; others wanted to get out of it.

What is subsistence?

The war against subsistence since 1945

In the North and, since 1945, increasingly in the rest of the world, everything that is connected with the immediate creation and maintenance of life, and also everything that is not arranged through the production or consumption of commodities, has been devalued. This includes all activities whose object is self-provisioning, whether in the house, the garden, the workshop, on the land or in the stable. What doesn't cost or doesn't produce money is worthless. This devaluation of self-provisioning work cannot be understood, if measured only quantitatively. It indicates at the same time a degradation of and contempt for the person who still performs such work. 'Housework? what drudgery! Agricultural labour? Shame, peasants stink!' (See Chapter 3.)

This barrier of disgust, which today surrounds all unpaid, essential-for-life subsistence activities, has no relationship to the content of this work. Such activities are suddenly recognised as decent professions, not only for women but also for men, if they are carried out by industrialised waged labour, particularly if based on a labour contract. The present-day high esteem for wage labour obviously rests on the high evaluation of money and on its myth. Not the image of money as a simple medium of exchange or measure of value, but of the money that creates ever more money which then becomes the basis of life, security for life and the hope for progress, emancipation, culture and the 'good life'. *He/she who has no money, cannot live.* Most people in the industrial societies today believe this statement. The myth of money is connected with the myth of wage labour. *He/she who does not work for wages cannot live.*

If life depends, in a material and symbolic sense, on wage labour and the acquisition of money, a perspective that speaks of subsistence work as hope can only be regarded as romantic, as backward-looking, or even as the threat of death. How did this alienation between people and their work develop to the point that the most lifeless thing of all, money, is seen as the source of life and our own life-producing subsistence work is seen as the source of death?

Contempt for subsistence is not all that old. Most people of the industrialised countries, rural as well as urban, were in one way or another occupied with subsistence activities until after the Second World War. Small peasants were more or less self-sufficient and produced only in part for the market. Workers in the industrial cities often had small animals, a cow, a pig, a goat, chickens and a garden; women produced a variety of foodstuffs for their daily needs. Many consumer goods were not bought but traded, self-produced or bought second-hand. A well-functioning network of neighbourhood help existed as well as mutual aid, the values of the old peasant 'moral economy' which survived also in the cities.

On the one hand the subsistence orientation of wage labourers was necessary to supplement their low wages; on the other, it provided a piece of freedom, of self-determination and self-realisation, some joy, a piece of home in an alien and alienating industrial world. Subsistence work also maintained the community, even in the cities, because it relied on cooperation and mutual help.

According to Torry Dickinson, the subsistence orientation lasted until after the Second World War in the USA. Only after 1945 did the systematic and rigorous war against subsistence begin (Illich 1982). It was identical with the new paradigm of development. Under the New Deal, wage labourers in the north of the country received higher wages than they had ever before enjoyed. Subsequently, they abandoned their diverse subsistence activities because they were no longer worth their while. Simultaneously the consumer market expanded, now supplying cheaply what women and men had previously produced themselves.

> As the economy expanded, US-based business paid high wages to so-called skilled laborers, which served to further widen the domestic market. Between 1945 and 1970, development created images of a wage-labor monoculture, monolithic state and corporate power, insatiable consumerism, growing unions and secure wage pacts for men, with middle class housewives confined to private life. (Dickinson 1995 p. 168)

The consequence of this expansion of industrial production was a decline of subsistence:

> As large-scale production grew, traditional means of subsistence declined, particularly in urban areas. The cultivation of large vegetable gardens, raising chickens and goats, canning, and bread making occurred less frequently. Households purchased more food and non-food items and engaged less in 'producing' and transforming food for direct household consumption. (Dickinson 1995: 169)

Those of us older than fifty remember similar processes in Germany. We all learned to accept them as quasi-natural, necessary processes of 'development', 'progress', the 'development of productive forces', and 'modernisation'. We did not ask if it had to be that way (see Chapter 3). Only in the last few years, with the collapse of the wage labour monoculture due to high unemployment, have a few people in the North begun to realise that there could have been and could be a life before, during and after the wage labour system, and that this life would not be just disgusting, weary and burdensome. It is not a new, voluntaristic whim when we talk today of a subsistence perspective: it connects with a history which many of us still know. We want to free the subsistence orientation of the stigma that the discourse of progress has attached to it and that now sticks to it like pitch. We don't want to change the Pitch Mary of the fairytale totally into Gold Mary, but we do want to emphasise that it is us, the people, who create and maintain life, not money or capital. That is subsistence.

Ivan Illich stated as long ago as 1982 that the war against subsistence is the real war of capital, not the struggle against the unions and their wage demands. Only after people's capacity to subsist is destroyed, are they totally and unconditionally in the power of capital.

This war is a war not only to colonise subsistence work but also to colonise language, culture, food, education, thinking, images, symbols. Mono-labour, mono-language, mono-culture, mono-food, mono-thought, mono-medicine, mono-education are supposed to take the place of the manifold and diverse ways of subsistence. A subsistence perspective means resistance against mono-culturisation and putting an end to the war against subsistence.

The concept of 'subsistence'

We reflected a great deal about this concept. We know it is awkward, not easy and smooth. It demands explanation. But that is just right. Because we want to avoid it being immediately treated like small change, like so many of the new, meaningless, 'plastic' terms, which can so easily be coopted for totally opposite purposes. This has happened, for example, to the concept of 'sustainability'. We have decided to adhere to the term 'subsistence' for several reasons. Here are some of the most important ones.

- It expresses most inclusively all we expect of an alternative social orientation: freedom, happines, self-determination within the limits of necessity – not in some other world but here; furthermore persistence, stamina, willingness to resist, the view from below, a world of plenty. The concept of self-provisioning is, in our opinion, far too limiting because it refers only to the economical dimension. 'Subsistence' encompasses concepts like 'moral economy', a new way of life in all its dimensions: economy, culture, society, politics, language etcetera, dimensions which can no longer be separated from each other.

- For us, not only does the concept of 'subsistence' have a history, but it also expresses the historical connectedness that exists, through colonisation and development, between us in the industrial countries and the countries of the South. In both cases modern development happened and happens by means of war against subsistence. Today there comes to pass for the countries of the North what we have observed for years in the countries of the South.

- The term 'subsistence' is used in all modern languages and has the same meaning everywhere.

- Beyond the historical and geographic–political continuity, the concept expresses also the contradictory nature, the Janus face of this modern history, which is dependent on the perspective of the observer. For the men and women who profit from the war against subsistence, 'subsistence' spells backwardness, poverty, and drudgery. For the victims of this war it means security, the 'good life', freedom, autonomy, self-determination, preservation of the economic and ecological base, and cultural and biological diversity.

- The concept of 'subsistence' also expresses continuity with the nature within us and around us, and continuity between nature and history, the fact that dependence on the world of necessity is not to be seen as a misfortune and limitation, but as a good thing and a precondition for our happiness and freedom.

- The more the current crisis hits those who up to now have benefited from the war against subsistence, the more the attractiveness of the subsistence lifestyle will be rediscovered. The concept includes many things that are subsumed under headings such as regionalisation, local economy, self-sufficiency, new communes, alternative lifestyles, a caring economy, the living economy, the 'third way'.

- We adhere to the concept 'subsistence', because it offers a perspective, in particular for today.

We have emphasised for years not only that subsistence or production of life will not disappear as a result of modernisation, industrialisation and the consumer economy, but also that it is, on the contrary, the constant opposite as well as the basis of modern industrial society and of generalised commodity production. 'Without subsistence production, no commodity production: but without commodity production, definitely, subsistence production.' Until the beginning of the industrial age, subsistence production secured the life and survival of the people. If the people of the world had had to depend on generalised commodity production and universal wage labour, on the capitalist commodity market – which today is hailed as our saviour from poverty and underdevelopment – they would not have survived until today.

Inside the industrialised societies subsistence production is being continued, mainly in the form of unpaid housework. The reproduction of the workforce is guaranteed and kept cheap through unwaged housework. Therefore we defined subsistence production as follows:

> Subsistence production or production of life includes all work that is expended in the creation, re-creation and maintenance of immediate life and which has no other purpose. Subsistence production therefore stands in contrast to commodity and surplus value production. For subsistence production the aim is 'life', for commodity production it is 'money', which 'produces' ever more money, or the accumulation of capital.

For this mode of production life is, so to speak, only a coincidental side-effect. It is typical of the capitalist industrial system that it declares everything that it wants to exploit free of charge to be part of nature, a natural resource. To this belongs the housework of women as well as the work of peasants in the Third World, but also the productivity of all of nature. (Mies 1983)

Originally we introduced the subsistence concept not only in order to be able to explain the exploitation of women's unpaid labour under capitalism, but also to find a way out of the dead end of industrial society with its ecologically unsustainable production and consumption patterns. Already twenty years ago, we saw that the utopia of scientific socialism, which presupposed the highest degree of development of the productive forces as the precondition for overcoming capitalism, was based on the same development model as capitalism (Ullrich 1979).

The concept of subsistence does not only have the negative connotations that are often attributed to it. On the contrary, as Erika Märke has shown, it means the 'attitude of independence', 'existence by one's own effort'. Märke enumerates three attributes of subsistence: (1) independence – in the sense of autonomy; (2) self-sufficiency in the sense of non-expansionism; (3) self-reliance, in the sense of cultural identity (Märke 1986: 138). This positive concept of subsistence is decisive for us when we speak of the need for a new social perspective.

We associate another image of the 'good life' with the concept of the 'subsistence perspective'. Recent developments and insights in the field of ecology have shown that the subsistence perspective is not only an approach to overcoming exploitation by capital, patriarchy and colonialism, the basic structures of the modern industrial system; it also constitutes a liberation of nature within us and around us from the self-destructive growth logic of capital.

The process of capital accumulation – the transformation of life (living work and nature) into commodities, money, and steadily increasing capital – is polarising and irreversible. In other words, money and capital can grow out of life, but no new life can grow out of capital and money. Life always has to be added to capital in order to make it palatable and bring it to life. Money that 'breeds' more money out of itself (as through interest) is a myth.

We call subsistence or life production that which has to be added to dead money/capital. If we truly want a future for ourselves and for nature of which we are part, life production has to be delinked from the production of capital. It has once again to become the centre of our concerns. In other words, colonised and marginalised spheres of reality (nature, women, and children, etcetera) have to become the central focus of economic activity, and the earning of money has to become secondary and peripheral again.

The subsistence perspective is not only practically and theoretically necessary, it is also possible and it has already begun. It has started with those who do not want to be 'developed'. These are people who know they will have to pay the price for modernisation, but will never reap its benefits. They are the people of the Third World, women, indigenous peoples who fight for the continuation of their autonomous subsistence basis. In such movements this other concept of 'good life' is promoted which we describe as 'abundance', another synonym for subsistence.

But new reflections on a different concept of economy, other than the present dominating one, are also beginning in the industrial countries of the North. Not only are there thousands of initiatives for the founding of communes, eco-villages, self-governing enterprises, producer–consumer associations, self-help and communal projects in deindustrialised cities and regions. There are also systematic beginnings in the development of an economy other than that of global – and, we add, patriarchal – capitalism.

Naturally, not all these initiatives are to be equated with a broad and general rejection of the dominant capitalist production and consumption model or with a revolutionary movement. The old concept of revolution, that is, the mostly sudden, violent overthrow of state power and of social relations, does not fit our understanding of subsistence orientation. After so many failed or abrogated revolutions, we no longer have confidence in the power which comes out of the barrels of the guns of the international warriors.

The changes required for a subsistence approach do not presuppose a political avant-garde. Nor do they have to wait until the situation or the productive forces are 'ripe'. They can be started by every woman and every man here and now. But they do need a different perspective, a different vision.

Women in subsistence societies have no problem with the development of such a radically new perspective, but the women of the middle class, who consider the cage in which they are sitting a paradise, do have a problem. For that reason, we would now like to give voice to women of the South, who belong to the lowest level of the exploited, to express their analysis of the dominant economic system. Their vision of a different economy and society is far clearer than that of most feminist academicians in our countries.

Many women of the South no longer appreciate or accept the currently dominant economy. This was clearly expressed during a women's workshop in Rio de Janeiro in 1992. Women rubber tappers, fishers, nut gatherers, peasants, and coconut cutters, and women engaged in urban small trade conducted this workshop in connection with the UNCED conference in Rio de Janeiro. It had the theme 'With courage and competence: women in subsistence, in agriculture and gathering economies' (Viezzer 1992). In this workshop women described their life and work. They analysed the economic and ecological consequences of the industrial model for themselves, for nature and for the future as well as for the women of the North.

After the women had listened to each other, they recognised what diversity and abundance nature was providing and what riches they themselves had created through their productive work. It was a wealth, however, of which the capitalist economy had totally robbed them. If they no longer exported this wealth to the rich countries and classes, if instead they traded among themselves, they would not only help and protect nature, but they all would be enabled to lead a full and happy life. At the end, after their stories, analyses, recommendations and role playing, they formulated the slogan *'Stop the capitalist economic model! Long live abundance!'*

NOTES

1. After the Second World War the term 'Trümmerfrau' was used of the women who cleaned up the rubble in the ruins of the bombed German cities.
2. The expression 'blood and soil' (*Blut und Boden*) refers to a slogan of the national-socialists who considered race and land as the basis of the German people.

2

Globalisation and Subsistence

My father, Professor Weizenbaum and the 'black hole'

Some years ago, the Trierer Initiative für angewandtes Denken (Initiative for Applied Thinking, Trier) organised a symposium to celebrate Karl Marx's 175th birthday (Marx was born in Trier). They invited several well-known professors and the keynote speaker was Josef Weizenbaum of the Massachusetts Institute of Technology (MIT). I, Maria Mies, was supposed to represent the 'feminist perspective' in this all-male circle. Josef Weizenbaum had converted from a computer specialist to one of the most prominent and radical critics of computers and particularly of artificial intelligence (AI). In his keynote he castigated the state of science in the USA. He not only refuted the common notion that computers had saved time, labour and money, he also said that computer science and technology had largely been financed by the US Defense Department. He stated, moreover, that today practically all research carried out in institutions like MIT is paid for by the Pentagon. He regretted that young scholars who were keen on their careers obviously had no problem with this state of affairs. Asked whether there was no opposition from students to this militarisation of science, Professor Weizenbaum said the curricula were such that students had no time for political activities.

He closed with the remark that the biggest problem of our time was no longer the threat of atomic annihilation but the population explosion. Scientists should devote all their efforts to curb population growth.

At the end of the symposium there was a panel discussion. The speakers had been asked to present their own perspectives on the future; and one by one these learned professors painted an absolutely bleak picture. I looked

---

at the audience: all young people with worried faces. They had come on this Sunday morning to get some orientation from these famous speakers for their own future. But they only painted an apocalyptic picture of gloom and hopelessness. The gist of their presentations was that there was no alternative, that we could do nothing. I could not tolerate this pessimism any longer and said, 'Please, don't forget where we are. We are in Trier, in the midst of the ruins of what once was one of the capitals of the Roman empire. An empire whose collapse people then thought would mean the end of the world. But the world did not come to an end with the end of Rome. The plough of my father, a peasant in the Eifel, used to hit the stones of the Roman road that connected Trier with Cologne. On this road where the Roman legions had marched grass had grown, and now we grew our potatoes on that road.' I wanted to say that even the collapse of big empires does not mean the end of the world; rather, people then begin to understand what is important in life, namely our subsistence.

This was too much for Professor Weizenbaum. Angrily, he turned to me and said it was the utmost naïvety to believe that after the catastrophes that were imminent even a single blade of grass would still grow. It was irresponsible to think that life would simply go on. 'No, the only thing necessary now is to realise that there is just one big black hole in front of us. After that there is nothing, no hope.' After this he continued attacking me, the feminist: 'By the way, you women have not done anything to prevent those wars. You have not even organised a sex strike.'

That was enough for me. I replied that it was strange that he now blamed women for wars whereas the day before he had told us that the MIT was totally financed by the Pentagon and that one could do nothing against this militarisation of research. We women were fed up with this kind of male logic. We were also fed up to be the eternal *Trümmerfrauen*, ready to clean up the mess after each macho war and see to it that life goes on. After that, I stood up and went. I left the men sitting in front of their 'black holes' in their apocalyptic mood.

This episode taught me an important lesson, namely that there seems to be an interrelation between a mania for technological omnipotence and political impotence. Josef Weizenbaum is one of those prominent male scientists who, at the end of their lives, are horrified when they look at themselves and their works, and when they realise that the God to whom they have devoted their whole life – scientific progress – is a Moloch who eats his children. Some of these men then convert from a Saul to a Paul. But they rarely give up the whole megalomania of the project of modern science. If they can't solve humanity's problems by almighty science and technology then at least the catastrophe has to be total and all-encompassing. Not even a single blade of grass is allowed to grow on the ruins of their deeds. When the big patriarchal project comes down with thunder and lightning then the whole world has to come to an end too. Its future and everything has to be sucked into an abyss of nothingness. Anyone who, in the face of such an apocalyptic scenario, still talks of life, potatoes, subsistence, hope, future, perspective, must be attacked as an enemy. Mania of omnipotence and of impotence are two sides of the same coin.

The image of my father behind the plough on the old Roman road stands for another philosophy, another logic. For most male – and also some female – scientists this subsistence logic is difficult to grasp. It is neither expressed in the slogan that 'life will go on by itself' (nature will regenerate herself, grass will grow by itself), nor by the attitude that we humans can control nature and repair all damage done by our master technology. The difference between a subsistence orientation and scientific omnipotence mania is the understanding that life neither simply regenerates itself, nor is it an invention of engineers; rather we, as natural beings, have to cooperate with nature if we want life to continue.

The 'black holes' of the globalised economy

After this episode, I discovered a number of 'black holes' in front of which people in the industrial world stand, feeling helpless and hopeless. Most of them are due to the globalisation of the economy. They have been visible since the beginning of the nineties. The phenomenon is particularly noticeable in Germany, where the euphoria after the breakdown of socialism in East Germany was soon followed by a deep sense of pessimism, in both the former East and the former West Germany. This was largely due to the dramatic rise of unemployment rates in the reunited Germany. They are the highest since the Second World War. In January 1998 the official number of people un-employed was almost 5 million, a rate of 13 per cent (ÖTV Hintergrund, Info-Dienst für Vertrauensleute und Mandatsträger, June 1998, p. 14). The highest unemployment rate was observed in the former East Germany. In 1989 Chancellor Kohl had promised that East Germany would reach the economic standard of West Germany within three years. Since then the government has had to admit that this goal cannot be reached and that it will take at least twenty years to close the gap between West and East. Not only leading economists but also politicians say openly that the era of full employment is over for good, even in Germany. For young people, for women and for older people the prospect of finding secure long-term employment with sufficient income is drastically reduced. They must be happy if they find casual jobs, part-time employment or a job through the Employment Promotion Scheme (Arbeitsbeschaffungsmassnahmen – ABM).

Indeed, the black hole of decreasing waged work can be found in all the rich industrialised countries. It can be compared to Professor Weizenbaum's 'black hole': feelings of absolute impotence, hopelessness and lack of perspective had been preceded by fantasies of global power and omnipotence following the globalisation of the economy.

What is 'globalisation of the economy'?

Although the globalisation of the economy is as old as capitalism, the modern use of this concept refers to the period that started around 1990. 'Globalisation' is part of neoliberal economic policy, which aims at abolishing protectionist rules, tariffs and regulations by means of which the free flow of goods, services and capital to all nooks and crannies of the world could be hampered by national governments. This policy has resulted in the integration of most national economies into one global market. This process has brought about a rapid qualitative change in the economy, in politics, in social life, a change that most people are not able to understand fully. Three phenomena made this rapid change possible: first, the long-term political strategy of those who wanted to replace post-1945 Keynesian economics by neoliberalism; second, the new communications technology; and third, the breakdown of socialism in Eastern Europe.

Tony Clarke and others have shown that the economic theory and policy followed from the end of the Second World War up to the end of the seventies in most industrialised countries did not disappear automatically but was systematically abolished by the think-tanks of the big transnational corporations (TNCs) (Clarke and Barlow 1997: 19ff.). Milton Friedman of the Chicago School of monetarists launched his attack on the Keynesian welfare state already in the 1970s. He advocated privatisation and the establishment of a 'free market place', unhampered by government intervention, regulation and protectionism. But this neoliberal theory was not put into practice until Pinochet's coup in Chile in 1973. Chile was the first country that carried out these economic 'reforms' under the conditions of a dictatorship. In the eighties Ms Thatcher in the UK and Mr Reagan in the USA followed the example of Chile. Then, with the beginning of the nineties, neoliberal policy was universalised and stabilised by global treaties such as the General Agreement on Tariffs and Trade (GATT) which in 1995 was institutionalised in the World Trade Organisation (WTO). The latest effort to globalise and legitimise neoliberal dogma for all time is the Multilateral Agreement on Investment (MAI) (Clarke and Barlow 1997).

Through computer technology, the second promoter of globalisation, data can be transferred from one continent to another at the speed of light. Space and time fall into one. While employees of a TNC in Manhattan sleep, their colleagues in Hong Kong continue to work on the same task. Due to this speed of data transfer, the stock exchanges in New York or Frankfurt can realise profits by capitalising on differences between exchange rates that exist only for minutes. This example hints at two aspects of modern globalisation: (1) concentration of capital in fewer hands and the domination of TNCs, (2) the growing role of finance capital.

Today half the world's trade is carried out between financially interrelated TNCs, 90 per cent of which are based in the North, while the 100 mightiest among them dominate at all levels. Owing to the globalisation of the last few decades the national economies in particular of the seven most powerful nations – the G7 countries – have undergone definite changes. Visible transfers, that is, the trade in goods, have lost their importance *vis-à-vis* invisible transfers like banking, transport, insurances, tourism. Finance transactions play the most important role in this shift. In the USA, where this restructuring is most advanced, the proportion of the finance sector in GNP grew from 18 per cent in 1970 to 25 per cent in 1990. A large part of this increase comes from international finance transactions or speculations. Financial markets, which ought to be only the oil to lubricate world trade, have become independent markets. They can hardly be controlled by national authorities (Decornoy, *Le Monde Diplomatique*, 25 September 1996).

The breakdown of socialism has resulted in the G7 nations dividing the world up into their spheres of influence, where big capital can operate without any restrictions. This policy had started already after the Second World War when the World Bank and the International Monetary Fund (IMF) were created. Throughout their history, but particularly after 1989, the World Bank and the IMF have promoted the neoliberal policy of free trade and globalisation.

The end of East–West confrontation has led to a new trilateral structure of the world economy: the USA, the EU and Japan with their respective spheres of influence: Latin America, Africa and Asia. The core countries have only 12 per cent of the world's population, but 60 per cent of the world's production is concentrated in them and they control 51 per cent of military expenditure worldwide (SEF 1993/94).

It would be wrong, however, to believe, that economic globalisation is a new phenomenon. As Wallerstein (1974) pointed out, right from its beginning the capitalist economy has been a world system, based on colonialism and the marginalisation and exploitation of peripheral countries and agriculture. This colonial structure was and is the basis for what became known as 'free trade' in the eighteenth and nineteenth centuries. But this world structure was not only ̣orical phenomenon, without which capitalism could not have established due to its inner logic of permanent growth or accumulation capitalism *has to* strive towards universality and globalism. This means, as Marx observed, that this system is structurally condemned to encompass and transform all areas of the globe and of life. What is new today is simply the destruction of the illusion that the globalised economy would be the harbinger of universal equality, justice and welfare for everybody (Altvater and Mahnkopf 1996).

People in the South, who were the victims of this global system from its beginning, understood earlier than people in the North that the globalisation, deregulation and privatisation imposed on their governments by the World Bank and the IMF for the benefit of TNCs were a fraud. Therefore, in a number of countries in Asia and South America the new neoliberal regime was opposed by peasants, women and trade unions. In India large peasant movements fought against the GATT, against Trade Related Intellectual Property Rights (TRIPs), against TNCs like Pepsi-Cola, Kentucky Fried Chicken, Monsanto and Cargill who are keen to integrate Indian agriculture into the 'free' world market (Mies and Shiva 1993; Mies 1996c; Shiva 1996b).

One may ask why resistance against the neoliberal policy of globalisation was much stronger in the South than in the North. One reason is that the Northern welfare states are still, in spite of being under attack, in a position to provide a certain standard of social security to the unemployed and the growing number of the poor. Another reason is the illusions that are held about the nature of the 'market economy', namely, that in the long run it will create a 'level playing field' and that the wealth accumulated by the rich will eventually 'trickle down' to the poor. Those who have looked at this economic system from below, from the perspective of women, of children, of people in the colonised South and of nature, have developed a more comprehensive understanding of what capitalism really has been from its beginning. This understanding is corroborated today by the processes of globalisation worldwide. Before we take a closer look at the various 'black holes' in the globalised economy we want to present the main points of this analysis from below, as we developed it from the late 1970s on (Mies, Bennholdt-Thomsen and von Werlhof 1988).

Colonising women, nature and foreign peoples

It is usually assumed that progress is a linear, evolutionary process starting from a 'primitive', 'backward' stage and, driven by the development of science and technology, or in Marxist terms of 'productive forces', moving up and up in unlimited progression. In this Promethean project, however, the limits of this globe, of time, of space, of our human existence, are not respected. Within a limited world, aims like 'unlimited growth' can be realised only at the expense of others. Or: there cannot be progress of one part without regression of another part, there cannot be development of some without underdeveloping others. There cannot be wealth of some without impoverishing others. Concepts like 'unlimited growth' or extended capital accumulation, therefore, necessarily imply that this growth (progress, development, wealth) is at the expense of some 'others', given the limits of our world. This means that 'progress', 'development', etcetera must be seen as polarising processes, following a dualistic worldview (Plumwood 1993).

Rosa Luxemburg has shown that capital accumulation presupposes the exploitation of ever more 'non-capitalist' milieux for the appropriation of more labour, more raw materials and more markets (Luxemburg 1923). We call these milieux colonies. Colonies were not only necessary to initiate the process of capital accumulation in what has been called the period of 'primitive accumulation' at the beginning of capitalism. They continue to be necessary even today to keep the growth mechanism going. Therefore we talk of the need for 'ongoing primitive accumulation and colonization' (Mies, Bennholdt-Thomsen and von Werlhof, 1988: 15–17).

Some theses on global capitalism

1. There is no colonisation without violence. Whereas the relationship between the capitalist and the wage labourer is legally one of owners (the one of capital, the other of labour power) who enter a contract of exchange of equivalents, the relationship between colonisers and colonies is never based on a contract or an exchange of equivalents. It is enforced and stabilised by direct and structural violence. Hence, violence is still necessary to uphold a system of dominance oriented towards capital accumulation.

2. This violence is not gender-neutral; it is basically directed against women. It is usually been assumed that with modernisation, industrialisation and urbanisation patriarchy as a system of male dominance would disappear and make way for equality between men and women. Contrary to this assumption, it is our thesis that patriarchy not only has not disappeared in this process, which is identical with the spread of the modern capitalist world economy, but the ever-expanding process of capital accumulation is based on the maintenance or even re-creation of patriarchal or sexist man–woman relations, an asymmetric sexual division of labour within and outside the family, the definition of all women as dependent 'housewives' and the definition of all men as 'breadwinners'. This sexual division of labour is integrated with an international division of labour in which women are manipulated both as 'producer-housewives' and as 'consumer-housewives'.

3. With the global world system getting more and more into a crisis we can observe an increase of violence particularly against women, not only in the South but also in the North. As this violence is part and parcel of a political–economic system based on colonisation and limitless growth it cannot be overcome by a strategy aiming only at gender equality. Within

a colonial context equality means catching up with the colonial masters, not doing away with colonialism. This is the reason why feminists cannot be satisfied with an 'equal opportunities' policy but must strive to overcome all relationships of exploitation, oppression and colonisation necessary for the maintenance of global capitalist patriarchy (Plumwood 1993).

4. When in the late seventies we began to ask about the root causes of the ongoing oppression and exploitation of women, of the ongoing violence against women even in the rich, democratic, industrialised societies of the North, we rediscovered not only that patriarchy continued to exist as a social system but also that it is intrinsically linked to the capitalist system with its aim of ongoing growth of goods, services and capital. We realised that the secret of such ongoing economic growth was not, as is usually assumed, the intelligence of scientists and engineers who invent ever more labour-saving machines and thus make labour ever more 'productive' and by the same mechanism ever more redundant. Nor could permanent growth or accumulation be fully explained, as Marx had explained it, by the fact that the capitalists pay back to the workers only a share of the value they have produced by their work, namely only that share that is necessary to reproduce their labour power (Mies, Bennholdt-Thomsen and von Werlhof 1988).

We discovered that women's work to reproduce that labour power did not appear in the calculations either of the capitalists or of the state, or in Marx's theory. On the contrary, in all economic theories and models this life-producing and life-preserving subsistence work of women appears as a 'free good', a free resource like air, water, sunshine. It appears to flow naturally from women's bodies. 'Housewifeisation' of women is therefore the necessary

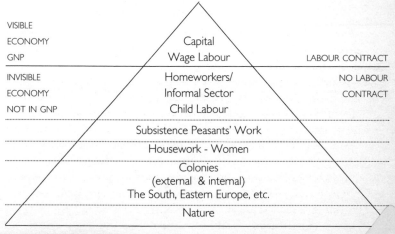

Figure 2.1 • The Iceberg Model of Capitalist Patriarchal Economics

complement to the proletarianisation of men. We visualised this capitalist patriarchal economy in the form of an iceberg (see Figure 2.1).

We began to understand that the dominant theories about the functioning of our economy, including Marxism, were only concerned with the tip of the iceberg visible above the water, namely only capital and wage labour. The base of that iceberg under the water was invisible, namely women's unpaid house-work, caring work, nurturing work, or, as we then called it, the production of life or subsistence production.

But as we had lived in Third World countries for a long time, we immediately saw that women's unpaid housework and caring work was not the only component of this invisible base of our economy; it also included the work of small peasants and artisans in still-existing subsistence economies in the South, the work of millions of small producers who produce for local needs. All work conceptualised as 'informal sector' work is part of the invisible economy (von Werlhof 1988: 168 ff.).

And finally we saw, that nature herself was considered to be a 'free good', to be appropriated and exploited with no or little costs for the sake of accumu-lation. Therefore we called all those parts of the submerged 'hidden economy' which are under the water in our iceberg metaphor – nature, women and colonised people and territories – the 'Colonies of the White Man'. 'White Man' stands here for the Western industrial system (Mies 1986b/1999; Mies, Bennholdt-Thomsen and von Werlhof 1988).

With regard to the growth paradigm it is our thesis that permanent economic growth or capital accumulation can only continue so long as such 'colonies' exist which can be exploited free of cost or at very little cost. These are the areas for the 'externalisation of costs'.

Patriarchy, colonisation and housewifeisation

In our feminist analysis of capitalism the concepts of patriarchy, housewifeisa-tion and colonisation play a central role. They are also important concepts in our analysis of the globalised economy today. If we want to understand the functioning of this economy, we have to step back and take a brief look at the history of our societies. Let us look at the emergence of patriarchy first.

Patriarchy as a system of male dominance over women emerged some 5,000 –6,000 years ago among certain tribes living in the central Asian steppes north of the Black Sea. According to the research of the late archaeologist Marija Gimbutas, the men of these tribes, whom she called the 'Kurgan people', were able to make warfare and conquest of other tribes and their territory the main source of their wealth. The secret of the success of these Kurgan tribes was not their superior intelligence or culture, or some kind of genetic superiority, but mainly their more efficient means of transport, namely tamed horses and camels, and their more efficient means of destruction, namely bows and arrows and spears and other long-distance weapons. The monopoly over these arms gave the men of the Kurgan tribes a power over foreign men, women and their territories that did not grow out of their own work but out of violence and coercion. It is the power over life and death. This monopoly over efficient means of destruction, however, changed not only the relationship between those tribes and other tribes, but also the relationship between humans and nature and also, in particular, the relationship between men and women. Whereas formerly men were dependent on the women of their own tribes and clans for sexuality and reproduction of the people, now they could steal and enslave the women of the conquered 'enemies'. Moreover, this relationship between the conquering men and the women who then became part of the loot also changed the relationship between these men and their 'own' women. It also changed the whole conceptualisation about the originator of human life. Whereas before it was clear that women were the beginning, the *arkhé*, of human life, this logic could now be turned upside down. A new logic could be created, namely that of 'He who kills is.' That means, he who is capable of killing determines who can stay alive. He 'gives' life to those whom he has not killed. From then onwards archaeologists find not only arms and bones of horses and of female slaves in the big tumuli where the 'leading men' are buried; we also find new myths of origin in which a male god–father or culture hero is the origin of all things, including women. 'He who kills is' has remained the core of all patriarchal logic until today (Mies 1986b/1999; Keller 1990). It is also the secret of the 'success' of European civilisation, including its modern industrial phase, of colonialism, capitalism and the nuclear family. It is our thesis that patriarchal ideology and structures are necessary for the continuation of this system. But there are not only continuities, there are also differences and modifications of these structures and the patriarchal ideology.

Housewifeisation

One important difference between the 'old' patriarchies and the modern, industrial one is the new definition of the concept of labour and of the sexual division of labour. According to this new conceptualisation the man is the 'breadwinner' for 'his' family. He has to sell his labour power for a wage (a salary) with which he then is able to 'feed' a family: wife and children. The woman is defined as his housewife who has to do the unpaid work to reproduce his labour power and the future generation of wage workers. This new definition of the division of labour between men and women is not a result of some inborn male sadism but is, as was said before, a structural necessity for the process of extended capital accumulation.

The concept 'housewifeisation' was coined by Maria Mies on the basis of her research for *The Lacemakers of Narsapur: Indian Housewives Produce for the World Market* (1982). She found that poor rural women in South India were crocheting lace in a home-based industry based on the putting-out system, and this lace was then exported to Europe, Australia and the USA. These women earned a small fraction of what was considered the minimum wage for an agricultural labourer. Their exploitation was justified by the lace exporters – who meanwhile had become millionaires – by the argument that these women were 'housewives' who were anyhow sitting idly in their houses. By making lace they could use their time *productively*.

Housewifeisation, then, means not only the *wageless reproduction* of labour power but also the *cheapest kind of production work*, mainly done by women in homeworking or similar work relations.

The housewifeisation of women's labour is not eliminated when women do enter the wage labour market as full-time workers, or even when they are the only breadwinners of their family. The difference between male and female wages continues to exist. In Germany it is 30 per cent. It is justified by the argument that women's earnings are only a supplement to the male breadwinner's wage.

Colonisation

The analysis of the process of housewifeisation would be incomplete if we did not look at it within the context of colonialism. In the first phase of globalisation, the processes of colonisation and housewifeisation did not only take place simultaneously; they were also logically connected. Without the conquest of colonies and their exploitation and plunder, European entrepreneurs would not have been able to start the Industrial Revolution; scientists would not have found capitalists who would have been interested in their inventions, and the bourgeois class would not have had enough money to have 'non-working' housewives. Colonialism was/is the material precondition for the development of the productivity of human labour which made/makes the modern industrial expansion possible .

A typical colonial and housewifeised labour relation is the work relation in world market factories (WMFs), where Northern metropolitan enterprises produce with very low labour costs commodities for the world market, mainly for markets in Northern countries. The reason for these low labour costs in the South is not only the fact that these countries are generally poor and have a large pool of unemployed, but also the fact that by far the majority of workers in the WMFs and EPZs are young, unmarried women.[1] One of the main reasons for hiring young women is the housewife ideology and the skills they have already acquired for housework: they know how to sew and knit. They are supposed to have 'nimble fingers' and to be 'docile'. Moreover, when they get married and have children, many either leave the job or are fired. This is a result of the housewife ideology owing to which women's wage is seen only as a supplement to the man's wage. As most of these women come from impoverished rural or urban households, they accept appalling working conditions with a

working day of up to twelve hours, inhuman work speeds
practically coercive labour discipline, and safety and health
be permitted in Northern countries (Mies 1986b/1999, Els

The three phases of globalisation

As was said before, the globalisation of the economy is an intrinsic characteristic
of capitalism. But this globalisation has not always been the same. We want to
differentiate between three different phases of globalisation:

1. the colonial phase proper, which lasted till the end of the Second World
   War, when most colonies became politically independent but were made
   economically dependent by development colonialism;
2. the phase of the so-called new international division of labour which started
   around 1972–73. It is characterised by the relocation of whole branches of
   production like textiles, electronics, toys and shoes from the old industrial
   centres to so-called cheap labour countries like South Korea, Malaysia, the
   Philippines, Mexico and Taiwan;
3. the present phase. Its main features are the universalisation of the neoliberal
   dogma as the only possible economic theory, the elimination of all
   protectionist barriers to trade and investment, not only in the South but
   also in the East and North. The World Bank and IMF control national
   economies through structural adjustment programmes (SAPs), by promoting free trade and free investment, deregulation, privatisation, globalisation and further commodity production and consumption.

In what follows we shall skip the first phase because we have written about
it earlier (Mies 1986b/1999; Mies, Bennholdt-Thomsen and von Werlhof
1988). We shall concentrate on the second and third phases.

Globalisation without a human face

The third phase of global restructuring began with the recession around 1990.
It is characterised by an unprecedented penetration of all regions of the globe
and all areas of life by the logic and practice of capital accumulation,
epitomised as global 'free trade'. In this stage most of the changes brought
about in the earlier stage of the restructuring of the world economy were
continued, but there are quantitative and qualitative differences. Thus, the
system of relocating manufacturing industries into low-wage countries has
been vastly expanded and includes today not only practically all the poor
countries of the world, but also all the erstwhile-socialist countries, including
Eastern Europe, Russia and also China. The closing-down of labour-intensive,
environmentally polluting plants and their relocation to cheap-labour
countries has now affected more industrial branches in the rich countries, like

..eel industry, coal mining, ship and car production etcetera. It has led to assive lay-offs of skilled workers, mainly male, in Europe and the USA. Moreover when, as a result of workers' protests, wages rise in one of the cheap labour countries, companies move to other countries which are even cheaper, for example from South Korea to Bangladesh (Elson 1994).

Until recently the women workers in these EPZs had hoped that through heroic struggles they would eventually at least reach minimum labour standards as they are prescribed by the ILO. But now they must realise that the TNCs for whom they had worked close down and move on to even 'cheaper' countries. From one day to the next they lose their jobs without any warning, compensation or alternative. Or, in Hong Kong, the companies hire even cheaper women workers as casual labour from mainland China.

In 1995 the Committee of Asian Women published a book with the title: *Silk and Steel*, in which the consequences of this new global restructuring for women in EPZs in South Korea, the Philippines, Hong Kong, Singapore, India and Bangladesh are analysed. From their data the authors conclude that sexist job discrimination has increased: for permanent jobs men are preferred, while women get casual and part-time jobs from which they can be fired at any time. Married women are practically excluded from the labour market, because 'the managers want to save the costs for maternity leave and other benefits. They usually argue that married women have too many family obligations and hence could not concentrate on their work' (CAW 1995: 31).

But this does not mean that all married women are provided for by an earning 'breadwinner', and therefore need not themselves work directly for capital. The further relocation of EPZs to other, cheaper labour countries has resulted in an increased casualisation of jobs: permanent jobs are changed into part-time, insecure, unprotected jobs; full-time jobs are changed into casual jobs; factory work is put out into homeworking. Homeworking in particular is mainly done by married women who have lost their factory job. It allows them, as we know, to combine family obligations with 'productive' work for the global market. Many of the women who were suddenly fired now do casual work in some newly established service enterprise: 70 per cent of unemployed women found casual labour in this sector.

That means they work for a few hours at McDonald's, Spaghetti House, Maxim, in supermarkets, as sweepers, maidservants and also as sex-workers. In Hong Kong such sex workers have recently formed an association, a kind of trade union, to protect themselves against increasing exploitation and violence (*ZiTeng Newsletter*, October 1998, No. 7). This is the kind of work in the 'service sector' that economists and politicians praise as the new job machine to solve the problem of unemployment.

The analysis of the situation of women workers in many Asian countries corroborates what we wrote in 1988 about the tendency to further housewifeisation of labour under the impact of the crises brought about by global capital. *Silk and Steel* gives ample data about the deterioration of women's work and living conditions as a result of this strategy. The authors also show that in the economic crisis men often simply leave their families so that the women are left alone to provide for their children, parents and siblings.[2]

Housewifeisation of labour is the optimal strategy for capital it seems, to realise comparative advantage in a globalised economy, because women as mothers and caretakers are the cheapest and most exploitable of 'cheap labour'. For women this strategy is a catastrophe.

The process of restructuring the global economy in the direction of ever more export-led industrialisation, both in the South and the East, is driven by the big TNCs. More and more capital and power are concentrated in their hands. They continue their neoliberal strategy although it has resulted in financial and economic crises in Asia, Russia and South America.

This neocolonial structure of the global economy is upheld by a few global institutions like the World Bank and the IMF, by the GATT, and nowadays by the WTO, the MAI, and similar agreements.

GATT is an agreement by which trade barriers that countries have set up to protect certain areas of their economy and society have to be removed, thus obliging the countries to open their markets to goods from all over the world. This new free trade policy assumes that all trading partners are equal, and that by using the principle of comparative advantage all trading partners will benefit. But in practice the weaker partners, above all Third World countries, will be forced to accept regulations that threaten their national sovereignty. They have to make their agricultural sector dependent on the TNCs and they have to abandon their policy of food self-sufficiency. They have to allow Northern firms to set up their 'dirty' industries in their territory. They have to open themselves up to Northern banks and insurance companies and above all, through the GATT clause on Trade Related Intellectual Property Rights (TRIPs), they have to allow foreign companies and scientists as patent holders to privatise, monopolise and commercialise their biological and cultural heritage and common property (see pages 39–40).

TRIPs are particularly dangerous for the Third World in combination with the development of biotechnology, gene and reproductive engineering. This technology is expected to change the world more than any technology before it. Biotechnological TNCs are trying to get monopoly control over all life forms, plants, animals, even human genes, particularly in the South. This will affect women in particular, who in many countries are responsible for the preservation of seeds (Mies and Shiva 1993; Akhter 1998).

But in the North also biotechnology – the genetic manipulation of plants, animals and eventually also of human beings – will have detrimental consequences. As most consumers in the North depend already now on the

TNCs for their food, they will lose the freedom to choose food that is not manipulated. As biotechnology is seen as *the* growth industry, ethical considerations are more and more pushed aside. In these processes women and their capacity to generate new human life are of strategic importance. Reproductive technology is being expanded all over the globe. It opens the way for eugenic, racist and sexist manipulations, and treats women's bodies increasingly as reservoirs of biological raw material for scientific experiments and bio-industry (Mies and Shiva 1993; Mies 1996a).

Another consequence of globalisation is an increasing polarisation of the rich and the poor in the South. One reason for this is the structural adjustment programmes (SAPs) which are imposed on indebted Third World countries in order to bring their economies under the discipline of the 'free market'. These SAPs have had disastrous consequences, particularly for poor women. Whereas in the second phase of globalisation the poor could still hope that the state would eventually take care of them, this illusion is now no longer possible. The poor and particularly poor women are virtually left to fend for themselves, to survive or to die. They are in practice expendable, both as producers and consumers. That is the reason why poor women are the main target of population control.

On the other hand the new global restructuring has improved the situation of the elites in the Third World, so much so that their lifestyle is more or less similar to that of the middle classes in the North (Sklair 1994). In fact, in this phase the fastest-growing economies were some of the Newly Industrialising Countries in Asia (NICs) like Thailand, Indonesia and also China and India. Their middle classes are keen to buy Western-produced consumer goods, and according to an analysis by Pam Woodall they helped 'to pull the rich world out of the recession of the early 1990s'. According to an OECD estimate, consumers in India, China and Indonesia will number 700 million people by the year 2010 (Woodall 1994: 13). But the author argues that the gap between these elite consumers and the poor in their countries will further widen.

A similar situation can also be observed in the North. Not only has the relocation of industries to 'cheap labour countries' led to increased unemployment, reduction in wage and poverty in the USA and Europe, but the strategies used to 'solve' this crisis are similar to those applied so far only in the Third World. This means deregulation and flexibilisation of labour – housewife-isation and informalisation of hitherto formal labour relations, an increase of homeworking, are the main methods. The creation of cheap labour sectors within a country, particularly for women, and the gradual dismantling of the welfare state follow the same pattern as SAPs in the Third World.

As a result of all these measures poverty has returned to the rich countries of the North, and it is mainly female poverty. Also in the North the polarisation between the poor and the rich is increasing. Global restructuring has not brought, as its spokespeople maintain, more wealth and happiness and development to all; on the contrary, the global capitalist economy can only grow so long as it maintains and re-creates inequality both within individual countries and in the world as a whole. This was clearly spelt out by Pam Woodall in the conservative *Economist*:

> The benefits of international trade come from allowing countries to exploit their comparative advantage, not from requiring them to be identical. And much of the Third World's comparative advantage lies, in one way or another, in the fact of its poverty, in particular, cheap labour and a greater tolerance of pollution. (Woodall 1994: 42)

The neoliberal free trade strategy promoted by the big TNCs has not only resulted in 'black holes' as far as the work situation is concerned, particularly for women in the EPZs and *maquiladoras* in Asia and Central and South America. It has also led to mass pauperisation of peasants everywhere in the South, to the taking over of vast areas of agricultural and food production by TNCs from the North, and to the destruction of policies of food self-sufficiency in the South and North. These so-called economic reforms have affected peasants and poor women in the South most dramatically. In order to understand whether the 'comparative advantages' of which the neoliberal dogma speaks are really creating a level playing field and really benefiting those at the bottom of the iceberg economy, it may be useful to look at some of the main features of the neoliberal strategy and their effects on women, children, farmers and nature.

GATT, the WTO, regional trade blocks and food security

In 1986, in the so-called Uruguay Round,[3] neoliberal free trade policies were expanded to include the agricultural sectors of the nations that signed the General Agreement on Tariffs and Trade. Until then, agricultural trade had been exempted from free trade policies in order to protect local farmers. The Uruguay Round talks lasted eight years, and were concluded in Marrakesh in 1994. Food and agricultural trade were thereby globalised and liberalised. This meant that the countries that had signed the GATT agreements had no longer the possibility of protecting local farmers or consumers by forbidding foreign corporations access to their markets. The main goal of agricultural production was no longer to provide the native population with food, but to produce trade goods for international export as needed by the market. Furthermore, the liberalising of agricultural and food trade meant that giant TNCs could invest in other countries without restrictions. As a result, for instance, Kentucky Fried Chicken, to name one company, could attempt to establish their fast-food chain all over India.

The GATT regulations contain a clause regarding Trade Related Intellectual Property Rights (TRIPs). Behind this abbreviation is mainly hidden the attempt of rich industrial nations and their TNCs to gain free access to the genetic diversity of the Southern tropical countries, and to the traditional knowledge of the local communities concerning plants, animals, the earth, and health. This knowledge will then be used to industrialise, to commercialise, to privatise and in the end to monopolise that genetic diversity (Shiva 1995b). This is made possible because the TRIPs under the auspices of GATT allow researchers and concerns to patent biologically or genetically manipulated plants and animals. The patenting of life forms was not possible until a short time ago.

The results for local farmers and small merchants were recently made clear by the Indian farmers' movement against GATT and against the patenting of products of the neem tree. These products had been used in India for thousands of years as natural disinfectants and pesticides, and the quality of neem products is common knowledge in India. Tony Larson, an American, acquired the patent for all neem products and sold it to the TNC W.R. Grace; he had discovered nothing new, but had made the ancient Indian knowledge his private property and then sold it. After this, Indians who wished to produce anything from neem had to pay licence fees to Larson and W.R. Grace. Vandana Shiva and Jeremy Rifkin fought successfully against this bio-piracy before the US Patent Office (*BIJA*, No. 15–16, 1996: 32). Similar processes are going on especially in the seed sector, where huge TNCs have expanded their global control to include seeds and biogenetic resources, and are supporting their commercial interests against the farming population with international laws.[4]

After the closing of the GATT talks, in January 1995 the complete set of regulations was transferred to the WTO, which now regulates world trade according to the free trade principles described above. At the same time, large trade blocks such as the EU, NAFTA, APEC (Asian–Pacific Economic Cooperation) and MERCOSUR (Mercado Comun del Cono Sur) have been or are in the process of being established. They are the result of competition in a global economy, competition for markets, investments, production and services. The FAO is trying expressly to achieve the goal of 'world food security' within this GATT/WTO framework. The analysers of the global free trade in the agricultural sector expect profits in OECD nations to reach US$25 billion per year (FAO Technical Paper No. 7, 1996: 10).

Whether this gain in profits means a gain in food security is completely open to question. It is going on the wrong track to expect food security from those very institutions, interests and theories that have done so much to destroy food security for so many in the first place. We formulate the following thesis:

Universal food security is impossible in a global market economy that rests on worldwide liberalisation and deregulation of agricultural and food trade, and on the neoliberal dogma of comparative advantage, universal competition, profit maximisation and permanent growth.

Let us now take a look at the results these neoliberal trade doctrines have had up till now for the poor of the world. The poor, as is well known, are mostly women. The effects on women of globalisation in the South and in the North have been differently analysed and criticised. Not only is it the case that 70 per cent of the world's poor are women; neoliberal developments have led to an increase in female poverty in Germany as well (Bennholdt-Thomsen 1996b). What does this mean for food security?

The global doctrine of free trade is mainly based on David Ricardo's theory of comparative advantage. This theory states that goods should be produced where the natural conditions are most favourable and production costs are lowest. For example, the Portuguese should produce wine and not textiles, and the English should produce textiles and not wine. Both countries could then profit from trading these goods. Applied to agricultural and food production within the framework of GATT/WTO, this doctrine means that food should be produced where the wages are lowest, and where environmental protection laws are most lax. In addition, this means that the local farmers no longer provide for the needs of their own population, but instead produce for an external market where higher profits beckon.

To this end, for example in India, fertile ricelands along the east coast are bought or leased by international firms to make shrimp farms. The shrimps are exported to Europe, Japan and the USA, and can now be bought cheaply in our supermarkets. In order to set up the shrimp basins, salt water must be pumped onto the land, which spoils both the land and the drinking water.

The environmental, economic and social costs of this 'growth' are paid by the local communities, as proved by Vandana Shiva, above all by women. While shrimp exports appear in national and international growth statistics, the destruction of the local food and water resources remains unmentioned. Above all, the women of the local fishing and farming villages, who have lived from rice paddies and fishing for ages, have been robbed of their basis of sustenance. They are the ones who are most actively protesting against the shrimp farms. Vandana Shiva quotes Govindamma from the village of Kurru in Tamil Nadu: 'First they drove us from the coast, and we had to seek work in the country. Now they build these shrimp farms on the rice paddies.... There we have also lost our work. How shall we earn our living?' (Shiva 1995a).

The delta areas of India's east coast are especially suited for rice growing. Today, this basis for local self-sufficiency has been destroyed. The financial gains from shrimp export can never compensate: first, these gains are claimed by mainly private, foreign and domestic firms, and, second, the wages of the few people who find work in this industry are so low, that they can hardly guarantee food security as defined by the FAO. These cheap wages are part of the comparative advantage of the shrimp companies; without them they might have established their facilities on German or Japanese coasts. In addition, more jobs are destroyed than are created by these industries. Moreover, it is also known that these shrimp farms can only operate productively for a limited time, as the shellfish succumb to disease and new coastal areas must be sought. Child labour is part of the comparative advantage as well, as shown in the video 'The Violence of the Blue Revolution'.

The example of shrimp farming could be further supported by others, such as flower and strawberry production for export in West India, where land that had previously been available for local food production is now used for luxury goods for the already overfed consumers in the lands with higher purchasing power.

The doctrine of comparative advantage was developed at a time when the mobility of labour and capital was still limited by national borders. David Ricardo clearly stated that capital would seek absolute and not comparative advantage if it could move freely across all borders. Then, national governments and parliaments would no longer be able to obstruct the search for absolute and not comparative advantage. Today, this situation has been reached.

And the final costs are carried by nature, the poor, children and women. The search for absolute advantage in the agricultural and food sectors means that the survival of the farmers and food security for the impoverished countries of the South is sacrificed in the interest of capital growth. Vandana Shiva writes that in India the prices of rice and wheat have risen due to these export-oriented policies. Simultaneously, the poor farmers in poor regions were robbed of their own market by the import of cheap millet (Shiva 1995a).

That there are only winners in the global, liberalised market of agricultural production if there are losers somewhere else is confirmed by the following statement from a US agricultural politician: 'before the US can achieve its main economic objective, namely dramatic increases in grain sales [to Europe], they must firstly destroy the European food security policies that encourage domestic production' (quoted by Shiva 1995a). This statement expresses the true relationships in the global agrarian market. For certain countries and TNCs to realise their comparative or absolute advantages, local self-sufficiency elsewhere must be destroyed. The USA has been following the strategy of using wheat as a weapon since the early 1970s. That this is currently a conscious strategy of the TNCs as well is shown by the example of Pepsi and *Bikaneri bhujia* in India.

The Bikaneri bhujia *case*

Bikaneri bhujia is a traditional snack produced in cottage industries in Bikaner, Rajasthan, India, and currently provides 2,500,500 persons, mainly women, with an income. Pepsi, with its capital, is now mass-producing this snack and using this traditional name in its advertising, in order to underbid local producers and therefore destroy their market. Pepsi has introduced no new recipe to produce this snack. This US TNC, which after the economic liberalisation can now operate freely in India, has appropriated the common knowledge and the traditional method of food preparation of millions of simple women, and thereby destroyed their basis of living. These women, from town and country, educated and uneducated, married and widowed, gained an income from this cottage industry which was perfectly suited to the region which gave this snack its name. The moth lentil, used for preparing this snack, grows only in the deserts of Bikaner and Jodhpur. The cottage industry had a secure local market and supported not only the women but also the farmers in these desert regions, where not much else grows. A further ten thousand women are employed in the preparation of *papad*, a snack which is eaten together with the *Bikaneri bhujia*. And hundreds of thousands of street vendors live from the sales of these popular traditional snacks.

At the conference on 'Intellectual Property Rights, Community Rights, and Biodiversity' held in Delhi on 20 February 1996, it was reported that almost the entire population of Bikaner was involved in the production and distribution of *Bikaneri bhujia*. Now Pepsi has announced that it will remove this product from the cottage industry sector and relocate it in the high-tech sector. This will be a catastrophe for the people of Bikaner: Pepsi has stolen the traditional trademark name in order to destroy the market of the little people (*BIJA*, No. 15–16, 1996, pp. 29–30).

In India, in support of these policies, farmland necessary for the feeding of the local population is now planted with export food products, such as tomatoes for ketchup for Pepsi in place of rice in the Punjab, sunflowers instead of rice and millet in Karnataka, flowers, strawberries and fruits for export in Maharastra instead of basic foodstuffs. Corn is grown for animal feed, to be exported to Europe. The large food corporations turn the farmers into contract producers, who provide them with raw materials for the manufacture of 'novel food', which they then sell where there are social classes with the necessary purchasing power.

The results of these free trade policies are already being felt in India. The export of agricultural products, above all grain, has risen 71 per cent in recent years: from a value of 21.98 billion rupees in 1988–89 to 37.66 billion in 1992–93. Since the Indian government, according to the new economic policies, no longer has a right to influence the prices of basic foodstuffs, food prices rose 63 per cent in the same period of time, which led to an immediate drop in daily consumption from 510g. to 466g. per person (Shiva 1995a). In other countries of the South, the picture is similar.

On the basis of free trade, how can food security for all be guaranteed – for the economically weakest, the impoverished women and children? Regarding India, Vandana Shiva writes: 'When food is available solely at world market prices as required by the liberalizing of trade, hunger is the only certainty for the majority of the poor, who did not even have enough to eat before the economic reforms' (Shiva 1995a).

The corn farmers of Mindanao

A further example of how globalised free trade produces hunger is that of the corn farmers of Mindanao in the Philippines. These small peasants lived mainly by maize production, but the free trade policy of GATT/WTO drove them into poverty and starvation. When the USA began to export maize to the Philippines at a price far below the producer price of the corn farmers they could not compete and had to give up farming. The pauperised peasants then either moved to the slums of the cities, which are already overcrowded, or tried to find casual jobs on the plantations of food TNCs like Del Monte, which had bought up the peasants' land at a cutthroat price.

> Instead of growing food for themselves on their own land, those who are lucky to find casual jobs on the plantations now produce pineapples, bananas, vegetables for Western supermarkets on this land. And all this will be celebrated as a further victory of the theory of 'comparative advantages' and of free trade. After all, why should you grow your own food when you can buy it at a cheaper price? And cheaper than from the USA you can't get it these days. Since there are no trade barriers any longer the maize grown in the midwest of the United States can be sold for half of the corn market price in Mindanao. (Kevin Watkins, *Guardian Weekly*, 16 February 1997)

The irony is that agrarian trade in the USA is not really free. It is subsidised by the government to the extent of US$29,000 per farmer. 'Free trade' does not mean, as is always proclaimed by its propagandists, that a truly 'level playing field' is created, but that there are *winners* and *losers*. Winners are definitely the big agrarian and food TNCs. Losers are the small peasants, their women and children.

But what can we say about the consumers in the North? Do they not also belong to the group of winners? Weren't representatives of the G7 states right when at their summit in Lyons in autumn 1997 they stated that free trade would favour the consumers by making possible cheaper food prices? The international consumer associations welcomed GATT because of the lowering of all commodity prices. But consumers in Europe and the USA have hardly noticed the GATT negotiations. The majority do not ask why they can buy exotic fruits the whole year round for low prices and why T-shirts are getting cheaper every year. This kind of social ignorance regarding the real economy is part of the neoliberal strategy. It prevents people from beginning to question the food policy of GATT/WTO which sacrifices small peasants' existence and food security to boost TNC profits.

'Black holes' for women in the North

Although the countries of the North, particularly the G7 countries, have been the profiteers in the neoliberal globalisation process, the more this process goes on the more it becomes evident that poverty, hunger, social insecurity, misery and joblessness are found not only in the South but increasingly also in the North. In fact, in the USA as well as in Europe a process of social polarisation can be observed. This process has been most marked in eastern Germany where the reunification of Germany, first hailed as the beginning of a golden era, has led to a dramatic rise of joblessness. Two thirds of the jobless there are women. This happens in a country where women's waged employment was the highest in the world – 90 per cent – and where women were represented in all the professions. Today the old patriarchal strategy is used to send women home to 'Küche und Kinder' (kitchen and children) without any alternative.

In consequence of neoliberal policies, expenses for kindergartens and social security have been cut; women are the main victims of these processes. This is true not only for the former East Germany but also for the former West Germany and all the OECD countries, where all the governments follow the same neoliberal dogma. These governments consider it their main task to protect the interests of the big TNCs and not to protect the people. They cut public spending in the fields of social security, health, education, childcare and women's equality in order to promote the privatisation of public assets and to deregulate labour laws. All this is done to enhance the big corporations' competitiveness in the global marketplace and to attract foreign investors. This policy is justified by the argument that it will create more jobs. It is clear by now that this strategy will not create new jobs. Each rationalisation and innovation has instead destroyed jobs and produced what is known as 'jobless growth'. This strategy, however, has not been given up anywhere.

It is believed that what has been artificially produced is superior and more productive than living human labour power. 'Increase in productivity' - either by substituting this labour power by high-tech machinery or by relocating production to 'cheap labour' countries – is one of the key mechanisms used by the corporations to counter global competition.

Divide and rule

This neoliberal strategy is a disaster – not only for women in the South but also for women in the North. In Germany, for example, the proportion of social expenditure in GDP went down from 33 per cent in 1988 to 30 per cent in 1994. Of the women who work forty hours and more per week, 53 per cent do not have a sufficient income to cover their main costs of living – calculated to be DM1,800 (Möller 1991). In addition, women constitute the majority of workers in part-time and precarious jobs. The economic situation of single mothers and women-headed households has deteriorated since 1980, while the number of such households has increased by 1 million.

But this situation is not restricted to Germany. It can be found in the USA, in Canada, in the UK, and in most countries of the North. Of course, this feminisation of poverty, as it has been called, does not yet mean that many women are starving in these countries. What it is important to understand is that the present neoliberal globalisation process produces a new patriarchal subordination of women, both in the South and the North, not only by direct intervention or violence, but also simply by the fact that apparently value-free economic priorities, namely the commodification of everything and the maximisation of profit, are made the central goals of all societies. These goals appear as quasi-natural laws of all economic activity. Such a view of an economy is fundamentally hostile to women, to life, to humans as social beings, and to nature.

In recent years we have been able to observe a depressing erosion of solidarity in our societies. As a result of the principle of divide and rule and of the hierarchically split patriarchal society, women are the main victims of this erosion. The breakdown of socialism is not the cause of this shift, as is often assumed; it only aggravated it. The lesson we have to learn today - a historic lesson we have avoided for at least two hundred years – is that the question of whether capitalism or socialism was the better system is simply the wrong question. If people had asked this question from a women's perspective they would have known the answer much earlier: none of the two is preferable to the other.

The proletarian is dead, long live the housewife!

'The Proletarian Is Dead, Long Live the Housewife!' is the title of an essay that Claudia von Werlhof published in German in 1983 (English translation in Mies, Bennholdt-Thomsen and von Werlhof 1988: 168). This was at a moment when for the first time the end of the proletariat and of the 'work society' had been declared (Gorz 1983). Werlhof criticised this discourse by explaining that perhaps the male skilled worker, well protected by labour laws, trade unions and a labour contract, was no longer the optimal workforce for capital: instead the housewife was fitted exactly into the new capital strategy of that time, which demanded the flexibilisation of labour. This flexibilisation was propagated as the necessary consequence of the new work rationalisation brought about by the microelectronics and computer technology.

Whilst around 1983 the trade unions could still believe that flexibilisation was only a temporary strategy to tide capitalism over an economic slump, by now it is clear that this strategy has become the main method used to undermine the well-established and well-protected core labour standards in the industrialised countries. In the context of globalisation when corporations simply can move to other 'cheap labour countries', if trade unions in the core countries continue to stick to their traditional demands it seems plausible, from the point of view of capital, to flexibilise labour further. The former German minister of economics Rexrodt openly suggested the establishment of a cheap labour sector within Germany. Otherwise German capital would continue to move out to 'cheap labour' countries, mainly in Eastern Europe and Asia or South America. The minister was even explicit about the type of workforce to be employed in this 'cheap labour sector': women, housewives. He praised women for their capacity to combine housework, and care for children and the old with productive work – perhaps as homeworkers at computers.

Flexibilisation of work, in fact, means housewifeisation of work. Already in 1983 Claudia von Werlhof wrote that not only women's but also men's work would be 'housewifeised'. Because in capital's strategy the white, male wage worker is not the image of the future for all workers. The dream of all capitalists is the universalisation of work relations similar to those of housewives:

> There is no cheaper, more productive, and more fruitful human labour and it can also be enforced without the whip. I believe that the restructuring of our economy will involve the effort to re-educate the men and force upon them, as far as possible, the feminine work capacity. For the (male) wage worker does too little and knows too little. He can do only what he is paid for and what has been agreed upon by contract (von Werlhof 1988: 129).

If we look at countries that have apparently solved their job problem these days – the USA, Denmark or the Netherlands – we can see the correctness of the above statement. The jobs that have been created in these countries are housewifeised jobs. They are badly paid, part-time, casual, without the protection of labour laws, non-unionised, short-term, atomised. There is a lot of homeworking, the exploitation of which is nowadays camouflaged by concepts like 'self-employment' or 'entrepreneurship'. The deregulation of labour markets and the emphasis on a strong service sector follow exactly this line. Much of what is included in this service sector is nothing but commodified housework.

The 'black hole' of unemployment

As was said before, one of the attractions of globalisation for big corporations is the fact that they can save on labour costs. This together with continued rationalisation and capital concentration has destroyed millions of jobs in all industrialised countries at a rapid pace. Whereas the profits of these corporations have grown to fantastic heights, this growth does not lead to new jobs. 'Jobless growth' has become a normal phenomenon in the North. Even in Germany the official number of unemployed was 4.7 million in February 1997. This figure is higher than that of 1933, when it was less than 4.5 million (*Frankfurter Rundschau*, 3 February 1997)

Not only blue-collar workers are losing their jobs; highly qualified persons working in banking, insurance and industry are also becoming 'surplus' labour. For example, the fact that well-qualified persons in places like Bangalore or Hyderabad in India are able to do the same work in the software industry as

German or Dutch workers, but for a much lower wage, has led to massive closures or relocations of such industries in the North. Corporations like Siemens, Texas Instruments, Microsoft, Toshiba and Compac have relocated large parts of their software work. This has destroyed millions of jobs in the North. Martin and Schumann write that IBM, Digital Equipment and Siemens-Nixdorf eliminated more than 10,000 jobs by establishing daughter firms in Bangalore (Martin and Schumann 1996: 143). They estimate that of 200,000 jobs in the German software industry eventually only 2,000 will remain.

What is true for the computer and software sector is equally true for the service sector, for banking and insurance. The modernisation and globalisation of this sector – usually praised as the new job creator – will indeed destroy more jobs than it will create. Already the combined processes of globalisation, automation and rationalisation have abolished 40 million jobs in twenty-three OECD countries. The World Bank and other research institutions have come to the conclusion that 15 million people will lose their jobs in the EU. These numbers have to be added to the existing unemployment figures in the EU. After their analysis of the job situation in the OECD countries, Martin and Schumann are of the opinion that even in Germany the unemployment rate could rise from 9.7 per cent (in 1996) to 21 per cent (Martin and Schumann 1997: 146 ff.).

What is worse than the rising or stagnant figures of joblessness is the fact that politicians and economists have no idea how they should fill the 'black hole'. On the one hand they firmly believe in the neoliberal credo of globalisation, liberalisation, privatisation, rationalisation and competition, which destroys jobs, as they know; on the other they don't know how to create new jobs. So far they have no other solution to offer than the one that some twenty years ago we called the 'housewifeisation' of labour.

'Black holes' of financial warfare

One of the reasons why governments are cutting down on their expenses for social security, public education, health and environmental projects are the 'black holes' in their financial budgets. These 'black holes' are partly a consequence of the fact that banks and corporations that operate transnationally hardly pay taxes in their 'home' countries. These corporations can avoid paying taxes by moving their base to tax paradises. But they benefit at the same time from any governmental subsidy for industry. Thus a corporation like BMW in 1988 paid DM 545 million as taxes to the German state. In 1992 it paid only 6 per cent of that sum. From 1980 onwards the tax income of the German state from corporation profits sank from 37 to 25 per cent. Big TNCs pay less and less into the state's coffers (Martin and Schumann 1997: 271–2). That means that normal taxpayers have to carry by far the greatest bulk of the tax burden.

Since 1980 the taxes paid by wage workers and employees in Germany have risen by 163 per cent, while those paid by corporations and owners of private assets have risen only 33 per cent.

The scandal of 'black holes' in state treasuries is not only that they are a redistribution from the bottom of the iceberg economy to its peak but also that the nation-states see no possibility of controlling the free capital transfers of globally operating banks, corporations and speculators. One of the pillars of democracy and national sovereignty is the state's sovereign right to collect taxes. For global capital this sovereignty no longer counts. Neoliberalism has finally 'liberated' capital from all obligations and restrictions that democratically elected governments had used so far to control capitalism. Those who had believed that it is possible to 'humanise' capitalism must now realise that the neoliberal globalised market economy cannot be tamed by national governments. Capitalism now shows its true inhuman face, a face it always had shown to the colonies.

Globalisation has not only caused big black holes in state treasuries. The sudden financial crises in 1997–98 in Asia, Russia and Latin America sent waves of panic also through the guardians and promoters of the neoliberal credo. The irony is that the breakdown of the finance systems in Asia and Russia is not due to the fact that they did not follow their neoliberal teachers in the World Bank, the IMF and the think-tanks of the USA. They all followed obediently the free trade dogmas which demanded that all government controls over the free flow of capital should be removed.

Michel Chossudovsky has shown that the financial crises in Asia as well as those in Russia and in other parts of the world did not just happen like natural disasters – that they are the outcome of 'financial warfare' based on the manipulations of market forces by powerful actors, including transnational banks, the IMF and speculators. According to Chossudovsky this financial and economic warfare will lead to a 'recolonisation' of the world.

> No need to recolonize lost territory or send in invading armies. In the late twentieth century, the outright 'conquest of nations', meaning the control over productive assets, labour, natural resources and institutions, can be carried out in an impersonal fashion from the corporate boardroom: commands are dispatched from a computer terminal, or a cell phone. The relevant data are instantly relayed to major financial markets – often resulting in immediate disruptions in the functioning of national economies. (Chossudovsky 1998: 6)

In this warfare the IMF plays an important role, because since the Mexican crisis in 1994–95 the IMF bail-out operations for destabilised economies have not really rescued these countries but have instead opened up key sectors of their economies to be privatised and sold off to the world's largest merchant banks.

The world's largest money managers set countries on fire and are then called in as firemen (under the IMF 'rescue plan') to extinguish the blaze. They ultimately decide which enterprises are to be closed down and which are to be auctioned off to foreign investors at bargain prices. (Chossudovsky 1998: 8)

While 'vulture foreign investors' gain from these induced crises, national economies collapse, unemployment rises overnight, governments are unable to pay wages, poverty and hunger return all of a sudden to countries that have followed the neoliberal path to prosperity.

The leaders of the world economy have no explanations for the sudden breakdown of the economies in Asia, Russia and Latin America. They are afraid that the financial crises there could develop into a full-fledged worldwide recession which could also include the USA and Europe. But instead of giving up their faith in the neoliberal paradigm they continue to preach the same dogmas of privatisation, liberalisation, deregulation. They are unable to draw lessons from the reality, namely that their theories have just created black holes all over the world.

The great confusion: from theory to religion

The chaos neoliberalism has caused in the real economy has its counterpart in the confusion found in the theoretical explanations of 'black holes' yawning everywhere, and in the solutions offered to fill them. Economists describe how globalisation affects different sectors of the economy. And according to their standpoint they evaluate this positively or negatively. But they usually do not explain *why* in the industrialised countries of the North, after more than twenty boom years following the Second World War, the Keynesian model came to an end; *why* successful welfare states like Sweden all of a sudden could no longer continue as before; *why* the women in Sweden, who worldwide so far had gained most from this welfare state and were considered a model for emancipatory politics, were now relegated to the 'normal' European patriarchy.

The confusion is particularly remarkable when one looks at the solution offered to fill the 'black holes' of unemployment. The following statements may serve as illustrations for this confusion:

We still use the traditional concept of the full-time industrial labourer, although there are many people who are employed under labour relations which are different from these normal labour relations. These are not full-time wage labourers proper but have contracts on casual labour or are fake 'self-employed' who no longer work in a factory. I think we have to consider such new labour relations in our collective bargaining policy. (Walter Riester, IG Metall, *Frankfurter Rundschau*, 20 March 1997)

This statement made by a trade union leader shows that the trade unions have not yet started to develop a new labour concept which would include paid and unpaid labour – a task feminists had already done twenty years ago. Now, when flexibilisation and housewifeisation of labour is the main strategy of the TNCs for lowering labour costs, the trade unions have no theoretical tools to explain this process.

But the confusion on the part of the big corporations and their spokesmen is no less remarkable. Helmut Maucher, the chief executive officer of Nestlé and president of the International Chamber of Commerce (ICC), expressed this theoretical confusion clearly:

> Indeed, you can't explain to a normal person why the stock exchange prices rise day after day and yet more and more people are thrown out of their jobs. Yet it remains true, on the other hand, that competitiveness is finally the safest method to create jobs – even if the road towards this goal may sometimes be rough. (Maucher, quoted by von Werlhof 1998: 166)

Even though the belief in the dogma of the miraculous capacity of competitiveness to create more jobs does not stand the test of reality, even though this gap between dogma and reality is admitted by a leading figure of international capital, he still prefers to uphold his faith rather than draw a lesson from the real economy.

This example shows that the neoliberal theory is a religious faith rather than a scientifically tested theory. One of the dogmas of this religion says, 'Without competitiveness no investment. Without investment no jobs' (von Werlhof 1998: 166). The knowledge that this dogma is false does not result in the giving up of this religion. The reason for the incapacity to draw a lesson from reality is the firm belief that There Is No Alternative (TINA) to neoliberal capitalism – a belief spread all over the world since 1989, the Fall-of-the-Wall year.

That neoliberalism is indeed a religion and that commonsense rationality has given way to confusion and faith can also be seen in statements made by analysts and leaders of international finance capital on the financial meltdown in Asia, Russia, Latin America and the sudden crisis of confidence of international investors that followed. One observer describes the situation thus:

> One had the impression of being at the funeral of globalisation. But the mourners could not decide to accept the evidence of this death. They could not show any clarity of mind because they were locked into an attitude of denial. The breaking down of globalisation caused an intellectual crisis in them which resembled a religious crisis. (William Pfaff, 'The Crunch has a Message for Europe's Central Bank' *International Herald Tribune*, 16 October 1998, quoted by Bernard Cassen in the German version of *Le Monde Diplomatique*, November 1998, p. 8)

After the crash on the New York Stock Exchange on 31 August 1998 and later r the collapse of the speculative hedge funds on 23 September, panic seized en the mightiest banker in the world, Alan Greenspan, chief of the Federal Reserve Bank of the USA. He is reported to have said: 'I've never seen anything like that' (Bernard Cassen, *Le Monde Diplomatique*, November 1998, p. 8).

Panic, confusion, irrationality, religious dogmatism seem to characterise the leaders of the globalised economy today. But not only the national and international leaders of this economy, but also most of the 'normal' citizens in the rich countries of the North suffer from the same TINA syndrome as those at the top. 'There is no alternative' is the sentence most often heard when one tries to criticise the logic and the results of neoliberal capitalism. One reason for the widespread confusion, pessimism and religious attitude expressed in the TINA syndrome is blind belief in the axioms and basic assumptions, on which the theoreticians of the capitalist economy have constructed their dogmas.

The capitalist creed

At the meeting of the international campaign against the Multilateral Agreement on Investments held on 17–20 October 1998 in Paris, the following eight Articles of Faith of the neoliberal religion were distributed. They contain the quintessence of neoliberalism as it was formulated in the early 1970s, becaming known as the 'Washington Consensus' (Clarke and Barlow 1997: 14–15).

The eight articles of faith

1. There is no development without economic growth.
2. A growing national income automatically trickles down to benefit all members of society.
3. The integration of local and national economies in the world economy is a blessing to everybody.
4. The liberalisation of international trade enables every nation to make the best use of its comparative advantages in the international division of labour.
5. The liberalisation of international capital flows results in a better allocation of the means of production.
6. Technological innovation will compensate for the ecological flaws of the present production system.
7. Private property rights are not only the best system to deal with scarcity, but also suit human nature better than any other system.
8. The direct involvement of the nation-state in economic life always results in inefficiency and corruption.

We would like to add a few more to the above list of economic dogmas. They are the following:

a. Man is selfish. All economy is based on individual self-interest.
b. Nature is stingy. Economy has always to do with scarce resources.
c. Human needs are basically unlimited and insatiable.
d. A modern economy must permanently grow. Only 'productive work' is 'work'.

In what follows we criticise some of these dogmas from a subsistence perspective.

Man is selfish (articles a and 7)

If the fathers of capitalist theory (Hobbes, Smith, Locke) had chosen a mother instead of a single bourgeois male as the smallest economic unit for their theoretical constructions they would not have been able to formulate the axiom of the selfish nature of human beings the way they did. They would have realised that human beings can be both selfish and altruistic, both aggressive and caring. They would have seen that human life is not just 'solitary, poor, nasty, brutish, and short' and that the law of history is not only the 'war ... of every man against every man' (Hobbes); they would have been able to observe that people cooperate with each other, live in communities, can be peaceful and merciful and, in spite of hardships, enjoy and celebrate life.

Lieselotte Steinbrügge has shown that the Enlightenment philosophers of the eighteenth century were clearly aware of the difficulty the capitalist philosophy of the self-interested, competitive, rationally calculating, individualistic *homo oeconomicus* would create for society. What would happen, they asked, to mercy, peace, love, generosity etcetera?

They solved this difficulty by separating the public from the private sphere and creating two different kinds of ethics, one for the private, the other for the public sphere. The responsibility for 'private' values was then relegated to women, while men could pursue their 'war of all against all' in the public sphere of politics, militarism and economics (Steinbrügge 1987).

Resources are scarce (articles b and 7)

The anthropology of the lonely, egotistic, male human warrior fits well into the cosmology based on a concept of nature as principally poor, stingy, with permanently scarce resources. As Carolyn Merchant has plausibly demonstrated, before the Renaissance nature was conceptualised as generous Mother Nature, a female organism with inexhaustible wealth and resources (Merchant 1980). But the theoreticians of capitalist patriarchy, above all Bacon, turned her into a stingy witch from whom 'rational man' has to extract her treasures by coercion and torture.

From the Renaissance onwards all precapitalist and pre-industrial peoples have been looked upon as poor (backward), always busy collecting or producing the basic requirements for survival: food, clothing, shelter. They supposedly have no time for the 'higher' things in life: culture and education.

Concepts like 'natural man', 'primitives', 'Stone age people' express this valuation. In contrast to these 'primitives', capitalist industrial society appears to be
the creator of all wealth, culture and surplus.

Marshall Sahlins has convincingly demonstrated that 'Stone-Age economies',
both past and present ones, are the originally affluent societies. He defines an
affluent society as one 'in which all the people's material wants are easily
satisfied' (Sahlins 1974/1984: 1). 'Easily satisfied' can mean either that people
'desire little' or that they are readily able to 'produce more'. Capitalism has
chosen the second path. This is the reason, according to Sahlins, why it had to
introduce the concept of scarcity. This system is based on the assumption 'that
man's wants are great, not to say infinite, whereas his means are limited,
although improvable: thus the gap between means and ends can be narrowed
by industrial productivity' (Sahlins 1974/1984: 2).

Industrial productivity then, is the means to create affluence. But in order
to produce a wealth of goods, not only must the concept of scarcity be accepted
as the most basic economic assumption, scarcity must be factually created in
and by the very structures of the economy:

> The market-industrial system institutes scarcity, in a manner unparalleled
> and to a degree nowhere else approximated. Where production and
> distribution are arranged through the behaviour of prices, and all liveli-
> hoods depend on getting and spending, insufficiency of material means
> becomes the explicit, calculable starting point of all economic activity. The
> entrepreneur is confronted with alternative investments of a finite capital,
> the worker, (hopefully) with alternative choices of remunerative employ,
> and to the consumer ... consumption is a double tragedy: what begins in
> inadequacy will end in deprivation ... the market makes available a dazzling
> array of products: all these Good Things within a man's reach – but never
> all within his grasp. Worse, in this game of consumer free choice, every
> acquisition is simultaneously a deprivation, for every purchase of something
> is a forgoing of something else. (Sahlins 1974/1984: 4)

In the capitalist system, scarcity is structurally necessary and built into its
functioning. In a system that is driven mainly by the motive of constant growth
of money and because capital cannot say 'It is enough', there is no concept of
sufficiency. Because of this it is necessary that people *believe* that nature does
not provide enough and that the circle of work–money–commodities– consumption is the only way to escape scarcity, hunger or 'mere subsistence'.

According to Sahlins, 'mere subsistence' is one of the concepts by which the
myth of scarcity was created and is constantly being upheld. It serves at the
same time to devalue the subsistence economies of non-industrialised peoples
and also creates totally erroneous impressions of the life of past and present
'Stone Age people'. This impression is in no way corroborated by empirical fact.

Among the Aborigines in Australia or the Bushmen of the Kalahari desert in Africa, men and women do not have to work more than six hours a day to get enough and diverse food, rich in calories. Sahlins quotes the findings of Lee's study on the Bushmen. They 'worked' only 2.5 days per week. The men worked as hunters, the women as gatherers. On an average their workday was six hours for both genders. In spite of that short working day they consumed 2140 calories a day. What they did not consume they gave to their dogs (Sahlins 1974/1984: 20ff.).

Whatever one may think of the lifestyle of these 'Stone Age people' one thing is certain. They were not poor and they did not starve. On the contrary they were rich societies. They worked less than 'civilised' people, their food was healthier, richer in calories and diversity than the average for the 800 million people in the world whom the FAO defines as malnourished. According to the FAO, the average daily calorie intake of people living south of the Sahara is 1,300 calories (FAO 1996). This is much less than the calorie intake the pygmies of the Kalahari have obtained with much less work. At least so long as they were not colonised and subjected to modern 'development'.

In conclusion, we can say that hunger, malnutrition, scarcity and poverty are not caused by stingy nature or underdeveloped labour productivity. They are also not the result of unchecked population growth. They are the outcome of a mode of production that can never say, It is enough! Patriarchal capitalism is the father of scarcity, not mother nature.

But it is not only capitalist economics that is based on the axiom of universal and perennial scarcity. Marxism and socialism too have accepted the assumption of scarcity as the starting point for developing a new utopia.

Human needs are infinite (articles b and 1)

This article of faith stands in total contradiction to our daily experience in the 'real economy'. All our basic needs for food, clothing, shelter, warmth etcetera can be satisfied. They are not insatiable. Even so-called 'higher wants' – for instance for knowledge, culture, mobility, friendship, recognition, respect – love – are not infinite. They can be satisfied here and now . It is precisely one of the problems of the growth-oriented market economy that people's needs are so 'inflexible'. To solve this problem of finite needs in a finite world, capitalism had to transform needs into wants and addictions by producing ever more and ever more fashionable 'satisfiers' (Max-Neef et al. 1989). Only when thirst will no longer be quenched by water but only by Coca-Cola or wine or beer is it possible to extend the production of these and other beverages limitlessly. If such needs as thirst can be transformed into addictions and their satisfiers into pseudo-satisfiers, a limitless production of such commodified pseudo-satisfiers is possible (Mies and Shiva 1993).

But even in spite of these strategies to stimulate consumption beyond the satisfaction of needs, one of the main problems of globalised capitalism is the limits to further expansion of markets. This problem is not only one of overproduction *vis-à-vis* the lack of purchasing power of masses of people in the South, it is also that the classes with purchasing power, the middle classes worldwide, already have most of the goods, both material and immaterial, which the market economy produces. In order to overcome this limit the corporations spend billions on advertising their products. Trainer estimates that industry worldwide each year spends US$100,000 million on advertising. On the other hand they produce more and more throwaway articles or goods with inbuilt obsolescence.

In a subsistence society, on the other hand, all human needs would be really satisfied. This means that people would not have to turn to pseudo-satisfiers which at the same time stimulate further compensatory consumption because real needs are never satisfied. Pseudo-satisfiers and compensatory consumption lose their attraction if people and communities themselves produce what they need, and see in their own activity a connection between productive activity and consumption. These needs will not be infinite; they will be satisfied. True satisfaction always requires an element of self-activity. In a society where people are increasingly becoming mere consumers, without the satisfaction of producing (or doing anything meaningful), whole supermarkets full of goods and all the money in the world cannot buy true satisfaction. If people can see meaning in the work they do, the things they produce, if work is not only alienated wage labour, the supposed limitlessness of our needs will be drastically reduced.

The economy must permanently grow – only 'productive' work is work (articles d, 1 and 2)

This is the most prominent article of faith of (neoliberal) capitalism: without growth no development, without growth the whole economy will stagnate and collapse. Economists define growth as the increase of all goods and services produced and marketed in the course of one year in one country. The sum of this growth is measured in the GDP or GNP (gross domestic product, or gross national product). If, at the end of the business year, the GNP has not grown by at least 2 per cent it is said that the economy is in crisis. Joblessness grows and firms go bankrupt. Trainer has calculated what would happen by the year 2060 with a yearly growth rate of 2 per cent: we would have an output of goods and services eight times the one we have now. One does not need much imagination to understand what this would mean for the environment, for natural resources, for people in the South, for labour and for the relations between nations (Trainer 1996: 21).

But why and how was this indicator of growth, GNP/GDP, created in the first place? What does it measure, what not? Marilyn Waring has convincingly demonstrated that the bulk of the work done on this planet is *not* included in this indicator, namely the work of housewives and mothers, the work of subsistence peasants and artisans, most of the work in the informal sector, particularly in the South, and, of course, the self-generating activity of mother nature. All this production and work does not *count*. On the other hand all destructive work – like wars, environmental and other accidents, oil spills, arms production, trade and so on – is included in GDP, because it 'creates' more wage labour, more demand and economic growth. The oil spill of the *Exxon Valdez* along the Canadian Pacific coast some years ago has resulted in the biggest rise so far in Canada's GNP – because it required an enormous amount of work to undo the damage caused by this catastrophe.

'Destructive production' is not only a secondary component of GNP. Marilyn Waring found out that it was invented during the Second World War by the British economists Gilbert, Stone and Keynes. They had been given the task of finding out whether the war was economically viable. And they came to the conclusion that the war was good for the British economy. A war economy, contrary to what people thought, would have a positive impact on the national growth rate. After the war the indicator they had developed to measure this growth was adopted by the UN in the United Nations System of National Accounting (UNSNA). It was then used worldwide to measure the economic performance of all nations (Waring 1989).

This, however, does not yet answer the question of why the capitalist economy has to grow permanently. In order to find an answer to this question it is useful to remember the main goal of all capitalist production and consumption. In non-capitalist subsistence (Sahlins 1974/1984, Trainer 1996) *use-values* are produced for the satisfaction of limited human needs. When they are exchanged in the market, use-value is exchanged for use-value, for example, potatoes against apples. Marx called this the 'simple circulation of goods'. His formula is C–M–C:

$$\text{Commodity} \rightarrow \text{Money} \rightarrow \text{Commodity}$$
$$c \quad \rightarrow \quad m \quad \rightarrow \quad c$$

But the capitalist production process has a different beginning and aim. It starts with money and its aim is more money. This is achieved by using human labour to produce *exchange-values*. Exchange-values have no other purpose than to be exchanged in the market for a higher price than their production costs. The formula for this extended circulation is M–C–M':

$$\text{Money} \rightarrow \text{Commodity} \rightarrow \text{Money}'$$
$$m \quad \rightarrow \quad c \quad \rightarrow \quad m'$$

In the next production round the increased money (money') is again invested with the aim of again producing *more* money (money''). And thus ad infinitum. Use-value production and exchange-value production realise two different economic goals: the one life, the other money. The aim of use-value production – we also call it subsistence production – is fulfilled with the satisfaction of limited, concrete needs. It makes no sense to work longer once one has produced the things – or services – one needs for a good life. Exchange-value production, on the other hand, is by its very logic unlimited. Its aim is extended accumulation of ever more money, or abstract wealth. The formula for this extended, unlimited accumulation is:

$$\text{Money} \rightarrow \infty$$

In this logic lies the basic clue for the understanding of the capitalist growth mania, not in insatiable human greed, as some think.

The contrast between use-value and exchange-value production explains why, in spite of growing GNP, in spite of extended accumulation and in spite of rising standards of living the quality of life has deteriorated at the same time, even in rich countries. Daly and Cobb have shown that from 1950 to 1990 the GNP per capita in the USA doubled, but that in the same period the quality of life measured by twenty indicators like environment, loss of topsoil, etcetera, deteriorated (Daly and Cobb 1989: 420). In conclusion we can say that today there is a contradiction between standard of living and quality of life. The more the standard of living rises the more the quality of life goes down (Trainer 1996: 28).

A subsistence perspective, on the other hand, insists on the priority of use-value production. It is based on the recognition that, on a limited planet, limitless growth of money and commodities can only be destructive. To avoid this we must strive for a cyclic economy. It cannot be based on global free trade and investment. A subsistence perspective can be realised economically only in smaller, regionally limited, decentralised areas. Only in such regional or local economies can production and consumption be integrated in such a way that the interests of the producers and the consumers are not antagonistic.

The subsistence perspective also means a radical critique of the existing concepts of labour and labour productivity. In contrast to exchange-value production, only that work will be called productive that really produces, maintains and enhances life, not the work that simply contributes to money 'giving birth' to ever more money. Life will no longer be only a side-effect of extended accumulation; instead it will be the main goal of work. This life will be the outcome of mutual, respectful, loving, caring relations between human beings, between humans and nature, between old and young, women and men.

Such subsistence work need not be remunerated by a wage, it can also be exchanged directly. This necessary, life-producing work will get a new value, a value not based on money – if men and women share this work equally and if subsistence work has a higher prestige in society than wage labour. In this sense the subsistence economy would be like the old *oikonomia* (household economy) of the Greeks, but without slavery and patriarchy. It would have more prestige than *chrematistics*, the mere making of money for the sake of money, an activity that was despised in Ancient Greece. But such a change presupposes a change in the hierarchical, sexual and colonial division of labour.

It also presupposes the giving up of the belief that there is 'no life without wage labour', and instead the development of a new concept of labour and a new valuation of wageless labour. We have already talked about this unpaid labour in the context of the analysis of housework. In a subsistence society where this unpaid work is shared by men and women equally and where it is given a central place in society, the loss of wage labour would not be a tragedy. It would not lead to exclusion, depression and loss of perspective. This is because people would not depend solely on wage labour but also on non-wage-labour; and non-wage labour would be more important than wage labour (see Chapter 7).

This, however, cannot happen unless communities have been able to reclaim and recover control over their most important common resources: land, water, forests, biodiversity, knowledge. In such a society the present contradiction between the conservation of a healthy environment and the compulsion to destroy this environment in order to create jobs would no longer exist. At last places of work would be places of life.

Increases in productivity are desirable and infinite. Technological progress will compensate for all ecological damage done (article 6)

The articles of faith that an economy has always to grow and that our needs are infinite correspond with the dogma that productivity growth has no limits. Productivity is defined as output per worker per unit time. This productivity can be enhanced by science and technology. A worker who works at a robot in a car factory can produce more than a worker in an old-fashioned workshop. An increase in productivity means that less human labour is needed for the same output. Rationalisation therefore means the substitution of human labour by labour-saving technology. Computer technology has enhanced labour productivity in an unprecedented way in recent years and economists calculate that it will continue to grow 2 per cent per year (Trainer 1996: 23).

Productivity growth has the appearance of a natural law. One labour-saving technology makes an earlier labour-saving technology obsolete. Like extended accumulation, the process of science, technology and productivity is conceived as an infinite upward curve. It is assumed that it will continue to grow until hardly any human labour is needed to produce the necessary requirements. According to this assumption the ratio between human labour and technology, the organic composition of labour, as Marx called it, will tend to decline more and more, until it reaches a point where machines/technology do 100 per cent of the work and human beings 0 per cent – where dead labour dominates living labour.

If, however, we look at the real economy we see that this article of faith of permanently rising productivity is a Eurocentric, male myth. We see that the impressive labour productivity at the top of the iceberg economy has its dark underside in millions and millions of workers, many of them women, who continue to do labour-intensive necessary 'shit work' to keep the whole production and reproduction process going. The history of the emergence of computer technology, for example, reveals that hundreds of thousands of women worked in Silicon Valley and in Southeast Asia under most brutal conditions and for a small percentage of the wages Western male workers demanded to produce the first chips. If all these women in the global computer factory had had to be treated and paid like male skilled workers in Germany, we would not have had a 'computer revolution'.

What we want to point out is that 'increases in productivity' cannot only be understood as simply the new inventions of scientists and engineers. These inventions need the cheapest labour to turn them into mass consumer articles. The superexploitation of Asian women in particular has to be seen as one of the factors when one talks of the computer revolution and the growth of productivity.

The result of assumptions that there is no limit to increases of labour productivity is not only the 'dark underside' of progress, namely poverty and violence, but also the fact of the making redundant of the workers themselves by this progress. It is often argued that progress of technology is good and necessary because it frees people from hard and monotonous work and enables them to produce more in a shorter time. But this argument ignores that science and technology are not being used by capitalists to make work lighter and more agreeable for workers but to save labour costs, to have better control over the labour process and to beat competitors by means of higher labour productivity.

The often-heard critique that a subsistence orientation is 'anti-technology' misses the main point, namely that the logic of a certain production system is *inbuilt* into its science and technology. They are not system-neutral. In a subsistence perspective, science and technology will have to follow a subsistence logic and not an accumulation logic. There will be technology, no doubt, but it will be a different technology (Mies and Shiva 1993).

It is a fallacy that technology as such increases productivity, saves labour and is able to undo the damages created by technology. We also have to remember that much of the environmental destruction caused by the combination of technology and economic growth mania cannot be undone, cannot be repaired. This is the case with nuclear contamination, gene-manipulated organisms, the ozone hole, the desertification of whole areas, the destruction of biodiversity. Modern technology and capitalist greed are only able to produce big black holes. They are not capable of filling them again.

The need for an alternative perspective

We have carried our analysis of the existing capitalist–patriarchal world system to its logical conclusion not to end on a pessimistic note and to leave everybody depressed but rather to destroy the illusion that we can continue to eat our cake and have it too. If we still want to uphold our claim for a humane society and economy for all on a limited earth, then we have no alternative but to reject the whole destructive paradigm and search for an alternative.

And we think this is possible now – for two reasons: first, more and more people in the world rebel against the commodification and monopolisation of life; second, even the guardians of this system are at their wits' ends. To fill the 'black holes' neoliberal capitalism has created, they simply suggest more of the same.

But criticising neoliberalism, the IMF, the World Bank, the GATT, the MAI and TNCs will not help us to get out of the dead end into which this system has landed us. A mere demand to restore the *status quo ante*, to reconsolidate the welfare state through Keynesian economic policies and more public spending, will also not do. We need a much more fundamental change if we want to establish an economy and society in which women and children are the centre and in which nature is not destroyed for short-sighted monetary gains.

There is no ready-made blueprint of such a society or economy at present, and there is no country in this world where we could find such a new social vision in practice. But if one looks around one finds a surprisingly large number of individuals, groups, organisations, networks and grassroots movements where people are asking themselves the same questions we are asking here. And most of these individuals and groups begin to ask: What would an economy look like in which nature mattered, in which women mattered, in which children mattered, in which people mattered – an economy that would not be based on colonizing and exploiting others? It is perhaps no coincidence that such questions are often asked by women, and that such initiatives are often started by women – not always women who have studied economics, but always women who are concerned about the well-being of women, children and nature. They are scattered all over the globe, both in the North and in the South. Some are more involved in practical survival struggles, others in the women's and ecology movements; others in the peace movement, others are doing more theoretical work. What unites them all is the fundamental critique of the dominant economic paradigm and the endeavour to find new ways into the open.[5] And they mostly begin with the same search for an alternative economics.

Is sustainable development an alternative?

The iceberg paradigm of capitalist economy, with its pyramid of colonisation and its destructive consequences, leads us to formulate a few theses about 'sustainable development':

- 'Catch-up development' is not possible for all people. Historical ([ex]-colonies, [ex]colonisers and actual differences between various types of workers in terms of gender, race, ethnicity and age are used to set one against the other in an antagonistic relationship. Thus, wage workers in the

North who lose their jobs as a result of the globalisation of the economy tend to consider 'cheap labour' in the South and the East as their enemy. This in turn exacerbates racism and sexism and further diminishes the possibility of equality for all.

- 'Catch-up development' is not even desirable for the comparatively few on top of the iceberg economy.
- To preserve the foundations of life on earth, equality, justice and solidarity, new models of society and economy are needed that can lead towards true sustainability, or subsistence, as we prefer to call it.

We try to avoid the concept of of 'sustainability' because it is flawed right from the beginning. 'Sustainable development' is defined as development 'to meet the needs and aspirations of the present without compromising the ability to meet those of the future. Far from requiring the cessation of economic growth it recognises that the problems of poverty and underdevelopment cannot be solved unless we have a new era of growth in which developing countries play a large role and reap large benefits' (World Commission on Environment and Development 1987: 40).

In the meantime the original intention of integrating environment and development in one term has been totally perverted. Today the concept of 'sustainability' is most frequently used by TNCs to legitimise their neoliberal growth mania. They speak only of 'sustainable growth'. We want to stress, however, that true sustainability and permanent growth or capital accumulation are a contradiction in terms. For a new vision of an alternative paradigm we therefore prefer the concept subsistence.

Main features of a new subsistence paradigm

1. How would work change?

- There would be change in the sexual division of labour: Men would do as much unpaid work as women.
- Instead of wage work, independent self-determined socially and materially useful work would be at the centre of the economy.
- Subsistence production would have priority over commodity production.
- Today, subsistence production subsidises the market (money) economy. This must be reversed, liberating (decolonising) subsistence production so that wage labour and the market (money) economy subsidise the larger social productivity, the production of life.

2. What are the characteristics of subsistence technology?

- It must be regained as a tool to enhance life, nurture, care, share; not to dominate nature but to cooperate with nature. Technology should value the knowledge available among people.

- Technology should be such, that its effects could be 'healed' and repaired.

3. What are the 'moral' features of a subsistence economy?

- The economy respects the limits of nature.
- The economy is just one subsystem of the society, not the reverse. This calls for changes in economic relations based on cost-benefit calculations and competition.
- The economy must serve the core-life system.
- It is a decentralised, regional economy.
- The goal of a subsistence economy is to support the subsistence society in the production and regeneration of life on the planet as a whole.

4. How would trade and markets be different?

- Local and regional markets would serve local needs.
- The primary function of local markets would be to satisfy the subsistence needs of all.
- Local markets would also preserve the diversity of products and resist cultural homogenisation.
- Long-distance trade would not be used for meeting subsistence needs.
- Trade would not destroy biodiversity.

5. Changes in the concept of need and sufficiency

- A new concept of the satisfaction of needs must be based on direct satisfaction of all human needs and not the permanent accumulation of capital and material surpluses by fewer and fewer people.
- A subsistence economy requires new and reciprocal relations between rural and urban areas, between producers and consumers, between cultures, countries and regions.
- The principle of self-reliance with regard to food security is fundamental to a subsistence economy.
- The important concept and practice of the commons can be reclaimed to resist the injustice linked to privatisation and the commercialisation of nature.
- Money would be a means of circulation but cease to be a means of accumulation.

NOTES

1. EPZs, Export Processing Zones, are so-called because their production is not for a home market but for consumers in the North. At the border between the USA and Mexico they are called *maquiladoras*. The TNCs chose Third World countries as sites for their relocated global factories because of the great differences of labour costs. In 1994 a

production worker in Germany earned US$25 per hour, a worker in the USA US$16, in Poland US$1.40, in Mexico US$2.40, in India, China and Indonesia US$0.50 (Woodall 1994: p.42).

2. The book *Silk and Steel* was written in 1995, before the present financial crisis in Asia had broken out. From all we know this crisis has only exacerbated the tendencies described above. The situation of women has dramatically deteriorated in all the countries of Asia. Due to the practical breakdown of the economies there are not only mass lay-offs of male and female workers, but also increasing direct violence against women (Mies and von Werlhof 1998).

3. This round of negotiations is so named because it started in Uruguay.

4. The FAO conference on biogenetic resources took place in Leipzig from 17 to 23 June 1996, and was thought of as a preparation for the World Food Summit in Rome. At this conference, US interests took a stand against the resistance of primarily Southern environmental protectionists and farmers, who represent the right of the local farmers and communities to retain legal rights concerning their diversity of plant types and seeds, and who do not wish these rights given over to TNCs.

5. The most recent example of such movements is the one against GM food and genetically manipulated organisms. It started among Indian farmers but was taken up by consumers in the UK, the USA and several countries in continental Europe. It led to a questioning of the whole globalised economic system, particularly in the UK where the 'From Global to Local' campaign is explicit about its new economic goals.

3

Subsistence and Agriculture

Agnes and Lisbeth: land in women's hands

The following conversation took place in winter 1989 in Schönfeld. The participants in this conversation were the sisters Agnes Simon (A) and Lisbeth Reuland (L) as well as Sofia Bengel (S) and Maria Mies (M). Schönfeld is a small village in the Eifel with 150 inhabitants and 30 houses. It is approximately 100 kilometres south of Cologne. Up until the 1960s it was an autonomous community and all its inhabitants were peasants. Everyone, even the few families that earned their living as artisans, owned some land and was self-sufficient. Today, only four full-time peasants are left, and one who has an additional 'regular' job.

The Simon farm

A: My ancestors came to this farm in about 1850. They were my great-grandparents. There had been a wave of emigration from the Eifel then. My great-grandmother was from here, from Schönfeld. My great-grandfather was from Duppach. And they bought this farm then; I suppose that the people who had gone away from here had gone to America, that they needed money for the passage. Since that time we – that is, the Simon family – have lived on this farm.

M: How big is your farm?

A: At present, I have got 20 hectares of my own land. Now it consists only of pasture, I'm only doing dairy farming. Formerly we used to have sort of a mixed peasant economy.

M: Since when have you been doing exclusively dairy farming?

A: Since 1960, approximately.

M: How many cows do you have?

A: At present I have got twenty cows and 15 calves and ewes, and this is the average for me. Not more.

65

M: What machinery do you have?

A: I have a tractor, a mower, a loading wagon, a hay press and two hay machines to turn the hay and make it into rows. And I have a milking machine and a muck spreader. One milking machine is stationary and the other one is brought by tractor, when I go out to the pasture to milk the cows.

M: Is the farm in debt?

A: No.

M: When the machines become old, what will you do?

A: Well, I always have a basic stock of money as a precaution, for repairs or for when I have to buy a new machine. At times, I have been able to buy a used one which was still in good condition, so I could pay cash. I want to be able to think that – at least in a way – the income of each year, the gross earnings, is sufficient for my livelihood and for expenses for machinery.

Why Agnes chose to take over the farm

A: We were eight brothers and sisters, six girls and two boys. I, Agnes, was the seventh child, Lisbeth was the fifth. One of our brothers was supposed to do the farm work, he had attended agricultural college before the war and was to take over this farm in the future. This brother did not return from the war. And the other brother didn't feel like being a peasant. And then there was the flight from the countryside. Young rural people had been brainwashed into believing that the only decent and proper job was a job in urban industry. That such a job was better than farm work. You have your regulated labour time, a fixed number of hours only, and the free weekend and all those temptations. On top of that there were certain personal problems with this brother and his prospective wife. These two did not want to take care of our old parents. My brother even told our parents bluntly, 'You can go to our eldest sister.' Our parents, of course, refused to do that. And then he left the farm. What aggravated the situation was that we had already bought a tractor. My father had no driving licence, he was sixty years then, and we had already sold our horses. In this situation I had no choice but to get a driving licence for a tractor and start farming. It was spring; the fields had to be prepared and the crops had to be sown. At that time we had a mixed farm, we still planted potatoes, beetroots and other crops. My sisters helped me to hoe the potatoes, to weed the beetroot, to harvest the potatoes – in all that had to be done. And in between we had to do our garden. At that time my mother was still alive; she still had pigs and she bred piglets and took them to the market. That meant cash for us.

M: And that was a woman's job?

A: Pig farming and breeding piglets has always been women's work: that was my mother's work. That meant she had her own cash income. Of course, she also had control over money otherwise. My mother was an emancipated woman. A woman farmer, not a farm servant. But the financial burden on the farm was tremendous for us, I must admit. All personal wishes had to be postponed, because we had bought the tractor. Apart from this, in 1945 they had taken away all our cattle. We had no cattle stock any more – only four cows and two oxen in 1945. We had the French occupation here in our area after the war, and the French demanded regular delivery of cows and other goods. We simply could not manage to get a proper stock of cattle together. Because we had to live off the farm and we also had to sell cows and calves in order to get some cash.

The man–woman problem

M: You are a daughter who took over the farm. This is rather uncommon in this area. But even if it happens people expect that sooner or later a man will appear, a husband, to manage the farm.

A: Yes, that is what my parents also hoped, very much hoped.

M: But you did not get married?

A: No, I did not get married. I had known the father of my daughter for a long time before I had the baby in 1963. But because I had the farm now and was responsible for my parents I could not give up the farm. When I took over the farm I committed myself; it was not just a hobby one could give up easily. That was binding. But then I was already thirty and wanted a baby. And then I had this baby, Ute. At the time I gave birth to her we could not have married. And later, as life went on and things developed, I no longer wanted to get married. We had known each other for a very long time. He was a doctor, but he also had a farm. Afterwards we continued our relationship for a long time – we broke up only in 1980. We had tried to put our two farms together and have a common management. This we did for one year. And then the whole thing went bankrupt. We wanted to put our cattle together and shift over to dairy farming. He had only one cow and a calf. I had thirty-five cows. But during that year the debts grew over my head and we lost everything. And then we experienced the famous man–woman problem. Then I decided to go back to my own farm. I had only one cow left here in Schönfeld. From that cow we got milk and butter for our household. Slowly I made a new beginning here by breeding more cattle. But then the milk quotas policy started.[1]

M: What was that?

A: This policy started in 1983. Due to the loss of my cows in our experiment I had lost my milk quota. I almost went broke then. I had to fight with the regional government to get a quota back. I had practically to begin at point zero and slowly breed a stock of cows from my own calves. I did not buy a single head of cattle, none. Those were three bitter years. I lived literally from my garden produce. When I could sell a calf or a cow I was able to pay for necessary expenses. The milk we used in our own household. This one cow gave us enough butter and milk, for one whole year. This one cow!

M: Now I would like to ask you, Lisbeth, when did you return to this place?

L: I am married to a civil servant. His name is Norbert. He is a man who goes to his office regularly every morning and comes back in the afternoon. I found that this life is too monotonous for me. I was restricted to my flat in that city. I missed the contact with all the people which I was used to in Schönfeld. And then Agnes got her daughter. This was a very nice occasion for me to come back and get myself re-established here.

M: Where did you and your husband live?

L: First in Düsseldorf, then in Mönchengladbach. I always used to be homesick. But when I drove from Mönchengladbach to Schönfeld, and saw the sun rising behind Dahlem my heart would open and I felt at home immediately.

M: Yes. I know this feeling. The same happens to me when I come back here.

L: I can't describe how it is. When I had to go back I used to weep from Schönfeld to Mönchengladbach. I simply enjoyed being here. I enjoyed being with the animals. Everything is wide and free here. I need the contact with the village – yes, that's what I need. I need meaningful work. Yes. And then it happened that I simply hung on here. And now I won't ever go back.

From women farmers to housewives

M: But what do people think about you women managing a farm without a man?

A: Yes, they do sometimes ask, Is there not a man around on your farm?

M: What do you say then?

A: I answer, there are many men who work on our farm. But with them I never get the feeling that they do anything I don't ask them to do. It is clear right from the start, even without a word being said, that I am the one who gives orders here. But when I tell them to make a fence, they can make the fence as they like it. I don't interfere. Usually people who work with me understand this. I can rely on them.

M: Would it make a difference if there was a man on this farm?

A: Of course it would. Then I would not be the boss who gives orders and manages things. I have always been the boss here and don't want to change that.

M: But this is not common here. In most cases the man is the boss, not the woman.

A: This is because these women only say what they think their husband would want them to say. They themselves accept to play second fiddle because they feel that is what is expected from a woman.

M: Here in the Rhineland the traditional inheritance laws were such that daughters too could inherit land and a farm, not only sons. Many women here held on to their property in earlier times. But now we can observe that women are no longer interested in keeping the land in their own hands. Do these women still see themselves as women farmers as your mother did?

A: In our village there are only two women of my age who consider themselves to be farmers. They work in the same way as I do. The other women also do a lot of work on their farms as farm helpers. But certain jobs like taking cow dung and liquid manure out to the fields they won't do.

M: Do they drive tractors?

A: All the women here know how to drive a tractor. But certain dirty and heavy jobs they won't do.

M: Do they see themselves as housewives rather than farmers?

A: Yes, most of them. They think of themselves above all as wives. That is more important for them than being a housewife.

M: But all of them come from a farm and know the work. And what about your daughter Ute?

A: Yes, they do know all the work on a farm. And they know that this work starts early and ends late in the evening. That is what they dislike. My daughter likes to help on the farm. In the morning, before she goes to her job in a pharmacy, which starts at 9 a.m., she helps me to feed the cows in the stable, to clean the stable, and to milk the cows. At 8 a.m. she gets ready to go to the pharmacy. People do ask, of course, why she, who is even doing a PhD, still has to work in the stable. What kind of argument is this, I wonder? As if doing a PhD was incompatible with working in a cowshed.

'Peasants stink'

M: Where does this contempt for farm work stem from? Why do most young women refuse to marry a farmer?

L: Because farm work is looked down upon everywhere.

M: How did this come about? Did it happen automatically?

A: No. This contempt for farm work often comes from farmers themselves. This is what really annoys me. They do not have enough pride and self-respect, particularly the women. And they send their three-year-old children to the kindergarten. This means the children no longer learn how to handle a cow, how to touch the earth and to like and respect this work. Since children do not learn this from their early childhood on, they become alienated from the work their parents at home still do.

L: Here I must tell an anecdote our cousin Walter told us. Walter had been in a hospital in Trier when the following happened. There was an old man there, a sacristan from a small village. He was very old and the whole village loved him, and many people came to visit him. One visitor who came asked at the reception, 'In which room is our sacristan?' He got the answer, 'Just follow the stink from the village, where all those village women are, follow the stink!' This happened last week in the Friars' Hospital in Trier.

M: You say that the farm women themselves contribute to this devaluation of and contempt for farm work. Are there other institutions that construct rural women as housewives rather than as farmers?

A: Yes, this is done in part by the agricultural schools. Women who attend these schools are educated almost purely as housewives in domestic science. Their curriculum comprises nutrition, cooking, laundering, food, calories and health, etcetera.

M: You once told me that the Association of Rural Women propagates a similar image of women.

L: Yes, they conduct seminars on themes like: 'All around the apple' or 'How to rediscover old linen' – and they only had a few stupid patterns which they attached to old, often handwoven linen sheets. And their course 'All around the apple' was just a trick to recruit new members. They even recruited women of eighty.

M: What else does this Association of Rural Women do?

A: In my view this association isn't political enough. For example they do not teach the women how to oppose, how to resist. This is a strong organisation. They could mobilise women for many actions. It is not enough if their chairwoman, once in a while, poses for a photograph together with the district administrator.

M: Which issues should they take up then?

A: They should protest against the noise caused by those American war planes which use our area here as a test ground for their low-altitude flights. They should protest against the stationing of nuclear rockets here. They have stationed nuclear rockets all over our Eifel area here. Why doesn't the Association of Rural Women teach women how to resist this?

Relationships: old and young, neighbours, the village

M: I heard that many young rural women are of the opinion that many marriages fail because the old mother of the farmer does not give enough space to the young couple, particularly the daughter-in-law. They demand that the young couple should separate its household from that of the old people.

L: Yes, we know. But this suggestion is made more by the agricultural school than by the young women themselves. You hear it everywhere now that the young should have their own household, and the old theirs. This is not our concept of the relations between old and young.

A: I'm totally against this separating of the generations. I don't want to say that there should not be any free space for the young woman to retire to. A room of her own. But not like, This is *my* living room and that is *your* living room. On a farm there should be a common living room for all. I am also against the separation of the children from the grandparents. Children must learn how old people live and manage things. And the old people should have the small ones around them, the young, quick life. I am of the opinion that having small kids around them keeps old people alive and alert – being able to experience and see the joy of life of the children, their curiosity and zest for life. This is something the old people should have. And small children need someone into whose lap they can jump when they want to. This need not be the mother all the time. It can also be the grandmother. This would give the mother some rest, she could go away and have a nap herself. That is why I think the generations should stay together.

M: But you know that the modern trend goes in the opposite direction.

L: Yes, the grandmothers aren't even allowed to touch the children. You heard it yourself the other day when we visited Gisela. When one woman said she wanted to keep her children away from their grandparents. I was shocked when I heard this. I am of the opinion that grandmothers and grand-children belong together. Only thus is a basis laid for later, for the children to learn that there are several generations in a family and in society. So that social life is properly organised.

M: This touches already on the issue of future perspectives. This is a very important point. But let me first ask about the other social relations in this village, or relations with your neighbours. People always say that the village exercises a very strong social control on people. This is usually the case, I know. But you two are somewhat an exception in this village. You did not and do not follow the traditional norms and patterns. Did you have problems with your lifestyle in this village? How are your relations with your neighbours and the village? You do not fit the pattern of the typical housewife.

A: Our relationship with and in the village is very good. Also our relationships with our neighbours are excellent. This is an old, old neighbourhood. It was built up through many generations of children and grandparents. This always functioned very well. This is exactly what I mean. You must learn as a small child that there are borders you cannot cross. In your neighbour-hood also. But when we call out to the neighbour: 'Can you come and help us?' he or she will immediately stop the work and come over to us and help. And I do the same from my side when I am asked to give any help or service, no matter in what form.

L: Such good neighbourliness must be maintained when new young people come into a house through marriage. If someone calls, you go and help.

Otherwise you do not peep into their cooking pot. When we meet we stop and say hello and ask about good and bad occurrences. One tries to say a good word everyday when one meets one's neighbours. One does not simply run past them. There is always time for a few words.

Work – culture – joy in life – feminism

M: Can you tell me how you organise your day?

A: Our day always follows a certain rhythm. We get up at 5.30 a.m., then we put the milk from the evening before out to be collected by the dairy van. After that we drink a cup of coffee, then we tidy up the house.

L: And then we read. Reading, talking, for one hour. Or we talk about things we have to do during the day, how we shall organise our work. And we always have a book about which we talk. Sometimes we take only one sentence: 'Look what is written here: horrible! How do they formulate this!' Sometimes I get upset by one single sentence. Then we discuss this sentence the whole day.

M: What kind of books do you read?

L: At present we're reading Uta Ranke-Heinemann.[2] She has enlightened us about many things, for example about how badly women were treated by the Church in former times. We did know this before of course, but what were the reasons, what was the background? For instance the custom that women had to go to church after childbirth to undergo a special purificatory blessing by the priest. Before that they were not allowed to go into the street. We also read political books.

A: I sometimes like to read a good novel. Just now I'm reading *Grapes of Wrath* by Steinbeck. What he wrote fits exactly our situation now. I also like Heinrich Böll and Simone de Beauvoir. Novak is good for me. One sentence of his is sometimes sufficient to keep me thinking a whole day. I am also interested in knowing how I would act in a crisis situation. So I got myself a book called *In the Middle of Life*. I wanted to know why I react in one way and not in another. What do I like to read? Anything that makes me rebellious. For example Dorothee Sölle's books. Yes, I like her.

L: There are a whole lot of authors we like. For example there is Mitscherlich's *The Fatherless Society*. When I read such a book I think, My god, he's right: how clearly he has observed things. Or his *The Incapacity to Mourn*. The situation is really as he describes it.

M: This is true. And this has something to do with the old and new patriarchy. This will be our next theme.

A: Perhaps we didn't grow up in a traditional patriarchy. But in general one can say that we still have a patriarchal society. If you had seen yesterday's TV discussion, a discussion only among women … How they have to struggle in their careers. How they continually have to explain why they do things the way they do them. There was this policewoman who said that she too is at times astonished that she has to explain why and how she does a particular thing. That it is not simply accepted as a fact, as in the case of men.

L: If I meet acquaintances we immediately laugh, both of us. Because it doesn't take more than five minutes, never more than fifteen minutes, before someone asks, 'What has Norbert to say to this?' When I then grin, everyone around me knows what I'm thinking. And then I tell the person, 'You were fast. Only three minutes!'

A: The question for the man occurs very often when strangers visit our farm. Recently a car drove up into our courtyard – some agent. And he immediately said: 'My god – what a job! That is men's work.' I had to enlighten him there and then that there was no women's or men's work, but simply work as such. He looked at me stunned. Sometimes my brother-in-law helps us. I have observed that the male visitors immediately approach him when they want to ask something. 'Is this your man?' 'No, he isn't my man.' 'But then who is the man here? Don't you have a man?' 'Yes, I have several.' These are then …

M: Quite emancipated conditions! But do tell a bit more about your daily schedule.

A: We start our work at 7 a.m. Every day there is some specific work to be done. Today I had to take the liquid manure out, tomorrow it's the cow dung. We have to adjust our work to the weather, in the cold Eifel. And in spring certain work has to be done in the fields.

M: When do you stop in the evening?

A: Farmers stop when their work is done. That is usually around 7.30 p.m. Not always. In summer, when it is very warm, our work hours shift. Then I work longer in the evening, till 9.00 p.m., till everything is done. If we don't have to make hay we have a long siesta. We lie down in our garden, sun ourselves or do a bit of meditation.

L: Yes, we let ourselves virtually fall, in spirit, I mean.

M: What do you mean by 'let ourselves virtually fall'?

L: Fall into a deep hole. I must say, I enjoy this thoroughly, this stepping out of the everyday world. I also love to lie in our big meadow. There, I know nothing will come, from right or left – nobody crosses your meadow. If you lie in the midst of twenty acres of land, right in the middle, this is so marvellous, you cannot describe this feeling. Then I let the universe shine down upon me.

M: But then you have to milk your cows every morning and evening. Some people say you are tied to your cows, you are not free.

A: No, this is a wrong notion of freedom. I can even say that my work gives me ample opportunity to do all my gymnastic exercises for which other people have to pay: I kneel down, bend down, climb up and down a ladder, lift my arms, lower my arms, lift and carry things – all the movements I need for my bodily well-being. All of them I carry out in the morning while feeding our cows and calves. I press, I push, I lift, I run, I shout, I caress – all my personal bodily needs are thus satisfied.

M: And what about your feelings of success, of happiness?

A: For example, when a cow is sick and I manage to get her cured, this is for me a tremendous experience of success. There are so many such experiences of success on a farm that I cannot count them. But they are important. They encourage you to continue. For instance if you have prepared the field for sowing, or if the meadow is beautifully clean, or if I've worked on the fence and it is in order, this is just great.

L: Working in the garden also gives me feelings of success. You cannot describe it if you haven't seen it yourself, how wonderful it is when I have dug up the earth. The smell, you can't explain that smell of freshly dug up earth. You have to smell it. You have to take it in your hands, and feel whether the earth is cold or whether it is warm. And when you simply sit down on the ground and let the warm earth run through your fingers. What a lovely feeling this is. We did this already when we were kids.

A: That is happiness for me. It is happiness to see that what I've sown comes out beautifully, how the young plants develop. It is happiness for me when I lie down in our garden and let the sun shine upon my belly. Also, that there are so many people around us who like us, that also is happiness for me!

M: You said, Agnes, that you are free to decide what you want to do and when. But this concept of freedom is not the usual one, the one people have in mind when they say, 'I can do what I like.' Is it this kind of freedom you mean?

A: No, not like that. There are of course also necessities and compulsions. In my understanding freedom means that I can freely decide, even when I decide now to go and chop wood. That for me is meant by freedom.

M: That means within a framework of necessity you can decide what you do.

A: I decide freely about what to do with my income and about my expenses. This is also something I consider to be part of freedom.

L: Now, well, with your income you are not all that free. There the powers-that-be exert quite a bit of control.

Modern agrarian policy

A: This whole story started with the consolidation of arable land. That was the beginning. In our area this policy started at the beginning of the sixties. In this period some of the bigger farms were resettled outside the village. It took me quite some time before I understood what the aim of this measure was. Land was taken away from smaller farms and the argument was that these farms were no longer viable. This land then was given to the bigger farmers. The Land Consolidation Authority bought a whole lot of land from such small landholders and gave it to the big resettlers.

L: First of all, these new farms were relocated out of the village and set up at the border of the village land. This meant they could no longer directly sell their produce to the people around because nobody goes so far to fetch milk or eggs. They had to produce for an external market.

M: And the next phase?

A: The next phase started with the introduction of competition among the farmers. If I do not have fifty cows then my value is less than that of others. Envy also played a role. And the big tractors! The tractors played an enormous role in establishing new values in this process. For a young farmer, what tractor of what size he sits on is of crucial importance. I know that.

M: Do they really need these gigantic tractors? Or is it that these men need a big machine under themselves?

L: Yes, the young farmers want these big tractors; otherwise they will give up farming altogether. They do not consider their tractor to be a necessary machine. For them it is a status symbol. When they come along on such a tractor they sit very high – and they can look down upon people. They compete with each other for the biggest tractor.

M: And thus many get indebted, don't they? Can we now talk a bit about this later phase of the agrarian policy.

A: Yes, this phase brought the milk quota system. We mentioned it already. This system affected also the small peasants, even those with only two cows. The government had not fixed a limit; those who had only two cows got a quota for two cows only. They could not sell more milk. The big farmers were all indebted – those resettlers, tractor owners. The state had to bail them out otherwise they would have gone bankrupt. That was not the intention of the government, which favoured big farms. Therefore the big farms got a special subsidy.

M: How did you manage to keep your own subsistence farm in spite of this new agrarian policy, in spite of all those new laws and regulations? I know, for example, that you did not follow the rules of modern cattle breeding with artificial insemination and all that. You kept your own bull.

A: Yes, that is another thing that is not done any more.

M: Precisely, you do things that according to the new rules are not done. But tell me, how did you manage to keep your bull?

A: First we bought a young bull from good stock and let him graze with our cows. With artificial insemination it had always been difficult to know the right moment when a cow was in heat, and how to get her away from the herd, have her inseminated and then get her back again. And we noticed that using this procedure our cows often didn't conceive. It not only involved a tremendous amount of work, but also didn't function. The cows' heat got shorter and shorter. And the whole procedure had to be repeated again and again. And it was expensive: every time we had to pay DM100. The insemination station makes a lot of money. But often artificial insemination does not work. Moreover, our cows don't like some of the men from the station and then the whole thing is a failure. There was this insemination fellow from Gerolstein. The cows simply didn't like him. But with our own bull it's different. The whole summer he roams around with the herd. He is not wild, if you leave him alone. It is the same as in films about children in Africa who move around with cows and bulls freely, without any problems.

M: And there are no longer any problems now with your cows? Lisbeth, you know everything about cows?

L: Yes, for three days the bull follows a particular cow, in heat, he caresses her and tells her how beautiful she is or I don't know what he tells her. And when she is ready the thing is done. Really. And afterwards, when she doesn't want him any more, he leaves her alone. It's over.

M: Hence, there is never anything like rape.

L: No, never. It is such a stupid thing to say, 'He behaves like an animal.' Animals don't behave like that. No animal.

A: Because we do not follow the modern rules and procedures, we have beautiful cows and calves. Many people want to buy them.

Perspectives on the future

M: Your farm is not purely self-sufficient. You also produce for the market, don't you? You need cash and you must contribute to your old age pension. What are your plans for the future? Today one cannot expect that the young generation will continue farming, and that they will care for the old parents till they die. Your daughter, Agnes, became a pharmacist, not a farmer. What will you do when the work is getting too much for you?

L: Then we will simply stop farm work!

A: OK! – But where will the money come from for the pension fund? This is already my problem now. In the worst case my daughter would lease the farm. All I need is someone to lease the farm, otherwise I won't get a pension. And I would not like the farm to go to total strangers. If I could get my pension before sixty-five – prematurely – I would stop at fifty-eight. But then I'd need a successor. Or I would have to go in for the EU programme of taking land out of production.

M: But you would prefer your daughter to take over the farm?

A: Yes, I'd love that.

M: What is going to happen in the future? This private question is connected with the larger question, What is the future for agriculture in general? What would you want it to be?

A: Now, what I really want is generally that small farms like ours will continue and thrive. That is my wish. They preserve biodiversity, they practise mixed cropping – a small farmer will plant three rows of potatoes and three rows of beetroot for his animals. And they never talk of 'gainful employment' – what a stupid concept, 'gainful employment'! Usually this concept appears when they talk of women's work.

What is meant by 'gainful employment'?

A: Well, only what brings money is 'gainful' work. My mother always worked here in the house and I have always worked. Although I am the owner of this farm I am still treated as someone 'gainfully employed'. But my friend Maria works as much as I do but she is not 'gainfully employed'. That is because she does not have a job and does not work for a wage. But with her husband she earns their income.

L: All these small farmers here are basically 'gainfully employed', even though they haven't got any formal training as agriculturists. That's why it is important that they should remain here. It is not only the wage labourers who are gainfully employed, but also those who make their own living on their own subsistence farm. But in our economy they don't count.

M: Yes, they don't count. They don't appear in the statistics and in the GDP. It is the same with them as it is with housewives' work. I think the Association of Rural Women Association could make this one of their political goals, namely, to fight for another definition of work. To include all unpaid labour in the concept of work, or to do away with the concept of gainful employment and create a concept that comprises all work – all work that is important for the creation and maintenance of life, also the work for one's self-provisioning, one's subsistence.

A: Of course, also the so-called housewives are doing such work. They rear their children and they care for their families. Thus they are doing an immensely important job for society.

L: The Association of Rural Women could have thought about this issue long ago. Indeed they could have looked for adequate concepts and told the state, 'This is what it should be!'

Subsistence knowledge and feelings

A: If we don't want things to go the way they have gone in other parts of Europe – where you find only dead villages – something has to happen now. Isn't it madness that people allow everything to decay and disappear, so that young people don't learn any more how to sow lettuce, how to know when it is ripe and can be sold, how to make sauerkraut? And if they don't learn to grow or produce things in a garden, then eventually it will not be possible to bring anything to the market. All this would have to be learned from scratch again: how to make a kitchen garden, all the knowledge and skill needed to maintain it.

M: What are the skills and the knowledge you still have and what you consider necessary to be preserved?

L: For instance, I still know how to conserve meat, either by bottling it or by salting or smoking it. We still have a smoking chamber in our house. I also know how to make sauerkraut, and how to conserve beans in the same way, by fermenting them.

A: Yes, preserving fruit or vegetables in glass jars. I still do a lot of that. I make jams – we never buy any jam or jellies – and we make our fruit juices. We grow all our vegetables in our garden. We make our own butter. I can make cheese, and cottage cheese from buttermilk. Other cheese I could also make, but I haven't tried yet. I have no time for that now. I can bake bread, bread made from sour dough.

L: At present, we still could teach all these skills to the young ones. But in one generation's time all this knowledge will be lost. The young agriculturists only learn how to handle machines. They do not learn how to care for and nurture diverse plants and herbs.

A: They also don't have a proper relationship to animals any more, I dare say. Animals are only a production factor for them. They, of course, have no time to look after an individual animal. I heard from our vet that bigger farms no longer call for a vet when an animal falls sick. They immediately call for the butcher, that's less costly.

L: Yes, such an animal is then simply garbage. I feel, this relationship to the animals is the first relationship that needs to change. An animal is not a thing, it is life. And the same is true for the earth.

M: And that requires a caring and nurturing relationship?

A: Not only caring and nurturing but a loving relationship. I remember my father in my childhood, how he used to go over our fields. I can still see him before my eyes – I don't know how to put it … If I was to describe how God would go over the fields that was my father. Almost like that, when he went across the fields or followed the plough. How can I put it? Sometimes you see very old pictures, sometimes you see that man behind the plough. There is no hint of aggressiveness, there's a loving attitude.

M: Correct. I remember my father in the same way.

A: When these men were going across a field it was like the waves in a grain field.

M: Yes, yes, they had such a swing … a bit from left to right.

A: It would also be important to show how everything is connected with everything. This should be emphasised. The interconnections between our earth and us human beings on her. That should once again be taught to the people.

L: I always try to explain to the people I meet how wonderful this work, this life is. Why don't they see the beauty of the sunrise? Why don't they see and hear the birds, how they sing? There are some farmers in Schönfeld who still understand these things. One man in particular looks at all this in the same way as I do, and he also says, How great it is when the sun rises! And who also feels the same way I do. Because men too can feel these things.

Women and ecology

M: This, incidentally, was my last question. To see, feel and keep in mind and heart all these interrelationships, and to reflect upon the ecological problems of our time – don't you think that women's sensitivity is greater for all this than men's? What is your opinion?

A: In general you are right, I think. But there are men too, perhaps only few, who see this and feel about it in the same way. Who are as concerned about the ecological problem. For example that man whom Lisbeth mentioned. When we meet somewhere in the fields he stops and then we talk and talk, usually about these matters. He is lonely among his colleagues, of course, because he cannot talk to them about such things. They would immediately say: 'He's a bit crazy!'

M: I can imagine that those men whom you described just before, those men who need a big tractor under their behind in order to feel manly, that such men do not understand such feelings and thoughts.

A: Yes, they need to hear the noise of the tractor. Then they can't hear birds.

L: It doesn't even occur to them that they miss something. Two years ago, for example, the birds, the swallows came back too early. And then there was a spring frost and they didn't find any food. This is an ecological consequence of the fact that our weather has changed. The first batch of five young swallows died of cold. The parent birds managed to get the second batch to survive. I used to feed the swallows in our stable – they sat on the backs of our calves – with the flies from the walls. The flies were weak and tired because they had no food. Therefore one should not kill all flies with those sprays. Some of them have to remain so that our birds get food when they come back. The more we spray the fewer insects we have. We should think of this, even though insects may be a nuisance in summer.

M: Lisbeth, you have observed your cows so thoroughly. Can you tell me a bit more about them?

L: Of course, cows understand us. They greet us when we come to the meadow. When we say next morning we have to transfer the herd to another meadow, then the next morning they all stand at the gate and wait. They keep a special order when they come for milking. I only have to call one by her name, for example, 'Paula, come!' Then Paula comes. Moreover, they have their friendships among each other. Two cows will always be together. And I found that even their calves do the same. Therefore it makes me angry when people say, 'Stupid as a cow.'

M: You speak with your cows. But how is it then possible for you also to slaughter these animals?

A: I know that I am part of nature. I am not particularly a carnivore. That helps me. But I always say 'Forgive me' to the animal. It is a very strange thing. I can't describe it. In the beginning, when we slaughtered the animals here on the farm, I could never attend. I was not able to look the animal in the eyes. I always had to ask someone else to help.

L: It is particularly bad with calves. With pigs it is easier, I don't have such a close relationship to pigs. But that is the main reason we stopped rearing piglets. They are beautiful animals, but they are raised to be killed. Of course, it was also too much work. But slaughtering a calf whom I have known since the day it was born ... that was too much for me.

Postscript

On 1 February 1990 Agnes Simon leased her whole farm to a young farmer from the neighbouring village. This was the condition on which she was able to get her farmer's pension. The leasing contract is limited to ten years. She gave up farming on health grounds: with constant backaches she was no longer able to drive the tractor. After thirty years' work her monthly pension is DM613.

Land as the basis of subsistence

Capitalist patriarchy would like to make us forget our true origins, and to replace them with money, capital, machines and investments. We must therefore remind ourselves of the simple truths that *life comes from women* and *food comes from the land*. This is why the land and the way it is worked are for us the most important factors in an alternative ecological economy and society. Agri-culture (a culture centred around the cultivation of the soil) and the peasant economy are decisive components of the subsistence perspective.

In this respect we differ from most of the recent alternative approaches, whether their focus is on the 'local economy' (Technology Network in Berlin, and the work of Birkhölzer), the 'third sector' (Rifkin), the 'New Work' (Bergmann), or the concepts of the authors of the journal *Krisis* (Kurz *et al.*). All these contain elements of a subsistence orientation, but they do not take land and agriculture as their starting point. They have their roots in the urban milieu of wage labour.

However, once urban labour and unemployment are made the organising focus, it is difficult to recover the idea of the capacity for subsistence. In Britain in 1995, for instance, there were already four hundred LETS (Local Exchange and Trading Systems), in which some 20,000 members engaged in exchange (mainly of services) according to a subsistence principle, but there were only eight agricultural enterprises marketing part of their produce under the same system. The main reason for this, Tanja Loziczky suspects, is that 'it is not very easy for other members to offer a farmer services which he or she really needs, especially as unskilled assistance on the part of consumers often causes problems more than it lightens the producers' load' (1997: 32). In 1994, therefore, a 'LETS Eat Campaign' was started to encourage members to take up the growing and production of food and to teach them the necessary knowledge. For it was realised that a LETS could become a powerful alternative only if food was included within it (LETS Eat Campaign 1996, cited in Loziczky 1997). We would go even further and argue that without access to the land – either directly or through socially reliable mechanisms – dependence upon the world market, monopolistic corporations and their wage-paying jobs will continue to mould the lives of those who try to escape them by means of independent exchange systems.

But why is it so often difficult even for left-wing alternative approaches to take agriculture and the peasant economy on board? One major reason is that the peasant economy is seen, according to the spirit of the times, as a form of backwardness, as a dull tie to necessity, from which people are supposed to have freed themselves thanks to the 'developed state of the productive forces'. As the twentieth century draws to a close, there is thought to be no difference between the soil and any industrial raw material, as if agriculture were just one branch of industry among others. In our view, however, the soil or the earth is a very special 'material', which needs to be treated in a correspondingly different way.

This specificity was emphasised recently at a conference of the Protestant Academy in Tutzing, where the worldwide destruction of the soil was attributed to the fact that it is treated as just another industrial raw material. As a result of erosion, it was shown, nearly one third of the world's agriculturally useful land surface has been lost since 1960. In addition, the soil has been seriously damaged through hyperacidity (gas emissions from industry and transport), pesticide pollution,[3] oversalting as a result of water saturation, and soil compression by land and forest machinery. With this in mind, the earth scientist Stephan Raspe has demanded that the soil should again be regarded as a 'natural organism', instead of being treated as a 'lifeless substance'. And he asks rhetorically 'whether plant cultivation should be adapted to the soil or the soil to cultivation' (*Frankfurter Rundschau*, 15 April 1997).

As we see it, however, this question applies not only to plant cultures but also to social cultures. Which type of social organisation of agricultural production would treat the 'skin of our planet' with due care and attention? The maximisation economy of industrial farming is such that it inevitably destroys the soil, whereas the peasant economy has shown down the ages that it preserves the soil. In the rest of this chapter, we therefore draw out the differences between the two cultures, and ask what contribution the peasant economy can make today to a subsistence perspective, especially for women. Finally, we give some examples of subsistence-oriented agricultural projects and movements in the contemporary world.

Development of the productive forces versus agri-culture

Millions go hungry around the world – nearly one fifth of humanity. At the same time, immense surpluses resulting from hyper-technologisation are being held or destroyed in other parts of the world. Yet the UN's Food and Agriculture Organisation is not embarrassed to call for more technology (genetic engineering), and further moves to an open world market, as the way to combat hunger in the Third World. The reality, on the contrary, is that hunger is a result of technologisation (Mies 1996c). The US grain surpluses used for so-called famine relief have destroyed the indigenous millet market for African peasants (Imfeld 1975, NACLA 1976). The boring of deep wells in the Sahel in order to raise the productivity and therefore the profitability of cattle-breeding has dangerously lowered the water table and compounded the desertification effects of over-pasturing (J.O. Müller 1988; Comité d'Information Sahel 1975). The FAO's much-heralded Green Revolution, with its technologically generated maximum yields, has led in India, Thailand, Mexico and elsewhere to the concentration of land among those with the most capital, and to a veritable army of landless peasants (Shiva 1989; Paré 1979). If FAO president Diouff now admits that world hunger is a matter of unjust distribution rather than production shortfalls, and therefore a social rather than a technological problem, he is still only speaking half the truth. It would appear that technology and socially just distribution could be promoted in parallel and independently of each other. But in reality, technology is anything but socially 'innocent'.

Technology, or the level of the productive forces, is itself a social and cultural phenomenon. Yet most left-wing, supposedly alternative approaches take no account of this insight: they set up the achieved level of the productive forces as a kind of fetish, instead of making it the object of questioning. Thus, Gorz reacts with a classical faith in evolution to the subsistence-oriented proposal of an alternative economics, seeing it as a '*return* to *preindustrial* modes of production of *necessities*' and preindustrial 'craft production *for one's own needs*' (Gorz 1989: 166, emphases added; cf. Gorz and Hörl 1990). For his part, he wagers on the state and other organs of centralised power to effect a just distribution of 'socially necessary labour' within the framework of high-tech industrial production. For the sake of technology, then, he ends up with fantasies of totalitarian structures of power. We see socially necessary labour in a different way, as the labour that really keeps us alive. It should be organised not by a power stretching from the top down, but through relations of reciprocity from the bottom up – on the basis of access to the means of subsistence production, above all to the land.

Since the 1960s, *inter alia* as a result of development policy, the number of farmers in agriculture has been decreasing while hunger, malnourishment and food shortages have shown a marked increase. At least since 1978, when Joseph Collins and Frances Moore Lappé published their *Myth of Hunger*, it has been known that monocultural, industrial increases in production only lead to hunger. The idea that small-scale mixed culture cannot feed the world is, we also know, a deliberate falsehood.

Should we all go to live on the land?

Our stress on the importance of agriculture for the subsistence perspective often provokes spontaneous defensive reactions. Both women and men imagine with horror that everyone, themselves included, would have to go off to the country and grow their own potatoes. But this is a quite absurd idea, as we shall try to make clear in the following three points.

1. What we argue for is a subsistence perspective born of our own times. The conditions we seek to achieve are only ones that are feasible and livable for people in the world today; they are not to be achieved for some at the expense of others. We think that human beings today need to reinvent a subsistence-oriented form of economy and existence that is suited to conditions at the end of the twentieth century and to the reality of decolonisation.

2. A subsistence-oriented life and the development of a subsistence perspective are possible in cities also. Besides, the city is a historical fact. Our notion of subsistence, itself historical, is based upon analysis of real human life, and it is in this sense that it opens up a realistic perspective for the future. A static, 'stageist' concept, by contrast, ignores the subsistence-producing domains in the modern world – the very ones that we consider so important. For us, the whole point is to link up with what exists in order to work towards a feasible future.

3. The fact that modernity involves a generalisation of market and exchange means that historically older relations are imagined to be those of an autarkic subsistence economy, without either market or exchange. Conversely, modernity is pictured as the mere production of commodities,

without any kind of subsistence production. In reality, however, there have never been societies without exchange relations, above all in the case of cultivating groups. In today's world also, market and exchange do not have to be conceived in terms of cutthroat competition, as we have shown through our research in Juchitán (Bennholdt-Thomsen 1994). Subsistence-oriented exchange relations have also been preserved or reinvented in the core countries of the world economy (see Chapter 6).

Destruction of the peasant economy in Germany

When it comes to ways of linking up with other economic principles than capitalism, the peasant economy is a tradition available not only in the Third World but also in Europe. In Germany, it is essentially only since the Second World War that the peasant economy has been destroyed. In the West, it came under open attack with the Grow or Disappear programme of agriculture minister Josef Ertl of the German FDP (Liberal Democratic Party). Farms were supposed to become capitalist enterprises equipped with industrial technology; the rest had to disappear and their peasants had to be converted into wage labourers.

Whereas in 1949 there were still 1,647,000 farms on the territory of the then Federal Republic of Germany, the corresponding figure for 1995 was down to 524,800. Over the same period, the number of persons employed in agriculture fell from 3,742,000 to 571,000, with a significant acceleration in the rate of departure between the 1980s and the 1990s. 'In the period from 1981 to 1985, the annual rate of decline was still 2 per cent, but from 1985 to 1990 it went up to 2.6 per cent'; in the 1990–95 period it rose to 3.6 per cent (Deutscher Bauernverband 1997: 128).

Since the establishment of the single European market, this policy of driving out small farmers, analogous to the enclosures of the eighteenth and nineteenth centuries, has been pursued in every part of the EU (Wolf 1987; Krammer 1996; Hoppichler and Krammer 1996).[4] Farmers were also ruined by the allocation of EU subsidies, 80 per cent of which went in 1992 to a mere 20 per cent of enterprises (*Frankfurter Rundschau*, 11 November 1995).

Postwar industrialisation in both West and East Germany meant that as much labour as possible had to be shaken out of agriculture. The industrialisation of agriculture itself was supposed to raise output and cheapen food, with the result that wages could be lower than they would otherwise have been, or that a larger share of wages could be spent on industrial consumer goods. This trend has been making uninterrupted headway ever since. Thirty years ago in a middle-income household, DM30.70 out of every DM100 was spent on food items; today the figure is less than half, at DM14.20 (*Landwirtschaftliches Wochenblatt*, February 1997). As a consequence, the overwhelming majority of the population today rely upon wages and other money income to feed themselves.

For all the faith in money and economic growth, access to the land still evidently gives a feeling of economic security to people in Germany. Although the number of farms with an area of less than 20 hectares has fallen by 1,208,000 in the Federal Republic since 1949, and although the number of enterprises above 20 hectares has increased by 59,000, nearly half of all farms – 236,000 in total – are still below 10 hectares, and 65 per cent are below 20 hectares. In the new federal states in the Eastern part of the country, the total number of enterprises (most of them between 1 and 10 hectares) has been continually rising since 1991, as former farmers have made efforts to recover their land. Today these again make up nearly half of all farms (Deutscher Bauernverband 1995: 111ff, and 1997: 127ff).

A number of facts show that many small farms are being consciously maintained or restarted for the purpose of subsistence, without conforming to the dominant economic rationality. First of all, farms are often operated even when they do not secure anything like a reasonable price for their produce. One reason for this nowadays is the advantage that big farmers enjoy in the area-related system of subsidies which are given according to the number of hectares one owns. Those with a lot of land receive subsidies that alone are large enough for a family of several members to live on. Those with little land must find the necessary money by selling their produce. Medium-sized farms, in particular, have more or less the same machinery and buildings that larger ones have, yet they may receive in one year only as much 'state cash' as big farms net in a month. The smaller farms, for their part, often come away completely empty-handed. Many nevertheless managed to survive even the Ertl years, when they fell below the subsidy threshold and were expected to be forced into closure (Wolf 1987). Furthermore, many small farms are kept going as 'sidelines', which often involves their subsidisation by non-agricultural paid labour. In the old states of the Federal Republic, half of all units fell into this category in 1996.

A lot may be learned – not least for how things can continue in the future – from the mechanism underlying the death of farms: that is, the shift from a subsistence orientation to a profit orientation. The farms most likely to disappear have not, as a matter of fact, been small ones but medium-sized ones. It is these that have tended to believe the promises of agricultural association advisers, going into debt for the sake of investments that are supposed to turn them into profit-making enterprises. The farm thus ceases to be the basis of existence and becomes an object of speculation. Many farms have indeed had to shut down because they became too burdened with debt. They have gone into receivership. Farms that allowed previous generations to make a good living must now give up agriculture, because, it is said, 'you can't get by any more with such a small farm'. And nowadays, a 'small' farm means one of up to fifty hectares! The area necessary for a farming business to make a profit is, typically enough, known as the 'growth threshold'. 'The growth threshold below which the number of farms decreases, and above which the number increases, has risen since the beginning of the nineties to 50 hectares of agricultural surface area (AS). At the beginning of the eighties it was still 30 hectares of AS' (Deutscher Bauernverband 1995: 112). In Schleswig-Holstein, this threshold is now at 100 hectares, and in North-Rhine Westphalia it is 75 hectares. The lowest figure is 40 hectares, in Bavaria (Deutscher Bauernverband 1997: 128).

Peasant economy

In Germany as well as in Austria, Switzerland and other European countries, all agriculturalists, that is, all those who have direct access to the land and do not receive an agricultural wage, are called peasants (*Bauern*). In this concept, women are not included or, depending on how we look at it, they are silently subsumed. Besides the fact that this disposes of a proper word in German for the woman working on the farm (*Bäuerin*), the woman is also usually spoken of only in the sense of a farmer's wife, not in terms of independent female spheres of production. We shall look more closely at the patriarchalism involved in this invisibility of the work of the women on the farm. But first let us consider the ideological blurring that is already involved in the identification of all agriculturalists as peasants. Especially in German politics, this serves to cover up the distinction between big and small landowners, and to hitch the real (small) farmers to the waggon of those for whom agriculture is a profit-making business. The best example of the injustice this does to small farmers are the area-related subsidies that ruin small farms and provide the larger ones with extra profits.

What is distinctive about the true peasant economy is that it is carried on not for the sake of accumulation but for the reproduction of the farm and of the people living on it, to whom it has been handed down through generations. It is a question of a particular way of life, part of which is a culture of modest living. The peasant economy is guided by a different world-view from that of growth economics: it recognises the finite basis of economic activity in land, water, forest, plants and animals, and the need to operate with corresponding care and restraint. In principle, then, if not in every detail, the farm economy is also an ecological economy. The landscapes we love so much – heaths, meadows, fields with boundary hedges or ditches – are products of farm culture and not of the untouched nature that a naïve conservationist mentality imagines. Here we can see just how misleading the term 'peasant' is for agro-industrial businessmen whose activities are destroying the peasant landscape.

The peasant economy also involves a form of social behaviour different from the cutthroat competition of the modern world. An awareness of the limits of the world and of material goods entails knowledge that people are related to one another, and that everyone is entitled to have a place, as I have one myself. 'Live and let live' used to be the motto also in German villages, despite the (always only relative) differentiation into big and small pesants. People helped one another and came to agreements about things, conscious of the community as a living force. Of course, this also involved social control that stopped anyone deviating from the normative structure. Young people especially rebelled against this narrowness of village life, without realising the positive function of social control in preventing the enrichment of some at the expense of others.

Lying behind the 'live and let live' formula is the principle of 'moral economy'. In contrast to the economics of competition and growth, this means that every human being is allowed access to the necessary requirements for production so that they can maintain themselves in existence. All members of society feel an obligation to conduct their economic affairs in such a way that others also are able to survive, drawing assurance from the knowledge that their own basis of existence will always be safe. Social behaviour is thus determined not by competition but by reciprocity.

Here, a remark on the different concepts of 'peasant', 'farmer' and 'agricultural entrepreneur' is needed, and, at this point of the argument, also possible. In day-to-day English language the term 'peasant' has been replaced by 'farmer', to the extent that the term 'peasant' is an insult. But this illustrates only how contempt for those who take care of the basic necessities of life has penetrated modern thinking – be it contempt for the mother who cleans the shit of the baby or be it contempt for a peasant who deals with soil. But, beyond this modernistic ideology and taking into account historical facts, we come to another understanding of the terms in question (see also Shanin 1971; Wolf 1966 or in general the *Journal of Peasant Studies*). Peasants are those who participate in a common culture, based on the world-view described above.

The borderline of the category 'farmer' is blurring. A farmer is a modern peasant who produces in order to accumulate but whose profit normally has to be invested inmediately in the farm, its equipment and its machinery. He continuously has to modernise, otherwise he would drop out of the competitive agricultural market. This is because there are always bigger farmers than he is, who can afford to rationalise more and to produce more, and above all farmers with cheaper prices, mostly due to the high subsidies they are given. The typical farmers nowadays own a middle-sized agricultural enterprise; they are the farmers who have suffered most of the development in agriculture since 1945. In the process of 'grow or disappear' they have tended to disappear, leaving mostly only small farms, that is, peasant farms, or big farms, that is, industrial agricultural enterprises. In fact, the farmer is the victim of modern agricultural politics in the North. Replacing the term 'peasant' with 'farmer' was meant only to obscure this fact; furthermore, the change was intended to obscure the fact that in the South the peasant way of producing and living still embraces the majority of the people. Systematically to call them 'farmers' is to support the ideology of developmentalism, according to which the peasant way of production is underdeveloped, whereas the farmer way would lead to a golden, developed future.

However, when in German the term 'peasant' is systematically used instead of saying 'farmer' or 'industrial agriculturalist', something else is intentionally being veiled, namely the fact that most German agriculture is exclusively oriented towards profit-making and very little is left from the peasant culture of caring for the soil, the plants, the animals and the reciprocity within the village. But if we want an agriculture that produces real life-sustaining food instead of mere commodities for profit, then the peasant way of producing has to be sustained.

With the help of Christa Müller's report on research undertaken at our Institute for the Theory and Practice of Subsistence, we would like to point out that the peasant tradition in Germany did not vanish as long ago as we commonly think.

The peasant economy of Borgentreich in Westphalia

Until well into the sixties, local exchange relations corresponding to the principle of reciprocity still often functioned even in a Germany industrially armed to the teeth. In Borgentreich, for example, a village in southern Westphalia with a population then as now of about three thousand, as many as 95 per cent of the inhabitants were until a few decades ago either craftworkers or peasant men and women. But nearly every craftworker family also had one or more hectares of land, which were cultivated for it by the peasants in return for the services of blacksmith or cartwright, saddler or carpenter, shoe repairer or dressmaker. Both craftworkers and peasants were self-sufficient: they grew rye and then had it milled and baked locally, the miller and the baker charging part of the crop or a small sum of money for their services. In addition, every family had a number of pigs, goats and chickens, as well as one or more cows. A large part of life's daily necessities was thus produced by the family itself or by others in the village.

Cash played only a secondary role. Calculations were made at the end of each year and often balanced out – which meant that each of two parties had worked or supplied as much as the other and no extra money had to be raised. Since little money circulated at all, attempts were made to keep economic transactions as cashless as possible. A peasant, for example, would hand part of his crop over to the baker and receive a whole year's bread in return; or a carpenter would make shelves for the grocery store and draw from the 'account' provisions such as salt, sugar, vinegar or oil, until the sum entered in it for the shelves was used up.

There were other cases, however – for example, the making of a suit with material that had to be bought from dealers outside the village – when a written bill would be presented. Peasants, who had the least cash of any villagers at their disposal, might sometimes find themselves unable to pay their bills; but instead of sending them anonymous demands, the craftsman would usually be prepared to wait, perhaps vainly, for his money.

After waiting in vain, the craftsman would sometimes go to the farmer and pick up a couple of sacks of rye or seed, or maybe a few piglets. But as one master joiner put it, 'We also simply forgot about a lot of it.' The baker said that most people paid their bills at the end of the year, but 'those who hadn't a penny to their name got their bread for nothing; in the end you couldn't just let people starve.'

In the local economy, no one could take the liberty of sending demands for payment or of getting a bailiff to collect the money from poor people (most of whom had many children and little or bad-quality land). Had they done this, they would have faced a huge loss of prestige. Since everyone knew everyone else, people's fates were directly bound up with those of other individuals; their own claims had to depend not only on the work they had performed but also on their customers' ability to pay.

The passage from a moral economy to a maximisation economy took place on a massive scale in the 1960s and 1970s, and it is still being insidiously completed today. The process as such was quite unspectacular. Scarcely had the first cars appeared in the village when people began driving into the cities to buy things 'more cheaply' and holding their own products in lesser esteem. Horses were replaced with tractors, wooden wheels with rubber tyres, massive cupboards with fitted kitchens, evenings together on the village bench with television viewing on small family armchairs, and the farmhouse with a small-town family home attached to an intensively operated cowshed. (Christa Müller 1998)

Resistance against development: the case of the peasants of Chiapas

Unlike peasants in Westphalia in Germany, the peasant men and women of Chiapas have resisted the policies of development and progress. They too were tempted by promises and subsidies to abandon the subsistence orientation, but

they soon realised that a growth economy would be the end of the road for
them. Besides, unlike their counterparts in Germany, they were unable to
participate in the colonial booty of the world market.

Chiapas peasants and the failure of development

In the area of Chiapas where the indigenous population has risen up against
the pillaging of their conditions of existence – the phenomenon known to
us as the Zapatista revolt – Veronika Bennholdt-Thomsen spent several
months of 1977 doing field research. She saw with her own eyes the effects
of a World Bank project to 'draw peasants from subsistence to commercial
agriculture' (McNamara 1973; see Bennholdt-Thomsen 1988a). Instead of
maize, beans and pumpkins for their own use, they were supposed to take
out loans to grow flowers and high-class vegetables for a tourist paradise
planned a hundred kilometres away. In 1982 their passive resistance was
helped by Mexico's debt crisis. Project funds, machinery and personnel
disappeared from one day to the next. But the peasants could be grateful
that they still had their maize and bean staples in storage.

The whole of rural Mexico is dotted with the ruins of development.
Here, in a region with adequate rainfall, one comes across a little dam that
was never needed for anything other than the never realised plan to grow
tourist flowers. There one sees a pigsty that was never maintained, because
the meagre land can only just support the people living on it. They cannot
even afford the luxury of draught animals. An oxcart was therefore foisted
on them, to talk them into growing vegetables. But it disappeared along
with the World Bank project. (Bennholdt-Thomsen 1982)

Development ideologues try to entice people into the debt trap and
thereby make them dependent. *Endrogarse*, getting hooked on drugs, is the
word people use in the Mexican countryside for falling into debt. Woe to
those who get caught up in it! The dealers vanish as soon as no more can
be pumped out of the addicts, and the latter are left with the shattered
remains of their basis for subsistence.

But in Mexico, peasants have learnt to distrust the capitalist lottery.
Above all, they no longer feel hurt by the contempt that is poured on them
because of their subsistence orientation, by the way in which they are
insulted as backward, stupid, impervious to reason, and so on. They were
the first to perceive the failure of the development road, presumably
because their old farming culture made them unsuitable for brainwashing
by the religion of progress.

The contribution of Peasant Studies

When Christa Müller presented the results of her study of Borgentreich, she was greeted with almost universal disbelief and rejection, with an unwillingness to accept that the shift from reciprocity to competition, and from a subsistence-farming orientation to one of profit maximisation, had taken place so recently. Somehow or other, people did not want to be personally or, if possible, actively associated with the change. The process of dehumanisation of the economy had to appear as something inescapably necessary that had happened by itself in the far-off days of barbaric early capitalism.

This was also the approach taken by agrarian sociologists and agricultural colleges in post-1945 Germany, where the main preoccupation for teachers was how to overcome the peasants' way of thinking as quickly as possible. Only after studies of the peasant economy in the Third World had led to a degree of rethinking was the true history of Europe rediscovered and the surviving elements of a peasant economy, including its subsistence orientation, given some value again. The Bielefeld discussions of the 1970s and 1980s, which we considered in Chapter 1, made a major contribution to this revaluation.

It was in the 1950s that the new sociological discipline of Peasant Studies began to emerge. Its anthropological or ethnological premiss was that people's way of life should be grasped in its own terms, in contrast to the ambition of development sociology to find reasons for, and ways of overcoming, so-called underdevelopment.

A major role was played here by the Russian dissident Alexander Chayanov, who in the 1920s developed the theory of an independent peasant economy with a social and cultural logic of its own. In opposition to the official Soviet proletarian-communist line, which sought to turn peasants into *kolkhoz* wage labourers, the agrarian economist Chayanov upheld the peasant economy on account of its ecological and social adaptability (Tschajanow 1923/1987). This view cost Chayanov his life in the Gulag Archipelago, but his theory has since become one of the foundations of Peasant Studies. As he explained it, peasant economic activity is geared not to profit maximisation but to necessities; it plays safe and steers clear of avoidable risks. The farm does not close down if it fails to reach certain profit targets, nor is its capital transferred to another sector where expectations are higher. When times are hard, people tighten their belts, work harder and consume less. Good times bring greater leisure, and surplus income is not invested but used for festivities. The main priority is to maintain what already exists, both economically and socially.

One of the lessons of Peasant Studies is that the peasant economy has similar structures throughout the world, and that – however great the local and regional differences – the same kind of cultural characteristics are to be observed (Wolf 1966; Shanin 1971; Sahlins 1972). For the subsistence approach, these are more than just suggestive conclusions. People have to feed and reproduce themselves in interchange with nature. If they do this in the form of settled agriculture, the human physique and the natural processes of coming into being and passing away do not leave scope for many major differences.

Apart from subsistence theory, our main contribution to the debate on peasant economy and culture is to argue that the social position accorded to peasants since early modern times is similar to the social position of women as housewives. Only this enabled us to understand the special relationship between modernity and the production of food and life's necessities (and therefore subsistence), as well as to grasp the connection between social subordination and proximity to nature (which by no means concern women alone). Since peasants and women both attend to the immediate everyday needs of human beings, they do not count for much in a world where the overcoming of the realm of necessity is supposed to open the doors to freedom. This attitude can be found on both the Right and the Left, among feminists such as Simone de Beauvoir (1974) as well as among notorious misogynists.

What we can learn from peasant economy for the contemporary world

This subhead is an allusion to the title of Shanin's book *Defining Peasants: Essays Concerning Rural Societies, Expolary Economies, and Learning from Them in the Contemporary World* (1990). Economies that exist outside the two poles of the socialist and capitalist economic systems – above all, the peasant economy – are described by Shanin as *expolary economies*. The concept already contains the critique. An ideological fixation on questions of power politics – which is the better of the two systems? – has brought with it a blindness to all other kinds of economy that exist alongside, within, below or even in association with one of the two dominant modes.

Shanin uses the image of 'Midas's finger' to denote the ideological perception intrinsic to the modern economy. Whatever that king touched was turned into gold. And this is just how the prevailing currents in social science, economics and politics perceive the maximisation economy and its various social mechanisms; whatever it touchs is supposed to turn into a glittering social system. But that is just fairytale romanticism. There is a well-known line of attack on pro-peasant theorising as romantic, but the real romanticism is an obsessive fixation on the two poles. In other words, expolary economies are not as nebulous as all that: indeed, they are at the centre of economic activity in most modern societies. Yet they are perceived, if at all, as only marginal or informal (Shanin 1990).

An analysis of these sectors which, instead of focusing on their deficiencies, took a positive interest in how they actually function and produce results could teach us much of importance for the burning questions of the contemporary world. For one thing is certain. In Germany too, the informal sector will continue to spread as unemployment rises and social provision is curtailed. The question is, which cultural and social model can we turn to? Will it be the model of the lumpenproletariat? Or wouldn't it be better if we turned to the model of the 'social economy' which we will be able to learn from the peasant economy? This is what we ourselves think, in agreement with Shanin (1990: 16).

Not only culturally but also in a directly economic sense, the peasant economy reaches beyond agriculture as such. Its outstanding feature is precisely its combination of gainful production and subsidiary income. Thus, handicrafts and peasant agriculture have always been closely bound up with each other, not least in the processing and marketing of agricultural produce (Shanin 1990: 13). If we do not follow modernisation theorists in conceiving the peasant economy only in terms of male agriculture and foreign trade, but see it instead as an independent, household-based way of assuring the existence of a group of people, then the figure of the peasant woman comes plainly into the foreground. For the sexual division of labour is the foundation of the farmhouse economy. 'Without a woman, there is no cow, no milk, no cheese, no poultry, no eggs': this was true for the peasant economics of the whole house (Bock and Duden 1976: 126; Brunner 1980). And, as we shall show in greater detail, it is also true of today's farm.

Wage labour is also, however, part of the combined form of the peasant economy, whether as sporadic migrant labour or as the permanent labour of one member of the household. When Immanuel Wallerstein and the House-hold Economies working group at the Fernand Braudel Center, Binghamton University, identify the pooling of household income as the typical form of the informal sector economy, they come very close to Shanin's, or Chayanov's, characterisation of the peasant economy (Smith, Wallerstein and Evers 1984).

Peasant women and the subsistence perspective

In all the conventional literature on the subject, the concept of 'peasant economy' is hardly distinguished from that of 'family economy'. In this context, as more generally in twentieth-century society, the expression 'family' does not mean anything good for women. For the collective term helps to make women's labour invisible, as do the facts that the farm in today's Germany or Europe, like the farm in Russia before, is usually the man's property and woman counts as his first maid. Even if the woman has inherited the farm – which is possible nearly everywhere in Europe – patriarchal convention ascribes decision-making power to her husband.

This has not always been the case, nor is it so today everywhere in the world. Nevertheless, in the countries of the North, the social deprecation of subsistence production reaches a peak in relation to the peasant woman, both because of her position as an agrarian producer and because of her being a woman. One may well ask, then, how the peasant economy can be part of any perspective for women and for feminists.

To answer this question, we think it important to consider women's real position and their concrete social strengths and weaknesses within the farming economy of German-speaking countries and elsewhere in Europe. But since deep-seated prejudices and ideology distort the perception of women's reality, we shall also have to try to remove the veils of ideological discourse. In our experience, three aspects play an especially important role in clouding people's vision.

First, views of the past are often marked by a romanticisation of economic growth according to which women and men do not work as much, and especially not as hard, as they used to do. All previous ways of life are supposed to have been shot through with toil and trouble. Yet, with the help of data collected by Sahlins, we have already refuted this preconception in Chapter 2 (Sahlins 1972). Precisely in connection with leisure, it should be clear that peasants' low consumption levels involve far less stress than the maximisation economy.

A further aspect in the clouding of people's vision is the way in which contemporary women relate to the history of their mothers and great-grand-mothers. Nothing in that history seems to them to be worthy of imitation. Since those forebears did not create the kind of women's world that now appears desirable (one all too often conceived simply in terms of equality with men), their struggles and their real strengths not only go unrecognised but are also run down and belittled. But this means that traditional elements in a woman's potential that might bind women together across generations in love and reconciliation are themselves also damaged.

These prejudices and misunderstandings naturally affect visions of the future. Many women, especially younger ones, can conceive of a future for women only as a paradise in which they will work as little as possible, enjoy equality without a struggle, and be subject to none of the constraints of everyday necessity.

This princess's vision of the future sees the past as full of neglected Cinderella figures, where peasant life was one long torment devoid of any rights for women. It is true, of course, that peasant women had to work hard, but they also, literally, held their life in their own hands. This is not the least of the reasons why joys and tribulations are so closely bound together in subsistence production, as we have seen in the striking case of Agnes and Lisbeth. Work, especially when you are in control of it yourself, can be a source of satisfaction and self-fulfilment. And it can also offer the prospect for women to achieve self-affirmation.

What is meant by 'peasant family economy'?

The simple question of what is meant by 'peasant family economy' leads us into the heart of the debate, and so an answer can only be given in context. Those who recognise the household *oikonomia* of the peasant farm as a genuine economy speak of 'peasant family economy' as synonymous with 'peasant economy' *tout court.* Those who do not see in it any economically productive potential emphasise the hierarchical split in the peasantry that is supposed to lead to its eventual dissolution. The latter tradition, deriving from Lenin and Kautsky, argues that capitalism penetrates the countryside through the separation of farms into capitalist enterprises and landless wage labourers. For a long time this tradition has not seen peasant women, peasant or family economy, but only agricultural producers caught up in a process of class differentiation.

In Mexico this position was held by the so-called *descampenistas* (Bartra 1974; compare the debate on rural classes in Paré 1979). In his 1976 article 'Y si los campesinos se extinguen ...' ('And if the peasants disappear'), Bartra once again predicted with satisfaction the end of the peasant economy, regarding it as the support for a reactionary political system and citing Marx's famous 1852 tract on the peasantry in the France of Napoleon III (Marx 1973). Claudia von Werlhof responded by entitling her book on rural Venezuela *Wenn die Bauern wiederkommen* (*If the Peasants Return*) (1985). According to the Mexican terminology, she belongs to the *campesinistas* who stress the importance of cooperation among the peasant population – not only the family in the narrow sense, but just as much the village or ethnic community woven together through bonds of kinship. This peasant population is subjected as a group to the capitalist market, and the point is to support its resistance struggles, not to argue the case for its proletarianisation (Bennholdt-Thomsen 1982).

The heart of the debate, then, is whether subsistence production is recognised as production, or if it is interpreted as mere reproduction and a mere reflection of the relation between capital and wage labour. Both approaches are patriarchal. And under patriarchal conditions, the concept of the family always tends to harbour a hostility to women. But in reference to the peasant family economy, it at least involves a recognition of subsistence production as a form of economy and therefore tends to be sympathetic to women. For not only is economic value not denied to women's labour, but men also, in cooperation with women, perform subsistence labour. In our view, this belongs to the subsistence perspective for the future: that men shall again undertake their share of subsistence production.

Various types of patriarchy

Women in general, and peasant women in particular, hardly feature at all in the debate we have been considering on the peasant family economy. Yet they and their labour are what is really at issue. We cannot shake off the suspicion that the modern dismissal of the peasant economy, both in theory and in practice, is largely due to the fact that women have too much independence within it – as in the preindustrial discussion of who wears the trousers (Bock and Duden 1976: 142ff.).

The pro-peasant line of argument in terms of a family economy cannot fail to include the contribution of women in its descriptions and calculations. But the theory of peasant economy does not seek to demonstrate the productivity of women's labour, and especially not in relation to men's labour; its main preoccupation is to retrieve the honour of the male peasant against those who can find nothing productive in the peasant subsistence orientation, and who also have no place for women's subsistence labour in their descriptions and calculations of agricultural production. Modernisers, whether capitalist or socialist in their inclinations, generate a discourse that de-economises subsistence production and the labour of both male and female peasants. In the case of women, this is a tacit procedure: they are not even mentioned.

In accordance with the 'divide and rule' maxim, the advocates of peasant economy or family economy both defend the economic value only of what the male peasant does. In the end, it is a debate between two types of patriarchy, the classical and the modern, neither of which even addresses the key question of the relationship between men and women.

In classical patriarchy, the father had authority over what happened in the farmhouse. With industrialisation and the spread of wage labour, this authority was replaced by the modern patriarchy of brothers. In so far as the father has control over the land basis of subsistence, passing it on to one or more of his sons, he keeps a crucial instrument of power in his hands. But wage labour offers those sons a way of emancipating themselves from their father. They become his equal as males, as members of the same sex, and no longer even need his consent to marry. In modern patriarchy, every man has the right to appropriate free of charge, as 'love', the now-invisible subsistence labour of women. The fact that this no longer requires the permission of the parental generation and of the woman's family group contributes to the invisibility and devaluation of women's labour, and is not necessarily to the young woman's advantage. In matriarchal traditions, the mother keeps watch to ensure that that labour retains its value (Bock and Duden 1976; Bennholdt-Thomsen 1987, 1994; Kandiyoti 1977).

The two types of patriarchy differ in their characteristic relationship between the generations and in their attitude to female subsistence producers, as well as in their relationship to nature. The man–woman relationship is the core that determines everything else. But these elements are not analysed in the (typically patriarchal) debate we have been considering. Even in women's research, too little attention has been paid to the ways in which the position of women and their relationship to nature have varied with different types of patriarchy. The field is still dominated by a monolithic concept of patriarchy and a romanticism of modernity (see also Lerner 1986).

Without peasant women, no peasant farms

In *Der bäuerliche Familienbetrieb zwischen Patriarchat und Partnerschaft* ('The

family farm between patriarchy and partnership') (1964), Ulrich
concerned himself with the question of peasant patriarchy. The book con
a lot of useful information, but it is handled from a viewpoint typical
modern patriarchy. Planck mainly examines the change in relations between
the generations. As to gender relations, he subscribes to the myth that men and
women become increasingly equal in the wake of modernisation (as does
Mitterauer 1980). Rather inconsistently, he cites a series of authors who, like
himself, maintain that peasant women in premodern times always had
'independent spheres of authority respected by men', which is only exception-
ally the case in modern farms (Planck 1964: 204). And yet, their contribution
to the economy is generally underestimated, as it was in Chayanov, even when
it ought to leap out from their own data (Spittler 1987: xx).

In contrast, Heide Inhetveen and Margret Blasche (1983) show for one
region in southern Germany today how crucial women are to the running and
upkeep of the farm economy, and how deeply concerned they are that it should
continue. This is one of the few modern studies that frees the labour of peasant
women from invisibility. And its conclusions strongly suggest that a decisive
reason for the economic and social problems of the farm is the deprecation of
female labour, the silence surrounding it in agrarian statistics, and the difficulty
that peasant women have had in asserting themselves and gaining recognition.
This is not, however, the conclusion drawn by the two authors themselves.

In our view, the persistence of patriarchalism is possibly the major problem
of farms today. For women are thought of and treated not as themselves
peasants, but as housewives who work in the home invisibly (because without
any monetary income) and merely help out as family members in the livestock
sheds and the fields. Little wonder that young farmers cannot find wives, when
the position of women in absolute terms has grown worse, not better, than it
used to be. 'Traditional patriarchalism', as Planck calls it, has thrown the gates
open to this tendency.

We firmly believe that this is one major reason why many farms, especially
medium-sized farms, have called it a day and why many more will continue to
do so. For they are failing in the very task they set themselves: namely, to
function as an industrial enterprise in which the farmer directs the machines
and is at the same time the one who brings the money home. This image
includes that of the dependent housewife, who is supposed to have nothing to
do on the farm and even less to say. (It remains an open question whether some
countrywomen, now as in the past, want to live like urban housewives at the
price of undermining their own position on the farm.) It may be the case that
many medium-sized units could survive as a farm with an integrated household
economy. But for that they would need a peasant woman rather than a
housewife. In this sense, the theorists of the peasant economy are completely
right in describing it as essentially a family economy.

...ived view of things, the position of the peasant woman
...n advance as one of subordination to a male peasant. In
...ther cultures, there have been completely different forms of
...abour. In sub-Saharan Africa, women do more than 80 per cent
...y agricultural labour – which has created a tradition quite different
...European one. Furthermore, the fact that a division of labour is
gender-based does not automatically mean that it is hierarchical. It is just such
a misunderstanding that leads women to seek salvation in the same work as
men's, giving up areas that would offer them autonomy and independence.
One such area of work in our own latitudes is doubtless the running of a farm
and the marketing of its produce. Today more than ever before, it is important
that women should keep areas of subsistence production at their disposal (see
Maria Mies 1996c), and that they should discuss and argue about the value of
their own position within the division of labour. The regulation of property
relations is another important aspect of life on today's farms. Conditions are
favourable for advances to be made in all these areas of farming, now that the
patriarchal order is running up against its limits. *The capacity for cooperation
and reciprocity, without which the peasants' integrated, cyclical economy cannot
function, will be decisive for its future existence.*

The housewifeisation of the peasant woman

One very clear feature of the peasant economy is that modern, industrial,
maximisation-centred patriarchalism has exacerbated not extenuated the
gender hierarchy; that the position of women has moved from relative independence to housewifely dependence. Precisely because the peasant, like the
nobleman, bourgeois or proletarian, wanted to have a 'nice piece of property',
the housewife, that did not appear to have to work, he set about turning his
farm into a business and thus ultimately ruined it. The patriarchal structures
affecting the 'whole household' (patrilinearity and patrilocality: that is, a male
line of succession and a wife's normal residence in the man's home) have
become still more pronounced, and cooperative work patterns shaped by the
subsistence economy have been converted into hierarchical work patterns.

Where the peasant economy exists within a matriarchal tradition, as it does
in Juchitán, it is much more resistant to the repressive mechanisms of
maximisation economics, even if the usual compulsion and violence are
screwed especially tight. In the case of Juchitán, the central government
built a dam and a number of irrigation canals as development measures in
the early 1960s, and arbitrarily redistributed the land. Subsequently, the
peasants were induced by various threats and promises to use the irrigated
land only for the growing of produce for export outside the region. But they

actually prefer to continue growing crops for regional consumption. This is important for the individual farmer, because then he can share his business and his life with a woman. The women of Juchitán, who are all independent traders and artisans, process and sell what the men produce. Without relations of economic cooperation, there can be no shared life with a man. It is as simple as that. (Holzer 1994)

In our part of the world, too, until well into the twentieth century, peasant women kept control over several areas of farm production, including the right to dispose of income from the selling of its produce. This right was successively taken from them by government action, so that today it is forbidden to market milk, butter or cheese directly, unless the farm has its own milk quota plus a direct marketing quota, and unless it meets the same so-called hygienic conditions that apply to industrial dairies using goods transported over hundreds of miles and stored for days or weeks on end (which is not at all the case on the farm). The marketing and production of others of the peasant woman's typical products – beer, schnapps, meat, poultry, eggs – have also been taken over by the state, often in the wake of preparations for the First or the Second World War, and consumers have helped to maintain and extend these acts of expropriation through their own consumption behaviour (Kolbeck 1985; C. Müller 1998).

This is how peasant women have increasingly become housewives. The separation between public–male and private–female has also penetrated the farm along the dividing line between paid and unpaid. A so-called 'outdoors' economy has come into being which is driven by men and brings in a lot of money. In contrast to the male part in the division of labour, peasant women have increasingly been confined to the four walls of their house, and their work became more and more oriented towards consumption like that of middle-class urban housewives. Since peasants have to pay for their machinery, they come under pressure not only to grow surpluses of subsistence staples but also to introduce production exclusively for the market – for example, sugar beet, rape seed, and now the so-called biomass. There are also all kinds of compulsory insurance payments to be met, as well as petrol, electricity and water costs, taxes, and refuse and sewage charges. Loans are especially common for the purpose of mechanisation, and these may well lead to an excessive burden of debt. But machines are also often purchased too hurriedly, because they offer to raise their owner from the position of a subsistence producer with low social esteem – one socially defined as female – to the position of a money-earning industrial producer – one socially defined as mostly male (see the story of Agnes and Lisbeth above). The subsistence-producing side of the peasant economy, now dismissed as being of little value, increasingly falls to the lot of women. And even if they slave away for the whole day, they are not believed to be doing anything essential. The peasant woman has been converted into a farmer's housewife.

Prospects of independence: the woman smallholder

It is in the world of small farms, which most closely corresponds to the traditional conception of a peasant farm, that new types of cooperation and production are opening up special prospects for women. These include various hybrid forms which are helping to overcome the patriarchal narrow-mindedness of the European peasant tradition. Many farms can, as one says, survive 'only' as a second occupation. In reality, however, this is a usual feature of the peasant economy: the farm is the subsistence-assuring basis from and around which other economic activities are grouped. Often a second occupation means that the husband engages in industrial wage labour, while the wife does the farming. The growing number of female small landowners shows that clever women are also making sure that they are nominally recognised as farmers. 'In farms below 5 hectares, 38.3 per cent of independent farmers are women; in farms between 5 and 20 hectares, their proportion already falls to 11.9 per cent; and in farms over 20 hectares, it is as low as 5.4 per cent.' Altogether, the number of female farm owners is increasing in Germany. In 1976 they accounted for 5 per cent of the total and in 1994 for 8.7 per cent, and in the age group up to twenty-four years for as much as 15 per cent (Inhetveen and Blasche 1983: 26; Grossenbacher 1996: 186; Schmitt 1997).

Another sector in which the farm economy is re-emerging is organic agriculture. Since this involves much more manual labour than conventional, chemical agriculture, and since small landowners can hardly afford to pay for wage labour, it is urgently necessary for them to look back to forms of mutual cooperation and partnership. For a long time, it was mainly small farms that made the switch-over. Instead of being undercut, ruinously subsidized and forced to close down by conventional competition, small farmers hoped that better bio-prices might yet enable them to make a living.

Organic farming: a wasted opportunity?

Meanwhile, tendencies to concentration in organic farming give reason to fear that this route, too, will soon be blocked for long-term relationships and economic communities on the land. First of all, sales to supermarkets by associations of organic farmers are already massively increasing in Austria, and a similar trend is in the offing in Germany.[5] This reminds us of the twentieth-century evolution of marketing and processing cooperatives, which increasingly escaped the control of the peasants themselves and eventually became big companies imposing industrial production methods and the functions of a corporate supplier. Given the highly monopolised structure of the food trade

– the ten largest food corporations account for nearly 80 per cent of the total market, and the four largest for 70 per cent – the supermarket road for organic produce means simply to give oneself up to the dictatorial market power of the monopolies (*Frankfurter Rundschau*, 15 March 1996). The rule by diktat of large centralised producers, involving purely commercial calculation and cut-throat competition among organic farms, is coming closer all the time. In Germany, moreover, this trend fits in with another phenomenon, namely the conversion to organic farming of many former collective farms in Eastern Germany whose very size (up to a thousand hectares) means that they cannot be run by individual farmers.

This competitive trend is actually encouraged by the associations (see note 5), the state and the EU, as well as by consumers. The reason is that the prevailing concept of organic farming is based on the purely technical idea of banning the use of pesticides and drugs; the social organisation of production is considered a matter of indifference. In reality, however, the very logic of the peasant economy includes the use of ecologically sound procedures, whereas the ecological principle cannot last long if that logic is changed.

But another reason is the patriarchalism of the organic farmers themselves. At the congress of one organic association, Veronika Bennholdt-Thomsen saw that most of the male farm representatives were arguing in favour of a super-market strategy because they wanted to get out of the 'organic farm niche'. In other words, they wanted to be where the real economic action is, to take part in the usual struggle for known markets instead of merely remaining in the pongy air of subsistence-oriented peasantry. Yet it is thanks to this niche that most of them have been able to survive up to now; and it is the difference between regions that has assured them of an income. Besides, one niche after another can cover quite a large area. Instead of living and letting live in this way, they are all now declaring competitive warfare on one another.

A further aspect of the supermarket road is even more startling. For a long time the organic market had to be built up virtually from scratch, with direct sales from the farm or through market stalls accounting for a large part of total sales. Typically, many women took charge of this side of things and recovered a sphere that had fallen prey to housewifeisation. The supermarket road thus implies that the possibility of earning an independent income will once again be taken away from women.

Peasant economy, regionalisation and the subsistence perspective

For us, the subsistence perspective means decolonising the three colonies of capital: nature, women and the Third World. The concept of a peasant economy is thus of central significance for our outline of an economic alternative, since peasant culture and economics do not have a colonialist structure.

This is not some wishful utopian notion but can be empirically demonstrated without difficulty.

Whereas Germany's factory farming and especially its livestock mass production are based upon cheap food imports from the Third World, independent farms not geared to profit maximisation are based upon integrated farming systems that sustain both farm and people. Mass livestock production, so utterly contemptuous of local life and animals, needs for its fodder a cultivated surface area twice as large as what is available. This is why it is said that German cattle graze beside the River Plate. The negative consequences in Third World countries – for example, through the cultivation of soya for export fodder – are already well known: destruction of areas traditionally used to feed the local population, concentration of the land and dispossession of the existing peasantry, chemical contamination of the soil and water. At the same time, the subsidised export of German and European beef to Africa leads to the collapse of stockbreeding there. Peasant farming on the contrary always only relies on its own region for the marketing of surpluses.

The relationship to nature can be decolonised through the peasant economy, which, unlike factory farming, is not based upon pillage of nature. Simple self-interest already dictates respect for the natural productive forces; the health of animals, soil and plants in a context of mixed agriculture is the best guarantee of the farm's survival, and a cyclical economy is also the cheapest method of cultivation for small farms. There is a yawning abyss between capital-intensive industrial farming and the agricultural production of peasants. They are two utterly different systems of production. Where the soil is not so rich as to offer huge profits, one tends to find (small) peasant farms – farms that convert most easily to organic production, because they have anyway been carrying on eco-logically sound practices. This preserves those varied landscapes of heaths, damp moorland, low-mountain forest and pasture that city dwellers think of as places for a relaxing holiday. But even areas cleared for livestock mass production could become habitable again through a return to the peasant economy.

The peasant economy is the basis for regional economic activity, not only for agriculture but for a way of life combining agriculture, crafts and other occupations. For in any event the farm and agriculture remain the centre from which other activities radiate in a kind of regional circle. Regionalisation – that is, production, exchange and consumption in and from the region – is for us integral to a politics directed against the colonialism of globalisation, and against the colonisation and incapacitation of our life in the North. Politics should here be understood as subsistence politics from below, as a self-authorising everyday strategy open to each and all of us. The simplest and always available measure, which is also an extremely effective one, is to buy produce only from the local region. This strengthens the peasant economy.

The biggest problem with peasant farming in Central Europe, however, is its patriarchalism. The gearing of agricultural policies to industry, together with a desire to participate in the 'honoured', militarised growth economy, prevents more farms in Germany from maintaining or rediscovering a subsistence orientation. The profit-and-consumption bacillus has infected men, and women as well. In our view, if people's hearts and minds are to be liberated from the patriarchal capitalist model, there must be a different organisation of society so that it breaks with the pattern of male breadwinner and female housewife.

New forms of social and economic organisation

Many farmers in Germany, both women and men, are creating new forms of social and economic organisation so that their farm can survive. Such inventiveness will also be necessary because very many farms no longer have children willing to take over the succession. Parents who cannot accept that the farm that still feeds them will when they die disappear as such, after centuries of existence, are reaching out for new models. None of the offers of quit or disuse payments, rental income or high purchase prices can induce them to pack up and go.

A dissident farmer

Farm A. is in a very fertile region in the centre of Germany. 'Power' agriculture – mechanisation, chemicalisation, mass livestock production – is far advanced here. Although the townspeople have traditionally cultivated smallholdings, the concentration of the land has increased enormously in recent years. Many farms have closed down and are rented out to so-called growth businesses. Not farm A. Farmer A has been running his farm for thirty-five years, and for a long time its 17 hectares have made it the smallest operational farm for miles around. Ten years ago he went over to organic farming, mainly because he could no longer bear the soil contamination and landscape destruction, or the way in which animals were being treated to extract the greatest profit. The farm's conversion earned him a lot of aggression from more conventional colleagues. A few blows of fate – the death of a wife who kept the home, a fire, and the children's lack of interest in agriculture and the continuation of the farm – led him to look for a different form of organisation. Eventually he decided that the integrated – which for him meant explicitly subsistence-oriented – peasant economy should be practised on the farm. Farmer A looked for and found people of like mind, two women and a man, and took them as partners in the farm. The small farm is divided into four still smaller tenant farms, which are worked in close cooperation. Each of the newcomers has the further assurance of lifelong usufruct over 2 hectares of land, as well as

transmissible tenancy rights. The farmer has issued legally binding
instructions that no part of the farm or its land should ever be sold, and that
any heirs must respect and endorse the agreements.

The varied search for new ways

Many farms are now taking new paths in order to survive: new property
dispositions, expanded circles of co-workers with corresponding rights and
duties (ordinary or limited liability companies, cooperatives, etcetera), and
producer–consumer agreements. It is not possible to say in general how far
these new forms are intended to secure a peasant economy, and how far they
may be a different path towards capitalist businesses with higher levels of
profit. But the latter is a rarer case, which has only appeared recently as a
derivative from alternative forms. Usually these new paths have started out
from organic farming, as we can see by reading magazines of the organic
association or the periodical *Ökologie & Landbau*. It is also apparent that such
new dispositions involve a different relationship to nature and between human
beings – as is the case with the production and marketing agreements.

JAPAN   The relationship between producers and consumers is especially close in
Community Supported Agriculture (CSA), which was originally based on an
idea of Rudolf Steiner and spread in the 1980s from Germany to the United
States and other countries. CSA is a type of pact between producers and consumers in which the latter provide finance and other assistance, guarantee
purchases, and have a certain right of say. In the United States there are already
more than three hundred CSA farms. Similar initiatives in Europe are less
uniform and less integrated, but they include the German and Swiss producer–
consumer cooperatives (PCCs), which operate according to the principle of 'cost
covering' and pursue an ideal of 'associative economics' (Hermannstorfer 1992),
as well as the so-called 'subscription farming' in Britain (Loziczky 1997: 22ff.).

The kind of farm help that may once have been provided by relatives from
outside the area in busy times and holidays is now often assured by the
organisation of 'elective affinities'. An interesting example is the Willing
Workers on Organic Farms (WWOOF) network, whereby organic farmers
offer places to city dwellers not previously known to them. As in CSA, those
who come out from the cities are people who find it necessary and desirable to
have contact with the land, animals and plants, and to work for a time on the
land.

Dropouts and returnees

The Austrian Mountain Peasants' Institute (Bundesanstalt für Bergbauern-
fragen), which concerns itself especially with the preservation of the peasant

economy, has conducted research on 'dropouts in country regions'. This term refers to those city dwellers who, since the early 1970s, have been going in increasing numbers to live and work on the land. The ensuing economic forms are as varied as the people involved. The dropouts are 'young people from the green-alternative scene ... who want to build an alternative life', 'artists, esoteric gurus', 'young academics', 'people frustrated with their work life so far (blue- and white-collar workers, managers)', 'prosperous freelancers who use farming (in a partner's charge) as a tax-deductible job', 'pensioners' with a piece of 'hobby land', 'unemployed people who cannot meet the expense of city living', others returning to their roots. Farms may become centres for the 'professional' growing and direct marketing of specialised products (herbs, sheep's milk produce, etcetera). Or agriculture may be combined with other paid work or may be used 'to provide oneself with especially nutritious food'. Barter ('a drum for a wooden step, a lamb for some grain') plays a central role (Groier 1997).

Especially in the case of 'lifestyle dropouts', the author observed a number of typical peasant's attitudes: 'Slackening of the strict distinction between work time and leisure time, moving in the direction of "life-time"', 'joint work, labour festivals', 'a stress on subsistence', 'work as a way of satisfying needs rather than of increasing capital'. There is also another feature characteristic of the peasant family economy in our part of the world. 'With regard to the division of labour and the allocation of roles between men and women, the same inherited patterns of behaviour (women have less free time, do most of the housework, and are less involved in farming work) can be observed in the dropout households that were interviewed' (Groier 1997: 180).

Nevertheless, as Michael Groier points out, most of the dropouts do not think of themselves as peasants. The same appears to be true of those who, having been socialised in the city, later return to their parents' farm. The reason first mentioned for this is the 'distance from the peasants' traditional-conservative view of life (socio-cultural narrowness)' (Groier 1997: 178).

We wonder how many prejudices of city people, who regard themselves as superior because more modern, still play a part in these attitudes of distancing, and how many times this distancing has triggered hostile reactions from the side of the locals. Nevertheless this situation could be a chance for urban dissidents and rural dissidents to join hands with one another. What is certain is that there can be no future without a history: without the peasants' know-ledge and culture, including the material culture of peasant women, it will not be easy to develop a different kind of farming that is neither geared to growth economics nor destructive of the environment.

Communes, eco-villages and much else besides

In the early eighties, a number of 'communes' based on shared living and finances came into being in rural Germany. They had a number of distinguishing principles: common economic arrangements, decision making by consensus, collective work structures, and an end to gender-specific structures of power within the small family. They linked up with the store of ideas and culture stemming from the experiences of communal organisation in the post-1968 urban students' movement (see Chapter 4). Of eleven communes that are presented in a recently published anthology, nine are in the country and only two in the city; one has only recently been established, two have just been through a painful break-up. We shall therefore consider the six well-functioning rural communes, one of which is in the Pyrenees. They all combine farming and/or market gardening with various handicrafts, often having a house for meetings and, more rarely, putting in some paid labour outside the commune (Kollektiv KommuneBuch 1996).

The largest of the communes is Niederkaufungen, which on its tenth anniversary in 1996 had 53 adults (24 women, 29 men) and 18 children and young people. Its work is discribed as follows:

> Ecological and social orientation of work, production and services: integrated and mixed-age day nurseries; building operations/planning, architectural office, carpentry, metalworking, revolutionary sewing and leatherwork shop, conference and meeting house, food provision for commune and conference house, organic vegetable farming, livestock farming, administration, typesetting, occupational pension scheme under construction, arrangements for short-term care being planned'. (ibid: 30)

As we were able to see personally during our visit, the commune is well integrated into the village of Niederkaufungen, in the sense that neighbours recognise how 'hard-working' its members are. Any misgivings have obviously faded away. Each year there is a festival at which visitors are shown around; it is attended by as many as two thousand people.

In general, the most prominent feature of the rural commune is not necessarily its basis in farming, but rather its everything-lumped-together economics and its form of social organisation centred on the community and not on small families. Moreover, the idea of subsistence or self-reliant farming is gaining ground in the context of communes. For a couple of years now, commune members have been organising events in German cities to inform people about their alternative to unemployment and drugs.

The eco-villages, for their part, were founded with the idea of subsistence directly in mind. This is how Elisabeth Voss puts it in the same anthology:

> What is meant by an 'eco-village' is not an ecological-organic settlement but a community that develops models of life and work for a larger number of people – forms that present an alternative to capitalism. The cornerstones are supposed to be: common ownership of land and buildings, production overwhelmingly for the needs of people in the village (self-sufficiency), and in general an ecologically and socially oriented way of life that lays more

stress on quality than on quantity, and that is less geared to consumption and more full of relish than is usually the case. This idea was advocated nearly ten years ago by the Heidelberg psychologist Jörg Sommer, who – not least to find people to put it into action – founded the Informationsdienst Ökodorf (IDÖF) (Eco-Village Information Service).

Since then, at least two projects have been developed along these lines, both of them in the new federal states of eastern Germany. In 1993 the initiative stemming from Heidelberg set itself up at the eco-village project centre in Gross Chüden (near Salzwedel), with the participation of sixty adults and children. The aim is to establish a 'village' with three hundred inhabitants. By 1996 the following project areas had been developed: 'accommodation and work groups, guest and seminar unit, self-sufficiency and economic operations, planning office, free schools, networking'. 'People are equally welcome if they want to live in families, in communal housing or in groups established in accordance with an ideal' (*eurotopia*, 1–2/96).

Unfortunately, the material available to us does not say more about the progress of self-provisioning farming and market gardening. But we learn that in 1996 the eco-village project received the Action-Prize of the Federal German Environment Institute for Communal Ecological Initiatives in the New Federal States, and that it can count on further support from the government of Saxony-Anhalt. Perhaps it is to this that we should attribute the developmentalist rhetoric in Dieter Halbach's appeal.

> The whole settlement offers a new cultural model with which to bring the world back into the village and the village into the world. ... Lasting regional development (soft tourism, natural conservation, direct marketing, crafts). ... We hope that the eco-village will also contribute something to the Altmark and other structurally weak regions ... it will help to raise the region's development potential and to offer advice on how it may be used.

Another project, the LebensGut Pommritz, whose subsistence philosophy was developed by Rudolf Bahro in connection with our feminist subsistence approach, made its debut in 1993 north of Dresden. According to the magazine *eurotopia* (Autumn 1994), 'The aim is to develop, to test and to run in exemplary fashion an ecological settlement with a long-term regionally oriented cyclical economy.' Bahro, who was in direct contact with the Saxon prime minister Biedenkopf, obtained funding from the state of Saxony. Instead of merely providing unemployment benefit and social security, the government was to help people gain access to the means of subsistence, particularly land, so that they could make an independent living for themselves.

> So [we] got farmland on a favourable lease from the state of Saxony. With this initial help we were supposed to develop over the medium term something like a model of a self-supporting, socially and ecologically sustainable

community based upon small-scale operations with a regional economic horizon.' (*eurotopia*, 1-2/96: 35).

The magazine *eurotopia*, which we have already mentioned a number of times, provides a good overview of communal projects as well as networking assistance, and encourages people to embark on similar ventures. Its pages speak of 'starry villages', 'survival islands', 'Mother Earth land', 'life gardens', 'Christian farming communes', and much much more. The impression emerges of a movement for the establishment of new communities in Germany and Europe which in nearly every case seeks direct access to the land because it wants to practise a different relationship with nature and sees self-provisioning farming as the basis of community. With this in view, a 'Long May' group demanded 'the impossible' after reunification: namely, that state lands held in trust by local councils should be handed over for use by the resident population. But 'Communalisation of the Land Remains a Utopia' (poster produced by the Longo Mai Cooperative in Mecklenburg, in 1996).

The networked communes have begun to create a bridge between 'spirituals' and 'politicos'. In our opinion, there is also need for a bridge between new-community-enthusiasts and those peasants who dissent from the growth economy and wish to keep their peasant way. For theirs is a mode of life and production resting upon an old cultural tradition, which could also help the new communities: (a) in dealing with self-provisioning within an everyday subsistence economy; (b) in instilling the pride and self-assurance that come from providing one's own necessities of life; and (c) in emotionally anchoring their autonomy from any superior authority.

NOTES

1. Milk quotas mean that farmers are allowed to sell only a certain amount of milk. These quotas are fixed according to the head of cattle a farmer had in 1983.
2. Uta Ranke-Heinemann is a feminist theologian. In a number of books she has criticised patriarchal ideology and institutions in the Churches.
3. Of the 30,000 tonnes of 'plant-protecting substances' (i.e., pesticides) employed in Germany, roughly half do not even come into contact with plants but end up in the soil or, sometimes quickly, in groundwater. *Frankfurter Rundschau*, 16 August 1994.
4. Of the economically active population in Greece, 30 per cent was still in agriculture in 1980, 24 per cent in 1990, and 20.8 per cent in 1994. In Portugal the figures were 27 per cent in 1980, 18 per cent in 1990, and 11.8 per cent in 1994; and in Spain, 19 per cent in 1980, 12 per cent in 1990, and 9.9 per cent in 1994 (*Landwirtschaftliches Wochenblatt*, 8 April 1993; Deutscher Bauerverband 1996: 124). We can only guess at the harsh personal dramas and the far-reaching cultural change concealed in these figures.
5. The associations in question involve an amalgamation of farms engaged in organic farming, which thereby undertake to submit to self-monitoring.

4

Subsistence and the Market

The women traders of Juchitán

In Juchitán, a Zapotec town in the Mexican state of Oaxaca with a population of eighty thousand, women have a strong social position. The men are peasants, fishermen, craftsmen and wage labourers. The women are traders. This social division of labour has operated for hundreds of years. Women have responsibility for the home and the children, for food, going to the market and certain craft activities. There are no housewives, but also no female entrepreneurs. Unlike in our part of the world, where the housewife is constituted by the fact that the division of labour decreases in the household economy while increasing in the industrial sphere, the division of labour in Juchitán is also very extensive within the household economy. Instead of households run by one woman, there are specialisations in many different kinds of product, especially in the cooked dishes or preserves that women take to sell at the market. Movement is free-flowing between the subsistence activity of housewives and the market activity of tradeswomen.

Women do not engage in trade or crafts to accumulate wealth or to have others work for a wage; their aim is to guarantee a living and, above all, to gain respect within the community and among other women. It is part of the reciprocity principle that prices are not fixed but vary with the degree of social obligation – according to whether a favour has to be returned, or whether one is expected in the future.

Surpluses are consumed collectively at great 'festivals of merit'. They are called this because material things are expended at them in order to gain something immaterial: respect or prestige. These festivals of merit, which are an essential part of the network of reciprocity, also keep the local economy going. Spending on clothes, food and drink, jewellery, music and presents reaches almost incredible levels. The social mechanisms of prestige economics and reciprocity here give the market a special character.

Nevertheless, it would be wrong to speak of a separate market economy of Juchitán. The same money circulates here as in the rest of Mexico. The town lies astride an important route linking North and South America, being on both the Pan-American Highway and the railway line from the Atlantic to the nearby Pacific port. The place is, so to speak, seamlessly integrated into the national and international market. And yet its market and trade are subsistence-oriented. In other words, at the end of the twentieth century the market economy is moulded here in a different way.

Juchitán society is organised matrifocally. The mother is at the centre of social prestige, and the mother–child unit is the basic family constellation. Socially and emotionally, the mother is the main point of reference for children. The father may take on certain obligations, but a woman is not respected less if she does not have a husband around. She attends to finances as she does elsewhere, but this task is not misjudged as if she was merely adding to what the male breadwinner brings home. Altogether, the women's or tradeswomen's economy – all women being traders in Juchitán – remains subsistence-oriented. Subsistence production counts as real social work; the separation between private and public spheres of production does not apply. The woman goes about her business for day-to-day living, for the children's education, and for a surplus that will win social prestige for herself (not, as in many other cultures, for her husband). The woman is not an object but a subject of events.

Trade in Juchitán is still today centred on food. As this is produced, negotiated over and consumed at a local level, it fosters independent regional circulation that makes Juchitán more prosperous than other Mexican towns of comparable size. To be able to procure food by careful management is an important element in women's self-esteem and in the respect shown to them. Unlike in Germany, where such activity is accorded little value and women are expected to be slim, corpulence is part of the ideal of feminine beauty. A major driving force behind Juchitán's independent model of the market is the sense of community deriving from the maternal line of descent. People are proud of their origins, as they are of their own mother, their mother tongue, their ability to speak Zapotec, their music, painting and food. This different cultural orientation is capable of making its mark even on the market economy of modern times.

The big employers or monopolies have not been able to find their feet in Juchitán, nor, for example, is there any real supermarket here. For many years the central government consciously targeted the region, aiming to create there a free economic zone along the lines of Taiwan or Singapore or *maquiladora* factories working for the world market, as on Mexico's northern border with the United States. But this process has failed to materialise. Despite a constant ideological barrage from the schools and media, the population has not gone all out to achieve the consumption patterns of the big brother to the north.

The people of Juchitán have not internalised the norms and rules of the modern market economy; they have a different morality. Sears, a North American retail corporation with many branches in Mexico which mainly sell clothing and consumer durables, once had an outlet in Juchitán too. But in the late seventies, when the people of Juchitán once again felt outraged at decisions being made by the central political administration, they stormed into the store and ransacked it. When the incident was later repeated, Sears thought it best to pull out, and closed the branch down. No such ventures have been attempted since then: trade remains in the hands of the local women.

Market and subsistence are not contradictory

Exchange relations have always existed; we cannot imagine a society in human history without them. This may seem a banal point, but it still needs to be made. For it is a peculiarity of modern ideology that it conceives of existing conditions as those of human beings *tout court*, and characterises as primitive any that are not found in the same or a similar form. In sum, it is thought that household autarky prevails wherever market relations are not general.

In reality, however, there have been and still are countless different kinds of exchange relationship, both outside the market altogether and in conjunction with the modern market economy. Some of these forms are: the exchange of gifts; ritual exchange; exchange within kinship groups; exchange between ethnic groups, on the basis of different geographical and climatic conditions (Andes, Sahel, Alps); forced exchange (in Spain's American colonies in the sixteenth and seventeenth centuries); and, finally, exchange conducted by trading peoples such as the ancient Phoenicians, who founded settlements for the purpose, or the Sinti and Romanies in parts of Europe today. There is trade in kind and trade with various types of money (conch shells in Polynesia and many parts of Africa; cocoa beans, quetzal feathers and obsidian in pre-Conquest Mexico). There are various mechanisms of price formation, and opinions differ about the conditions and the period in which it becomes appropriate to speak of a market system (Polanyi 1957). So far, there has been little analysis of exchange relations in modern societies which, though producing commodities, escape cost–benefit calculation or the M–C–M' schema of the passage of capital from money through commodities to a greater sum of money.

The generalisation of commodity production, to the point where the market and trade determine the shape of modern society, has had the result that not only are so-called traditional societies imagined to be subsistence societies without any market at all, but the market relations actually present in them are regarded as anachronistic relics of pre-industrial forms of commerce that can therefore be left out of account.[1]

Following Darwin, the idea appeared in the nineteenth century that peoples who do not have our 'civilised' constitution of society should be thought of as 'contemporary primitive ancestors'. This theory had its heyday in the development ideology of the period after the Second World War, when the 'primitive contemporaries' became 'underdeveloped peoples'. It is in this context that the concept of subsistence society has arisen in opposition to that of market society. As if there had never been such a thing as colonialism, or within individual countries a colonial relationship between town and country, leading sociologists in the US and elsewhere advanced a dualistic model for 'underdeveloped countries', with 'traditional subsistence society' in the countryside and 'modern market society' in the towns. Of course, the idea was to carry the 'subsistence society' out of its underdevelopment into the higher stage of market society.[2] But for our part, we have always emphasised that the two sides belong together, that both are part of capitalism, and that capitalism is different from how these sociologists claim it to be (see Chapter 2).

For there have never been societies without exchange relations; what there have been are exchange relations that follow a different morality from the one dominant in the maximisation society. In the present day, too, market and exchange are not necessarily geared to cutthroat competition, as we have shown through our research in Juchitán and elsewhere (Bennholdt-Thomsen 1994; Holzer 1995). Moreover, we are convinced that as soon as the profit-defined concept of the market is revised, a variety of subsistence-oriented exchange relations will also become visible in Europe, and the value of their contribution to the economy will be recognised.

Market is not just market

The prevailing blindness to other than maximisation-centred market relations derives from a widespread sense of fatalism. It is considered beyond doubt not only that there is just this one form of market but also that it is the only form there ever can be – that the market is necessarily so and cannot be otherwise. People feel impotent against such supposedly inherent laws, and this is why they bow to the much-vaunted policy of attracting investment and even to the erosion of the welfare state. They think that 'Germany' or 'Great Britain' (whoever that might be) must remain competitive, that this is a law of the market that has necessarily developed in the way that it has. We can do nothing against the waves of market globalisation supposedly breaking over us. That the GATT agreements and the role of the WTO are a political creation, that they are the latest in a long line of 'development policies', is largely unknown or ignored (see Chapter 2).

The idea that there can only ever be this type of market goes hand in hand with the legitimating belief that the market has nothing to do with morality. Indeed, other relations are eyed suspiciously or have their very existence denied, on the grounds that market behaviour can only ever be amoral (Rott 1989).

The myth of inherent laws of the market

Polanyi studied the process whereby the assumption that the modern market economy worked according to inevitable laws imposed itself in the history of ideas. Seeking to discover how the catastrophe of the Second World War came about, he saw as one crucial factor the belief in inherent economic laws. His book The *Great Transformation* describes how this ideology took root, so that in the course of the nineteenth century the economy became independent of society.[3] Polanyi regarded this as the great world-historic 'transformation' in economic thought and behaviour. For what happened then had never happened before: the economy came to determine society, not the other way around (Polanyi 1944).

Although a critic of the dominant thinking in the West, Polanyi assumed that the separation between economy and society or economy and culture, and the primacy of the economy within it, did accurately characterise modern market society. We, on the other hand, would argue for a different, feminist point of view. Still very much in the spirit of Polanyi, as it were, we think it more productive to apply his concept of the 'embeddedness' of the economy in society not only to premodern relations but also to the modern world.[4] Today, as in earlier societies, culture and economy are not separate from each other, for the modern economy also has its corresponding culture, and vice versa. *Thus, the ideology of inherent market laws is one of its characteristic cultural beliefs.* Polanyi's critical analysis of the phenomenon bequeathed to us the keywords for more extensive research. Nature, he saw, is robbed of its natural character and becomes a factor in production calculations, while the market is ascribed a natural character as if its mechanisms were beyond human influence (Polanyi 1944).

This analysis reveals the true driving force, in the history of ideas as in science and popular consciousness, behind the assumption of laws intrinsic to market economy; namely, the constitution of modern patriarchal domination. In this process, the understanding of market and subsistence underwent a fundamental transformation, so that it was now thought that the market *is* life, *is* subsistence. According to this view, subsistence disappears forever from the economy, from what is necessary to life. There is only one kind of economy:

market economy. And the primacy of the market economy sets the seal on male primacy and the warlike, amoral view of economics.

The reason why Polanyi, for all his clear-sightedness, was unable to grasp the unity of economy and culture in our society was his faith in the necessity of progress and in technological feasibility.[5] His only wish was that progress could be made more socially tolerable. But he failed to see the socially intolerable fact that the technologically progressive market economy ruins the subsistence aspect of the economy that is essential to life.

The question also arises of how far the development of modern technology can be even conceived without social injustice in the industrial heartlands and between them and the colonies. Technological development without capitalist, imperialist exploitation, and especially without the military technology that is its driving force, would certainly not generate progress in the conventional sense of the term. Progress, including technological progress, would then look different and be directed at conservation and survival (cf. Mies and Shiva 1993: 53f.).

The de-economisation of subsistence

The supposedly inherent laws of the market belong together with the warlike view of economics and the modern relationship between the sexes. Polanyi's 'great transformation' actually consisted in the establishment of this linkage in the culture and the economic structure. The economy is assigned its own intrinsic, materially based laws, which are supposed to make cruelty and ruthlessness inescapable. This domain is reserved for men because their biology forearms them for aggressive encounters, so that in one breath women are excluded from the economy and barbarous behaviour is legitimated within it. This process – which, beginning in the sixteenth century, slowly spread from the upper strata of aristocratic-bourgeois societies down to the lower classes – is what we call the 'de-economisation of female labour'.

It was inscribed in the economic structure through the modern sexual division of labour – that is, through the conversion of women into housewives. In social-psychological terms, however, the de-economisation of female labour is a necessary part of modern culture. The good, fine, nurturing and caring side of the economy was not simply wiped out; it was delegated to women and therefore remained present. Even in modern times, it does not seem possible to declare the whole of one's social formation to be inhuman and warlike. But the price, of course, is an extremely limited concept of the economy.

In Juchitán, by contrast, women's activities have not been culturally written out of the economy. Subsistence production remains socially necessary economic activity, which is carried out via the market.

The de-economisation of female labour and the de-economisation of subsistence are one and the same process. The former unity of the economy now breaks up into a public and a private part, with the result that subsistence production is for the first time separated off from commodity production for the market. Subsistence, not oriented to profit, thus becomes de-economised and allocated to women in the private sphere – or else, in the case of farmers, it is defined as economically irrelevant so long as its goal is 'only' farm reproduction and not increased profits. In the course of this process, the link between subsistence and market also disappears. From now on, by virtue of a capitalist–patriarchal definition, the market exists only for the realisation of profits. To the extent that this is not the motive, it is not an operation of the market economy that is involved. Of course, this 'definition' was not established all by itself; it had to be imposed by force. Just as the driving of women into the private sphere began with the violent persecution of witches and has continued in new forms up to the present day, so the destruction of subsistence markets is a process that has taken place under ever-changing guises. These range all the way from state action to suppress peasant women's markets to the closing-down of the neighbourhood-based small corner shop (in Germany the so-called Aunt Emma's shop, Tante-Emma-Laden) – again through state action, only this time in the shape of its economic policy.

Restoring the link between subsistence and market

'Subsistence markets' and 'subsistence trade' are for us processes of exchange in which the link persists between subsistence and market; that is, in which useful and necessary supplies – mainly food, but also clothing, household equipment, building material, furniture, etcetera – are traded as use-values.

For market and subsistence to be linked rather than separated, it is also necessary that the market process itself should not be the object of a hunt for profits, especially not of the monopolistic kind, as it is in the globalised supermarket. Subsistence trading, as in Juchitán, is itself a craft that requires participants to learn how to handle the social relationships network of exchange. It is a fine art that also creates obligations, so it cannot be replaced by wage labour. The logic of subsistence trading is precisely not one of profit maximisation without regard to long-term relationships among producers, traders and customers. Subsistence *relations* are just as important as the supplies themselves – and in any case, more important than money – for the survival of the participants.

Moreover, subsistence trading is closely bound up with the craft skills involved in producing the items for sale. Either the traders are themselves also producers, or the link between producing and selling is so close that *responsibility* for the skilfulness and wholesomeness of the product is never lost. Its use-value is not a matter of indifference for the seller, and so its content remains a meaningful factor.

The way in which subsistence and market are linked together varies according to the region and its history. Our aim is not to give a completely clear-cut definition – which is generally not possible anyway – but to clarify the general tendency of subsistence-oriented market trading, and to argue that, especially for women, it is important that the link between subsistence and the market should be restored.

Contrary to what Polanyi thought, it is not the *independence* of the economy from modern society that is the obstacle to peaceful coexistence between nations or between human beings and nature, and – what interests us most here – to the linking or relinking of subsistence and the market. The real problem, on the contrary, is that growth economics is *embedded* in every fibre of our society. The competitive, belligerent, profit-obsessed character of our economy, its need for cruelty and intransigence, have been internalised by most people in the North and the wealthier classes in the South, gaining their active consent in their day-to-day economic intercourse with one another. The claim that the market operates according to inherent abstract laws helps politicians, managers and bankers – and not only them – to protest their complete innocence; it allows individuals to wash their hands of responsibility for their everyday economic activities. Men and women declare themselves to have no power in relation to the market, thereby legitimating their own consumerism, their own environmental and market behaviour. This maintains the anonymity of the act of purchase – which, in our view, is one of the great obstacles on the way towards new subsistence markets and ecologically responsible behaviour.

The market sphere itself is not perceived as a site of responsible behaviour. It no longer occurs to anyone in our part of the world that traders and customers might have some obligations to one another. But subsistence markets do not establish themselves; they have to be put in place, as the global market too has been put in place. Traders, as well as artisans or peasants when functioning as traders, play an important role in all this – not least in preserving or destroying the job they have chosen for themselves.

If the marketplace as a scene of action has been a taboo subject, if there has been so little discussion of it as a process shaped by human beings, this can to a significant degree be laid at the door of Marxist theory. Its evolutionary faith in technology, its related proletarianism and disdain for the peasantry, its general failure to recognise subsistence activity as economic: these lead to the dismissal of exchange relations as belonging merely to the 'sphere of circulation'. In Chapter 3 on the peasant economy, we saw from the discussion in Latin America that Marxist theory regards exploitation in the modern market economy as located exclusively in the relation between capital and wage labour. Thus in Mexico, and not only there, the talk has constantly been of semi-proletarianisation of the peasantry and the desirability of their full proletarianisation. Anyone who points to the peasantry's impoverishment by the market is treated as a 'circulationist', since all that can happen in the market is realisation of the profit that the capitalist pumps out of wage labour. For socialists, moreover, the market seems to operate by itself: there are no market traders, no market actors – except for precapitalist profiteers – who might play a role in shaping the exchange process. Our view, however, is that the market is an economic activity which determines the course of the whole economy, at least as much as production and consumption do.

Women, the market and the safeguarding of subsistence

All over the world, women's dominance in the marketplace seems to be closely connected with the trade in food. Ester Boserup, in a transcontinental survey of the development of female labour, argues that this connection arises where women mainly work in or have worked in agriculture. What they sell is, so to speak, their own produce or that of their fellow women (Boserup 1970). Plausible as this may sound, and accurate as it no doubt is for Africa and even Germany until recent times, it is not how things are in Juchitán. Agriculture there is man's work, and seems to have been man's work as far back in history as we can trace it. On the basis of Juchitán, therefore, it becomes clear that exchange is in itself an important social act, and that trade is by no means necessarily inconsistent with a subsistence orientation. In this case, the subsistence orientation is derived not directly from agricultural production but from the way in which women conceive and define trade.

The coastline of West Africa is famous for its large number of strong and independent tradeswomen, and the topic of women and the market has loomed large in studies of the region. The main research interest, however – especially of female investigators – has been to show that here too women are impoverished and repressed. It is regretfully noted, for example, that since they only trade in basic foods, they have hardly any scope to achieve prosperity or a major expansion in their trade (Frey-Nakonz 1984; Cutrufelli 1985: 101 – quoting other authors, Ligan, Meillassoux and Bohannan/Curtin).

This assessment reflects the point of view of patriarchal growth economics, for which trade in foodstuffs is a lesser, insubstantial form. Amid the negative litany, it is thus difficult to find positive statements which appreciate the amazing fact that women here conduct the greater part (in Ghana 80 per cent) of trade (Boserup 1970: 82). How is it that women manage to dominate the food trade in such adverse conditions? Given the problem that adequate nourishment poses in Africa, the high value placed on food would seem to be a more relevant consideration. As in Juchitán in relation to neighbouring regions, the child mortality rate is significantly lower in West Africa than in other parts of the continent (Ware 1983: 10). Althabe recognises the connection and shows that it is thanks to tradeswomen that the urban masses are able to feed themselves. It is true that large numbers of women are involved, that they currently deal only in small quantities, and that prices are high, but the provision of the towns is nevertheless secured and a certain redistribution effect is achieved. 'This is one way that (increasing) poverty can be shared around', is how he immediately qualifies his positive assessment of the subsistence economy (Althabe 1972).

If we continue our search for an explanation of how women in some parts of the world manage to dominate trade, even though the surrounding conditions are very different, the basic reason does seem to be, as in Juchitán, an identification with the figure of the mother. Among the population of east and central Java, and among the Minangkabau of the west Sumatra highlands who appear in ethnological literature as a paradigm of contemporary matriarchy, women have a strong position in trade which corresponds to their strong social position (Tanner 1974: 135f., 145). The tradeswomen of West Africa also come from mother-centred societies, whether these are matrilinear (as among the Yoruba) or patrilinear (as among the Igbo) (Amadiume 1987; Tanner 1974: 148f.). And in the Caribbean – for example, in Jamaica or Trinidad and Tobago – women keep the food retail trade in their hands. The so-called 'Caribbean' (mother-centred) family is the rule here: the father tends to be absent, and a mother often has several fathers for her children. This has been interpreted both as abandonment of the mother and as a source of women's strength, since they have an independent basis of subsistence in what is called the 'mother's plot' of land (Gonzalez 1970; Smith *et al.* 1987). Whatever the reason why women keep control of the market, a kind of syndrome takes shape in which this female control of the market is associated with the strong social position of women and the subsistence orientation.

This is also applicable to Germany. When peasant production was still subsistence-oriented and only surpluses were sold on the market, the social position of peasant women was crucially better than in later times. An essential role in their conversion into housewives was played by their being driven out of the market, a deliberate policy consummated under the Nazis. The pretext came with the preparatory stage of the war economy. But whereas wartime restrictions were lifted after the end of the First World War, those imposed before and during the Second World War have remained right up to the present day. As early as 1933 processing and marketing (including the female domain of cheese and preserves) were taken out of the hands of small and medium-sized farms, ostensibly to make them more effective and to tighten the controls on food production. It was known that peasant women would not accept this without a struggle, and so the prohibitions were disguised as hygienic measures in order to set consumers against producers. In this way, women were deprived of the market that had provided them with an independent monetary income (Kolbeck 1985).

This last example suggests that, even in the twentieth century, women have a chance to control trade when it is a question of the means of subsistence, when the items being traded are useful and necessary for life. We interpret this as a link between the concrete material level and the symbolic order, which here flow together at an especially sensitive point. In the situation in question, the public space is mainly occupied by women – which is forbidden in patriarchal societies, because femininity and natural fertility have to be driven into the realm of the invisible. Only male, artificial production is supposed to be fertile – that is, to constitute the economy. If women are allowed to occupy the public marketplace, with food items moreover, their position as nurturers will be emphatically underlined.

In Juchitán, the market is so 'female' that any man engaged in trade is regarded as a man–woman, as a homosexual. Even foreign men who do not know the rules – visitors from Europe, for example – are often nervous about entering this female force-field.

By virtue of the public position of tradeswomen as providers, disparagement of the female sex 'cannot' manifest itself in Juchitán – or at any rate, it manifests itself less, as is also true in the case of market women in bourgeois society. Even under patriarchal conditions, then, women are capable of defying a part of the symbolic order of patriarchy. In other words, the subsistence orientation makes women strong also in modern times. It weakens them only if they contribute to their own invisibility, by denying their autonomous power and belittling themselves as subsistence controllers and as mothers.

The resistance of market women

Let us first remind ourselves that it was women who stormed the Bastille and led the bread riots during the French Revolution. Not only in France, but elsewhere in Europe and the wider world, market women count as especially independent. Their ready tongues and their intrepidity in the face of power and authority are well known.

In Nigeria market women consciously use their traditional female-maternal strength to resist the oil multinationals. Terisa Turner and M.O. Oshare report two successful movements against the economic and ecological devastation resulting from the operations of Shell, Gulf, Elf and Pan Ocean, and against the local profiteers and supporters of the policy of globalisation. In the wake of the Structural Adjustment Programmes (SAPs) that as usual accompanied a loan from the IMF, there was to be an increase in income taxes, especially for women. This touched the traditional independence of women at a very sensitive point. Already in colonial times, when head taxes were central to the system of pillage in Africa, women repeatedly fought with success against attempts to tax them (Van Allen 1972). In 1986, women in the federal state of Bendel laid siege to the palace of a local potentate, who fled to the protection of the military governor in Benin City. But when the market women there threatened to close their stalls and to deprive the capital of food, the provincial government had no choice but to revoke the taxation of women (Turner and Oshare 1993).

The 'siege' is an old form of protest, which Judith Van Allen describes in her study 'Sitting on a Man' (1972). In 1984 several thousand women surrounded an oil extraction centre to demand compensation for soil contamination, as well as clean water and electricity for the villages and hamlets. For many hours no work shift was able to go in or come out. The women sang mocking songs and threatened to take all their clothes off. (This is the most insulting form of female protest, which has shamed men in Nigeria, Kenya, Trinidad and South Africa for the whole of their lives – publicly naked women using 'the symbolic power of motherhood, agricultural fertility and fertility *tout court*' to put a curse on men.) When the police arrived, the women carried out their threat and put all the men to flight, but eventually received an assurance that their demands would be met. The main concern of the US oil corporation was to avoid any mention of unrest in the press (and, above all, at the stock exchange); otherwise it would have had to steel itself for losses worth billions of dollars. The main concern of the women was with 'the soil, fishing grounds, markets, religious sites and their own living places, the whole underground of a thoroughly peasant existence' (Turner and Oshare 1993: 15).

The Nigerian market women, using specifically female means of power, initiated conscious resistance to the policy of globalisation. Unlike so many in our part of the world, they did not feel powerless in the face of the global economy and its market mechanisms. These women knew and felt that there can be no global market, or any kind of market, that takes global care of subsistence, but only ever a local marketplace and local market-trading – just as there can never be global common land but only local land attached to a genuine community that makes it common. One other reason given by the authors for the Nigerian women's success against the US oil corporation is that they refused to send representatives to meet and negotiate with representatives of the government. No, they stayed together in their thousands, stripped naked, and shamed the oil engineers and the police in the most direct way possible. Rightly do Turner and Oshare call them 'indigenous feminists'.

The image of the 'invisible hand' of abstract market mechanisms has made the market really invisible to us as a place of action. This is not the least reason why so few have realised that globalisation ruins concrete markets, and that the markets in question have mainly been women's markets. Thus the destruction of the retail trade through supermarket-driven globalisation does away with the jobs especially of female traders. Not by chance do Germans talk generically in this context of 'Aunt Emma's shop', for the tradeswoman used to be so well known in her locality that people called her 'auntie'. Children could go to her with a penny and buy a couple of sweets. She knew all the latest news about everyone and everything, being like a newspaper and agony aunt rolled into one. She brought to her work the typically female–maternal social skills.

If we think of the market and of trade as forms of human encounter, who other than women have the necessary competence within any meaningful sexual division of labour?

The market, of course, is especially prone to make the pursuit of money independent of the goal of subsistence. But the fact that in Juchitán it is women not men who have control of the market means that that kind of independence has not occurred. So we say: Subsistence markets in women's hands!

One conclusion: buying is politics

Exchange and market relations that are closely bound up with subsistence needs are capable, even in a market economy, of escaping the mechanisms of maximisation economics. For us, the phrase 'closely bound up with subsistence needs' refers to useful daily necessities, particularly food. It also means that people involved in these market processes are joined together in a social network, so that reciprocity is for them not only possible but necessary.

In Germany as in Europe generally, such conditions are present in binding producer–consumer associations. These have emerged out of social movements that wanted to put their ecological critique of society into practice and to build a new solidarity between town and country – Tanja Loziczky summarises her research in Germany and Austria. The producers are usually farmers unable or unwilling to fit in with the maximization objectives of industrialised capitalist agriculture, and keen to establish direct links with consumers who share the same principles. 'What is most important in the trading is not sales figures but the exemplary effect of solidarity between producers and consumers, which is intended to bring a change in people from self-interest (*Homo oeconomicus*) to group solidarity (*Homo cooperativus*)' (Baumhöfer 1983, quoted in Loziczky 1997: 12).

In other words, 'we need a new moral economy' (Mies 1992), one which every individual brings about by assuming responsibility. At the end of the twentieth century, the process of moral economy includes an awareness that *not only consuming but also buying is politics*. If, instead of driving to the supermarket, I shop at a consumers' cooperative, a weekly market stall or a peasants' stand, or directly from a peasant woman living nearby, I contribute to the workability of the peasant economy, to regionalisation and hence to the subsistence orientation.

Not only food but also clothing, furniture or building materials can immediately be supplied within a subsistence perspective. Tailors and carpenters can also make a living of their own as of now, if their skills are directly demanded in an economy that is being increasingly informalised anyhow. With regard to clothing and housing, however, there is still hardly any awareness that we can escape the machinations of world-market monopolies and breathe life back into regional markets.

Debatable though the action may have been against the offshore sinking of Shell's Brent Spar oil platform, the success of the boycott showed what power consumers can exercise through their purchasing decisions. The first step against belief in inherent market laws and individual powerlessness – a belief that, despite everything, is still with us – is for everyone to take responsibility for their own market behaviour.

NOTES

1. For a critique of such notions, see the contributions in Evers and Schrader 1994.
2. See the critical discussion of such notions in Frank 1966 and 1971.
3. Politics was supposed to follow the strategy that the economy should develop with the least possible interference. Polanyi criticised this policy on the grounds that a lack of social regulation is ultimately harmful to economic consolidation. (Looked at today, this again seems a highly topical debate.)
4. Once again it proves more productive for feminist theory to investigate the continuity, rather than the discontinuity, between premodern and modern society.
5. Left-alternative thinkers speak today in similar terms of the development of the productive forces. We have criticised this position in detail in chapters 2 and 3.

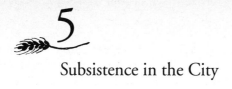

5

Subsistence in the City

Rachel L. Bagby reports how in Philadelphia in the eighties her mother, Rachel Edna Samiella Rebecca Jones Bagby, developed gardens in the middle of a neglected industrial area, and in the process, not only healed the earth and produced food, but built up an urban village community numbering 5,000 people. The author writes that the term 'village community' suits this settlement, even though it is situated in the middle of a city, because it comprises a group of houses, 'is larger than a hamlet, functions as a self-governing political unit, and has several half-acre plots that are worked by the community' (Bagby 1990: 231). Here is a summary of Rachel L. Bagby's story of her mother's city gardening.

Gardens instead of industry

Rachel Edna Bagby saw everywhere the empty, neglected areas covered in weeds, and she, who earlier had worked in the South on the land, said to herself, where weeds grow something useful should also be able to grow. She petitioned the city for this land and obtained it, approximately five acres. And then she asked three or four of the boys who were hanging around to dig it. They received three dollars per hour. They got horse manure as fertiliser from Woodside Park, where it was available free of cost, and needed only to be collected.

And then she planted, just as she had learned it, according to the moon calendar, all sorts of plants: carrots, red cabbage, herbs, tomatoes. She bought seeds and showed the boys how and when the different plants had to be seeded or planted. And the children learned from her. And so also did others in the community.

But Rachel's aim was not only to help the poor of the quarter to lower their living expenses. She wanted people themselves to start to plant the

---

neglected areas in the city with vegetables. Above all, she wanted to show them that it was possible, if they only wanted it. She organised meetings for the people of the neighbourhood, and more and more came. And Rachel Edna showed them how to preserve vegetables and fruit, so that they could enjoy the fruits of the garden during the winter too. She was also concerned to convey to the people the joy of putting seeds into the ground and then seeing how they sprout and grow – a feeling she still remembered from her childhood in the country.

> I know how one does that. I love it, it is part of me … I like to see things grow instead of wasting. And all these vacant lots! … but, you can buy a little dollar's worth of seeds and put it on them. Can't put houses on them, but you sit and eat stuff that comes from them. Look at the flowers that are so pretty. That sort of thing. So this is what started. And everybody, it's spreading, you know. (p. 238)

She also encountered resistance. Particularly from the young mothers, who sat in front of their TVs watching soap operas and had no desire to participate.

> People not wantin to work. They don't want to get their hands dirty … what I mean is you take a lot of mothers don't want to wash the greens, they don't wanna dig down and get the carrots from the ground. They don't wanna get the turnips from the ground. That's dirt. When they get it it's in the store and they clean, so to speak. So a lot of them rather go to the store and get it. I say, 'How long it's been in that store? You can get it right from here and clean it, put it right in your pot or eat it like it is. Put it in your salad and you get the real, all the vitamins.'
>
> So you have resistance, people say I can't bend down, can't bend over, or my fingernails too long. They don't tell you that but you look at the fingernails and know that they're too long to do any work. (p. 241)

Because of the mothers' resistance she likes to work with children:

> But I feel as though our children would better understand how to take care of things and would have a better feeling of the things around them … It begins when you're, you know, small really. (p. 241)

And that is why Rachel Edna works with the children and explains to them which are the weeds and which are vegetables, and that weeds are useful, too, because you can make compost out of them, and that everything that lives moves in a cycle.

The city – a parasite

The modern city is unable to exist on its own and cannot regenerate itself from its own resources. It requires a hinterland from where it imports the food for its citizens, the energy for heating, for factories and advertising signs, the raw material for buildings, clothing, and its whole production of goods. In addition, it needs a hinterland for the deposit of its refuse. This hinterland is by now the whole world, or rather the nature of the whole world. The city exports machines to this hinterland which serve to exploit nature even more, in order to maintain the city. The relation between the modern city and the country is structurally non-reciprocal, a unilateral, colonial, master–slave relationship à la Hegel, like the relationship between the First and Third worlds or that between man and woman in our society. Just as in the above-mentioned relationships, the dominant part is in fact and materially dependent for its life and survival on the part that is being exploited, devalued, dishonoured, marginalised, excluded from cultural and civil society. It is defined as 'wild nature'. Not surprisingly, therefore, contempt for subsistence production is deep-rooted in city dwellers, the consumers in this master–slave relationship. What is worse in these relationships, the exploited see the exploiter as the image of their future.

This parasitical relationship is further aggravated and globalised through today's neoliberal economic policy. The rapidly increasing urbanisation worldwide is not seen to be a consequence of the exploitation and bleeding to death of the countryside, but as a quasi-natural phenomenon, caused by the attractions of urban culture, which young people in particular are unable to resist. 'Explosive population growth' especially is blamed as the cause of this rapid urbanisation.

When we talk of subsistence in the city we want first to create an awareness about this parasitic relationship and look for a way out of it. From our analysis, it becomes evident that neither the liberation of women nor the decolonisation of the Third World nor the rescue of nature can be accomplished unless this relationship is basically altered. However, the cultural ignorance of those who profit from this relationship corresponds to their overbearing arrogance in respect of what already is happening, what already is reality. They are not able to see their own privileges as the result of historical colonisation; instead these are essentialised and universalised. (These postmodern terms seem indicated here). Therefore we will begin by providing empirical evidence that a subsistence orientation already exists in cities, before demonstrating why a subsistence orientation is necessary there. Only then will we deal with the concept of a different city, a different countryside, and a different relationship between city and country.

It has already started. Empirical findings

Subsistence in the cities of the Third World

We are immediately referred to the Third World when we ask where something like a subsistence economy or subsistence work is still or again practised in urban centres. Subsistence is what people are doing in the slums of the megacities in order to survive: garbage collecting, casual work by women and men, all sorts of repair work, prostitution, piece work, work as servants. But we also learn that people grow a few vegetables around their shacks, build their own huts, keep chickens, pigs and goats, in order not to be totally dependent on money income. Anyone who visits one of the large slums of Bombay or Calcutta or Rio de Janeiro or Mexico is surprised at the diversity of activity and the creativity with which people secure their subsistence.

Not only the procurement of the material necessities of life is guaranteed by this subsistence orientation, but frequently also a certain communal cohesion, the principle of mutual assistance, a slum culture – as was created, for instance, by the Samba Schools in the *favelas* of Rio de Janeiro – and often a certain community organisation. The slums are generally the first arrival point in the city for impoverished peasants driven off their land, who frequently still have a lot of rural subsistence capacity and an orientation towards self-provisioning.

This is particularly true for women, who try to secure their livelihood and that of their children through all possible kinds of work. The model of the nuclear family with the man as the breadwinner frequently collapses under these poor circumstances.

Naturally, the subsistence orientation in the growing slums of the megacities of the South is not a matter of free choice. Since cash income is small and the state or the city doesn't support these poorest of the poor at all, particularly after structural adjustment programmes, subsistence production is the necessary means of securing survival. For several years now, development specialists and economists have viewed the urban subsistence economy by no means only as an expression of poverty; they have also discovered in the many activities and methods of production a creativity that has long since been lost by the financially well-off people of the industrialised countries. In the meantime it also has become evident that the institutionalisation of a welfare state in the countries of the South is economically impossible. The survival of the poor guaranteed through subsistence production in the so-called informal sector is therefore for the state, for capital, and for the dominant classes the cheapest and most convenient method of keeping the poor quiet.[1] In addition, the informal sector represents an inexhaustible pool of the cheapest labour, which can be utilised when the need arises (cf. Chapter 2).

All that is well known. However, what interests us here now is less the exploitation of the people, particularly of women, in this informal sector, than the question of whether the subsistence orientation of the poor in the megacities of the South doesn't also contain structural elements of an economy that could become important if the informal sector was no longer parasitically exploited and colonised by the formal sector.

In connection with the UN Habitat Conference it was noted that some of the cities of the Third World produce up to 15 per cent of their food needs within their own borders (Uwe Hoering, *Frankfurter Rundschau* 10 June 1996). Since this urban food production is almost exclusively performed by women, it is statistically barely visible: it is 'shadow work', like housework. If you include with direct food production all the other varied forms of subsistence work – food preparation, bartering with food, all types of services, helping others, fetching and carrying water – then it becomes evident that the survival of the majority of the people in these cities depends on women's subsistence work. This subsistence orientation in the cities of the South is the result of exploitation, no doubt, but it can also become the basis for economic and ecological innovation.[2] This became evident at the Women's Day of Food held during the NGO Forum of the World Food Summit of the FAO on 15 November 1996 in Rome.

Monica Opole from Nairobi built a centre for indigenous knowledge systems and by-products (CIKSAP), where old food plants are collected which today are considered weeds. Meals are prepared, old recipes are popularised and disseminated. The aim of the centre is not only the maintenance of traditional ecological knowledge; it wants to give the poor access to these almost-free sources of nutrition, available even in the city.

The poor in the world have to become innovative and creative, to rediscover old subsistence knowledge, and to further develop it if they want to survive. They are faced by the fact that as a result of the structural adjustment programmes of the IMF, government funds for health care and food subsidies for the poor have been cut or eliminated.

Return to subsistence in the erstwhile 'socialist' countries

The big cities in several of the former socialist countries are in a similiar situation. They had been promised a rapid transition to the Western market economy. In reality, they were de-developed into neo-colonies of Western capitalism which, above all, found here a gigantic new market and, as in the Third World, an enormous supply of cheap labour. In order to survive, they have to accept similiar work conditions to those found in the informal sector in the Third World. Since the governmental supply systems have almost collapsed, and the market economy only functions in its mafia form, in winter the people in cities like Moscow or Sofia are threatened by hunger and cold. According to eyewitnesses, many people in Moscow have started to plant vegetables during the weekend outside the city or in the city (Meyer-Renschhausen 1997). In the autumn of 1996 university professors in Sofia had reached the point of considering moving to the countryside in order to find some food.[3] In Poland, the unemployed frequently return to the villages to winter there (Kindl 1995). In Cuba, as a result of the USA blockade, the government has asked its people to plant vegetables on every balcony, every empty piece of land and every roadside, and to revitalise old subsistence techniques (Rengam 1997). No thorough studies exist about the reintroduction of the subsistence economy in the former socialist countries and in Cuba. Above all, there is no study on how the people judge this necessary survival economy. Do they consider it a passing necessary evil, as a return to premodern times? Or are they able to recognise the subsistence economy as a new chance? Does it give them a sense of greater independence and security? Does it create new, satisfying neighbourly relationships? Are they able to see in this quasi-enforced subsistence production the beginning of a better economic system than that of the new mafia capitalism? These are open questions. We assume that the majority of people in these countries consider the return to subsistence as indeed necessary, but nevertheless as temporary, an interim stage which will eventually be replaced by a proper capitalist market economy or a return to erstwhile socialism.

In the cities of the South as well as in the cities of the former Eastern bloc, a subsistence economy is for many people necessary to secure survival. This does not mean that it necessarily appears as a subsistence *perspective*. The return to subsistence in the former Eastern bloc countries demonstrates, however, how quickly the basis of the industrial society can collapse.

Even though we don't share the opinion of some that a more or less automatically necessary collapse of industrial capitalism will follow the collapse of socialism (Kurtz 1991), we do believe that the present permanent crisis is going to confront people of the First World sooner or later in a similiar manner, and with it the question of securing their subsistence. More and more people are beginning to think about the subsistence perspective. This preoccupation grows out of the recognition that industrial society is, within the framework of its own paradigm and with the means at its disposal, unable to solve the problems it has created.

Subsistence as concrete utopia

The alternative economy

The beginnings of a new, urban subsistence orientation can be found in the students' movement and in its criticism of the profit-oriented capitalist system as well as of the state-controlled 'socialist' economy in the East. It was primarily for ideological reasons that the rebelling students, after 1968, founded communes and residential collectives, in which some of their principles could be realised: abolition of private property and authoritarianism, equality, self-determination, all doing the same work, living out of the same pot, direct democracy, decision-making by consensus, more autonomy. Besides, the communes and the residents' collectives there developed self-help projects like children's shops and parent initiatives. It had become evident that the welfare state did not provide the facilities for a great number of requirements. The more the women's movement spread in the seventies, the more self-run women's projects were started, which followed similiar principles: women's bookstores, women's publishing houses, women's artisan shops, women's journals, women's café shops, women's holiday houses, women's educational centres, women's communes and women's residents' collectives. During the seventies and eighties, they became part of the rapidly growing alternative sector, which consciously declared itself to be an alternative to the capitalist market as well as to state socialism. In West Germany there were, in 1989, 10,000 self-help projects with 80,000 activists, in addition to 4,000 projects of the alternative economy with 24,000 activists (Grottian and Kück, quoted by Sarkar 1987: 256 ff.). The majority were in the media or culture (24 per cent), followed by trade (18.8 per cent), and production like furniture making, repairs, printing (16 per cent) (Huber, quoted by Sarkar 1987: 260).

Even though these alternative enterprises started out explicitly with non-capitalist principles, many were caught up again in the capitalist market and are today almost indistinguishable from other enterprises (Sarkar, 1987: 261 ff.). A new study, on the other hand, shows that in the province of Hessen about half of the self-organised enterprises continue to adhere to their old principles after a period of ten years (Heider, Hock, and Seitz 1997).

The projects and initiatives that adhered to their political aims and principles are mainly those that had added to the principle of self-direction and self-determination that of self-provisioning. A good example of continuity of political aims and practice is Socialist Self-Help Cologne (SSK), which was described by Maria Mies (Mies and Shiva 1993), and Socialist Self-Help Mühlheim (SSM) which split from the SSK. These groups adhered over the years not only to the principles of self-government and provisioning, but also to socialist and ecological principles.

Several self-provisioning or food co-ops are also among the urban self-help and self-supply projects that originated in the mid-seventies. They, too, today still have the same political aims. The self-provisioning co-ops developed out of the ecology, anti-nuclear, and alternative movements of the seventies, while SSK and SSM had their origin in the student movement. Most activists had realised during the struggle against nuclear power plants that it is not sufficient to fight against the state and the nuclear industry, but that we need a fundamental change of production and consumption if we want to save the earth for future generations. In addition, they wanted healthy food, produced neither through poisoning the soil nor exploitation of the Third World.

Here is an example of the political subsistence orientation of an urban self-provisioning co-op, the story of the Bremen Self-Supply Co-op. It was founded in 1977. We quote from their tenth anniversary position paper of 1987.

Our aims

- Self-organisation of consumers and producers in order to harmonise production and manufacturing methods of food products; the consumers can aid and further the ecological supply and clean-up techniques; development of alternate techniques;
- avoidance of further alienation of city people from those living in the countryside; and elimination of the separation between living and working areas.
- Improvement of agricultural production by using ecological methods; avoidance of the increasing environmental problems in agriculture caused by artificial fertilisers and pesticides and the increase of monoculture.

The group declares as aims of producer–consumer co-ops:

1. 'reducing the anonymity' of the relations between producer and consumer. Mutual knowledge of their life situations and their needs.
2. 'quality control' – 'quality' primarily understood as the quality of human relations.
3. 'just prices', negotiated on the basis not of cost-benefit calculations, but of the financial possibilities of producer and consumer.
4. 'mutual reliance', that is, both the producer and the consumer carry the risks. Instead of competition, mutual care and intact human relationships.
5. 'healthy food': rejection of chemistry in agriculture, not only out of self-interest but out of concern for the ecology.
6. 'regional supply systems': food has to come from the region. Short transport chains with contact between consumer and producer.
7. 'seasonal supply': rejection of food from greenhouses or the Third World. Necessity to provide storage of food supplies for the winter.
8. 'meat only from animals who were raised according to their species' needs'.
9. 'the principle of not living at the expense or to the detriment of others and of finding our livelihood in our own country creates the precondition that other peoples also can find their livelihood in their own country'. (Selbstversorgungs-Cooperative Bremen 1987)

Producer–consumer cooperatives can be seen as a further development of self-supply co-ops or food co-ops. At the first federal congress of the food cooperatives in October 1986, the number of food co-ops in Germany was estimated to be between 400 and 500. By 1990 the number had risen to 800. At the time of the annual congress of producer–consumer cooperatives in Altenkirchen in 1987, 100 such co-ops existed in West Germany. We don't have definite figures for today. At that time producer–consumer co-ops

(PCCs) and food co-ops still saw themselves definitely as subsistence-oriented, self-provisioning, self-organised, anti-capitalist, basically democratic, eco-logical and internationalist, a training ground for an alternative economy. 'As politics in action, they put political demands into praxis and are "catalysts" for the dissemination of alternative values and actions in society' (Selbst-versorgungs-Cooperative Bremen 1987: 71). In 1989 the Wurzelwerk food co-op in Gütersloh, the first producer–consumer cooperative in Germany, restated the basic principles of the Altenkirchen declaration. Tilman Schröder writes in the Wurzelwerk newspaper:

> 'Wurzelwerk' is primarily an (economic) action concept which orients itself upon ethical criteria. It is important to realise, that an economic system that forgoes the exploitation of nature and of people is basically unable to compete with one based on exploitation, just as little as a merchant who pays a just price for his goods can compete with a fence.

> Our hope is based upon people: people who are prepared and strengthened by their still existing love to overcome the common split between that what they already know about the background of our neocolonial economic consumerist society and their daily economic behaviour; and who remain alert in the search for the victims wherever profits are made. And who not just buy what is offered cheaply. (*Wurzelwerk-Zeitung*, April 1989, p.14)

In the cities of the rich industrial countries, food co-ops and producer–consumer co-ops continue to be organised, but they are not quite as subsistence-oriented as they used to be ten years ago.[4] At the meeting of the PCCs in 1997 the members had to admit that 'green commerce' had pushed the political aims aside. Gila Zimmermann of Wurzelwerk reports that in the meantime broad international connections are developing between the PCCs. Wurzelwerk cooperates, for example, with PCCs in Greece and the Ukraine. New PCCs are started, among other reasons, because people reject gene-manipulated food.

In spite of the seemingly irresistible might of the capitalist market there continues to be an internationalising of the efforts to bring producer and consumer again into a non-alienating relationship. In Belgium so-called 'voedsel teams' (food teams) were founded in September 1996, following the model of the Japanese Seikatsu clubs. Jeannecke van de Ven, a woman activist of Aardewerk read in *Ecofeminism* (Mies and Shiva 1993) about these Japanese consumer–producer clubs, and immediately acted upon the idea.[5] Between September 1996 and April 1997, 200 such voedsel teams were started, each numbering 15 to 20 members, who cooperated with twenty biological farmers. According to Jeannecke van de Ven this is the first initiative towards the founding of producer–consumer associations in Belgium. The demand is great. Between urban consumers and rural producers a lively political discussion has developed touching also on other questions besides that of healthy food. More and more people realise that food is a highly political issue.[5]

In Canada the Urban Supported Agriculture movement has even gone beyond the mere change of consumer behaviour. Here urban people really cooperate with farmers and feel responsible for ensuring that they can continue with ecological farming.

Barter circles, LETS, local economy

Further urban attempts in the direction of subsistence are today mainly the different forms of barter circles, local exchange and trading systems (LETS), and a variety of local money circulation schemes. These projects also are searching for an alternative to the exploitative capitalist economy, but less through changes in production relations and more through a change in exchange relationships, which should replace capitalist market relations. Barter circles developed first in the USA. They were a reaction to the impoverishment of large parts of the population as a result of Reaganomics in the eighties. Barter circles function on the principle that work is exchanged for work or services. The unit of measure is time, recorded in a register. The person who has mowed somebody else's lawn for two hours has a claim for two hours of work from another member, regardless what type of work it is. In Germany there are at present some 300 of these barter circles.

While the barter circles simply use time as 'money' or as the unit of exchange, the LETS, which had their origin in 1989 in British Columbia, Canada, have invented a multitude of local currencies. These barter circles occurred on the European continent first in Switzerland where 'talents' were used as currency. Since then, many talent exchanges have sprung up in Austria, Switzerland and Germany. They all function on the same principle: If A works for B (for instance, he builds a shelf), he receives a credit of 400 talents from the time registry. A can receive for these 400 talents work or services from B, C, or D. In these exchanges the qualification of the worker and the quality of work make no difference. No interest accrues on the time accounts, but services can be exchanged for goods. The currencies have a great variety of names.

In England such barter circles exist in more than 200 cities and towns. They exchange not only services but food and other products as well. Totnes in Devon even has a weekly market for LETS services and goods. Ideally, the accounts are balanced: in other words, you spend as much time for others as they have spent for you. Sometimes, however, people have to overdraw their account – single mothers, for instance. That is no reason to terminate their membership, but they try to work out how their problems can be solved. In some cities even restaurants and supermarkets participate in such LETS exchanges. They provide goods, food and drink in exchange for work and services.

Strictly speaking these exchanges are not really new. They use elements of the pre-industrial 'moral economy', namely the principles of mutuality, reliability, and mutual assistance. They reject growth, interest and profiteering and aim for a local or regional economy based on use-values. Besides the barter of services and useful products they develop unalienated relationships. They want to re-create communities. For that reason a barter circle in Munich limits its membership to 3,000. People should be able to know each other.

Some of the barter and LETS circles pick up the theoretical ideas of Silvio Gesell who in 1916 formulated his theory of a 'natural economic order', the centrepiece of which is non-interest-bearing money. Gesell called this money 'free money', and his followers built on this the theory of the 'free economy'. They conducted experiments with 'free money' in Germany, Austria, Switzerland, France, Spain, and the USA, in order to fight unemployment. The Tyrolian community of Wörgl introduced 'free money' in 1932, and issued notes, which they called 'work confirmations', to the value of 32,000 schillings. All work was paid for with this interest-free money. Those who had not spent all their 'free money' at the end of the month were penalised by a user fee, a negative interest.

Within one year the 32,000 work confirmations had circulated 463 times and had thus made possible goods and services of the value of 14,816,000 schillings. Unemployment dropped by 25% during the year. But when 170 Austrian communities wanted to repeat the experiment of Wörgl, the Austrian government intervened and forbade the 'free economy'. The monopoly of the National Bank was being threatened. (Kennedy, 1990, 43)

The ideas of Silvio Gesell were again popularised in Germany in 1990 by Margrit Kennedy and in 1993 by Helmut Creutz. They believe that the monetary system is the main cause of the economic and ecological crises. The idea of local, interest-free money aims at transforming money again into a medium of exchange, which cannot be accumulated.

If we compare the self-support co-ops and the producer–consumer associations of the seventies and eighties with today's barter circles, LETS and talent exchanges, we realise that the earlier movements were based on a broader and more comprehensive political concept. They connected their self-liberation with the liberation of nature, an abolition of the city–country contradiction, the elimination of the exploitation of the Third World, and the development of non-alienating relationships among people and with nature. Above all, their view was not concentrated solely on the cities, as is largely the case with barter systems. The early PCCs and food co-ops put the main emphasis on the connection of the spheres of production and consumption. They were concerned not only with the *what* of production, but equally with the *how* and *how much*. The barter circles, on the other hand, are mainly interested in the circulation of goods and services; they don't ask *what*, *how*, or *how much*. The reason for this reduced perspective is that barter circles and LETS were primarily founded to fight unemployment and poverty. Their ecological, socialist, and particularly internationalist orientations are rather underdeveloped. In both approaches feminist ideas about non-sexist division of labour are largely ignored.

Urban gardening

What differentiates the projects of the seventies and eighties from those of the nineties is mainly the changed economic situation and the consequent general socio-psychological atmosphere. The urban alternative movement primarily aimed at a voluntary change of lifestyle as the basis for an ecological society and economy. Although there were already millions of unemployed, nobody could imagine in the early eighties that full employment could come to an end. Those who wanted subsistence, in city or country, took this step voluntarily.

Things are different today. The search for an alternative, local economy in urban areas originates mainly from helplessness in the face of rising unemployment, and from the realisation by many that full employment is a thing of the past. In addition, rapid technological development, globalisation and merciless international competition lead to more and more factories becoming redundant because they are no longer sufficiently profitable.

Many countries are full of such ruins of development and deserted industrial complexes, a consequence of neoliberal economic policies and the deindustrialisation of whole regions. This process of deindustrialisation began much earlier in the USA and the UK as a result of Thatcherism and Reaganomics. Cities that lived off one company were practically given up on and rapidly became delapidated when this corporation moved away. This happened, for example, to Detroit, Liverpool, Philadelphia and Chicago. On some of the fallow industrial lands, particularly in the USA, a *re-ruralisation* process begins to take place through a movement that calls itself City Gardening, or Urban Gardening. This tries to heal the earth and to create gardens to further self-provisioning in the city.

Gwyn Kirk reports on one of those grassroot movements for the re-creation of subsistence in Detroit, one of the cities most devastated by industrialisation. The aim of the movement is to rebuild, re-create, reinspire the city from the ground up. The movement does not want to repair the old capitalist city, controlled by General Motors or some other company, but wants to create a new city, which exists for its people and for nature. This 'clearing of a city' (analoguous to making land arable) abandoned by capitalism, in which violence, criminality, poverty, drug abuse, and hopelessness characterise the collapse of the social ecology is something different from that devised by landscapers and city planners who 'green' cities from above. The city administration of Detroit had offered General Motors tax breaks, had privatised communal properties, destroyed churches, small shops, dwellings, and hospitals, in order to develop new industrial centres, as we do in Germany. As a last resort, the city administration pushed gambling casinos in order to stimulate the economy. All this was without any success. The city degenerated more and more.

In 1993, the administration decided to close the inner city, because it was allegedly too expensive to supply it with water and electricity, and to collect garbage. In Detroit, one third of the total population and one half of all children live below the poverty line. We don't have to go to the Third World to see misery.

Nevertheless, says Gwyn Kirk, there is in Detroit not only devastation, poverty, violence and criminality, but also a multitude of initiatives and activities for the revitalisation of the community, the rebuilding of a local economy and new social relationships. One of these projects is the 4H Urban Gardens Project.[6] It was started by African-American women from the South who still had experience with farm and garden work. They call themselves the Gardening Angels, and they have, since 1994, created more than one hundred gardens, in which they grow vegetables, fruit and herbs for use and for sale. They pick up the knowledge and experience of the local population, use the land in an ecological manner, heal the ecological damage, produce cheaply and simultaneously create new relationships between the members of the community. Their main concern is the strengthening of self-reliance, self-provisioning, and personal strength. Besides all that, they teach the young how to garden and thus strengthen the ties between the generations and different communities. The urban gardening initiative in Detroit shows that economic, ecological, social and cultural aspects can be combined in one project, if it is subsistence-oriented.

This is also true of another project for the regeneration of Detroit, the Detroit Summer, which was started in 1992 as a multicultural, intergenerational youth programme. The project invites volunteers from the city and elsewhere to rebuild Detroit. They receive free board and lodging, and transportation to the workplace. They can also participate in a social and cultural educational programme and learn, for instance, how to build a new urban economy. These volunteers work together with women and men of the city and repair houses, paint, remove rubble, and build gardens and playgrounds.

The Detroit Summer goes back to the initiative of James Boggs, Grace Lee Boggs, and Shea Howell (Kirk 1996/97: 12). Their vision of a new city is a city independent of the investment decisions and the money of big companies, which have no responsibility for, and no loyalty to, the people. They want to build instead a local economy based on the principles of autonomy, self-help, and the creation and furthering of communal principles. They consider it important that young people who, in spite of a good education, are unable to find a job in industry acquire subsistence capabilities. An important part of this subsistence knowledge is that work is seen and valued differently. The experience of the volunteers in the Detroit Summer has taught them that the networks used by them to carry out their activities can also become the basis of a new economy in which relationships that satisfy mutual needs are more important than money.

'Urban gardening' in the USA is an answer from the victims of the neo-liberal policy of deindustrialisation of whole cities. Similiarly in England, more and more marginalised people with small incomes in the old, industrially deserted cities become involved in self-help, self-organising, and some also in self-supply. In contrast to Germany, however, such non-profit organisations in England are supported by the state, because they are a relief for the social services budget. The Community Development Foundation (CDF) in London supports, for instance, self-help groups or volunteer action groups in their efforts to exert pressure on the city administration to further initiatives for the regeneration of neglected and rundown urban districts.[7] The CDF is convinced that a third sector has to be developed between the private and state sectors: the community sector, which is the backbone of the local economy and, above all, represents a kind of life insurance for the poor. Most of the projects assisted by the CDF, for which it uses public and private financial sources, are urban projects: house construction, small trades, and urban renewal. But it also promotes the participation of the communities in public affairs, in direct involvement of the people in decision-making processes.

Nevertheless, the CDF remains, in respect of labour, obligated to the priority of wage labour, in other words – to the first labour market. Voluntary work for the community is good, but should not replace wage labour. It should, in time of crisis, help people to survive and to maintain their ability to work until the general economy is able to incorporate them again in the first labour market. According to the CDF, community sector and voluntary work essentially serve the purpose of bridging over crisis situations. But in the community sector there are also initiatives that go beyond crisis management. A citizens' initiative was started in 1996 in Salisbury called Greening of the Towers. In a fairly dilapidated area of high-rise flats, people had started to grow fruit and vegetables on the balconies of the tower blocks and on the neglected areas surrounding them. It started with just a few actions, then more and more people participated. For the first time a kind of community developed among the tenants through this communal food-growing project. The communal growing of plants led, as in Detroit and Philadelphia, to other communal activities, for instance, a café shop that served as a meeting place where the processed fruit was sold, and where future projects were discussed, where people learned how to deal with the bureaucracy and to find new sources of funding. The Greening of the Towers led to the 'greening' of a human community (Evans 1995). In the summer of 1996 the CDF filed an application to start such projects in all English cities with rundown areas.

The 'wild farmers' of Tokyo

'Urban gardening' in the USA and Greening of the Towers in England are responses to economic crises since the eighties. In Tokyo, people had already started in 1978 to carry out agriculture in the middle of the Tokyo megapolis. They call themselves 'yabo farmers' (wild farmers) and communally grow rice, vegetables and other grains on areas not yet covered by construction in the suburb of Hino and other areas. Recapturing self-sufficiency is their aim. Tetsuo Akemine was one of the first Yabo farmers. He is an agronomist who returned to practice. He talked in Cologne in 1997, at the invitation of Socialist Self-help Mühlheim (SSM), about subsistence agriculture in Tokyo.

The industrialisation of Japan took place in a very short time, virtually between 1960 and 1990. This meant not only that Tokyo became the most important industrial centre, expanding quickly into a city with a population of 11 million, but also that the government pursued systematic evictions of rice farmers. In 1970, the government introduced quotas on rice production, and imported cheap rice and corn from the USA. The Japanese learned to eat bread instead of rice and meat instead of fish. The corn was fed to animals. Japan had abandoned its policy of food self-sufficiency, which had been 100 per cent before the Second World War, in favour of building up the production and export of cars and computers. Today, Japan is dependent on the USA for 60 per cent of its wheat, 80 per cent of its soya beans, and 90 per cent of its corn. Since the signing of the GATT in 1993, Japan also has had to import rice from Thailand and the USA. Its self-sufficiency rate is only 46 per cent, the lowest of the industrialised countries.

The Yabo farmers want to oppose this neoliberal model, which is dependent on the import of food, with a subsistence model. Their aim is to make cities arable again. They work together and divide the proceeds among themselves. They do not use artificial fertiliser or pesticides. They grow fifty different plants, and keep chickens, pigs, and goats. They compost their kitchen garbage or use it for feed in order to maintain an organic cycle.

The Yabo farmers are not full-time peasants, but employees of publishing houses, single mothers, workers in computer firms and communication companies. They aim not for total autarky but for partial participatory self-provisioning. This they have accomplished for vegetables to 100 per cent, and for rice to 70 per cent. This subsistence agriculture is for Akemine an extremely important project, particularly now and in Tokyo. For Japan, Tokyo is the centre of global capital. All transnational corporations have been buying land in the centre of Tokyo during recent years. Land prices have exploded and people are more and more forced to the periphery. Until recently, fiscal policies have favoured the few remaining subsistence peasants in Tokyo. This has now changed. The owners of the land demand it now for construction. Thus the social project of the Yabo farmers is endangered. Akemine and his co-workers

are now trying to develop a national network of similiar urban part-time farmers in order to force legislative change. Under the present legal situation, self-suppliers and subsistence peasants are not considered to be farmers unless they produce for the market.

In Japan Tetsuo Akemine and the 'wild farmers' in Tokyo are not the only people who prefer subsistence agriculture to the scramble for money in the urban centres. Recently, according to the *Nikkei Weekly* of 18 January 1996, there has been a trend among young university graduates to return to agriculture, to a long-term self-sufficiency basis 'even if this means to deviate temporarily from the principles of free market economy'.

Farming in Tokyo and other cities is not a nostalgic hobby of urbanised rootless sons and daughters of peasants. It aims, as a social learning field, to remodel the dominant relationship between urban and rural areas. Not only is the responsibility of the city for agricultural subsistence production part of this, but also a new and different evaluation of the rural space. To make cities arable means in the end that the cities cease to remain the sole centres of culture, liberty, politics, social life and availability of work. They have to relinquish their parasitic existence, they have to become once again the site of production of the necessities of life rather than places of passive consumption only.

Making the cities arable will create a direct mutual relationship with a new, non-colonial culture of the countryside. When the countryside ceases to be just 'Hinterland' for the city, the present contempt for rural work will change. When young, well-trained people again desire to live in the country and, above all, when they are able to find work in the country, rural space will become attractive again. Then the country will also be a place of culture again. Our present concepts of culture and nature will have to undergo fundamental changes. We are going to have egalitarian, many-faceted, rich relationships, based on mutuality instead of colonial, hierarchical and dualistically structured relationships between culture and nature or city and country.

The examples show that subsistence in the cities is not a utopian pipe dream but is being practised in diverse ways.[8] The argument could be made, that we are dealing only with local, special cases which by no means represent a comprehensive alternative economical concept. True, these examples of urban subsistence production are not based on a theoretical overall model. The subsistence perspective cannot be forced into a rigid model. However, by now also more comprehensive theoretical approaches exist, suggesting how cities can be changed to subsistence communities. The Australian Ted Trainer is a theorist of urban subsistence economy. He developed the concept of a 'sustainable economy for cities'. His sustainable economy is largely identical with what we call 'subsistence orientation' (Trainer 1996). He rejects the three pillars of the expansive industrial system: permanent growth, capitalist markets, and profit maximisation. He opposes these with new principles:

- self-sufficiency in household, town, region, and nation
- simple lifestyle: people who are able to say, It is enough!
- cooperation and mutuality
- zero growth.

Trainer demonstrates that a subsistence economy in respect of food is possible even in cities, if the aim is self-supply. He proves that gardens could be created everywhere – between, behind and within appartment blocks – and that unused urban land can be used for food production. Studies in the USA have shown that 2,500 square feet (approx. 300 square metres of land) are sufficient to feed one person.

Subsistence-oriented cities would not be mega-cities. Trainer estimates that a town of 10,000 inhabitants would be able to self-supply itself partially, and that a periphery of ten kilometres would be sufficient to fulfil most of its basic needs. Trainer rejects the argument that in such a local/regional economy everything would be more expensive. There would most probably be more barter and less buying; long-distance transport would be eliminated, and local energy resources such as biomass and windmills could be used. People would produce much of what they need themselves. All this would drastically reduce the need for money but people would nevertheless live better. Like Akemine, Trainer is of the opinion that all these ideas make necessary a fundamentally new concept of the city and of relationship between the city and countryside, a concept that has said goodbye to the capitalist illusion of growth. However, if sustainability is not to remain an empty phrase, we have no other choice than the self-supply economy (Trainer 1996: 135–42).

With all the practical and theoretical attempts to make the city arable again, however, the question arises: are we dealing only with temporary crisis management, the attempts of people to survive in the ruins of the capitalist or state-socialist industrial systems? Such attempts may even be desired by capital and state, because they reduce expenses, they keep the population fit for further exploitation and accumulation, and they help to repair destroyed nature. In the face of the worldwide politics of structural adjustment programmes and the neoliberal destruction of social support systems by governments, the ruralisation of the cities with this type of subsistence production might be welcomed by the corporations. It might be welcomed in particular because it would possibly neutralise the anger and disappointment of the unemployed and marginalised, and guide this anger into productive channels.

Does that mean, in the end, that subsistence in the city is going to become only instrumental for the maintenance and subsidising of the capitalist system, just as the work of women, of small peasants, of the survival work in the so-called informal sector, has always done (Bennholdt-Thomsen, Mies and von Werlhof 1983/92) but on a broader basis?

We cannot answer this question with a simple yes or no. We have learned in our analysis of the functioning of capitalism not only that the accumulation of capital exploits and destroys subsistence, but that new cycles of accumulation grow upon the ruins of subsistence. The new ruins in the cities, however, are those of the industrial system itself, emerging from its own contradictions. When people, particularly women, produce and renew their lives and those of their children on and within this rubble, as they have always done, without depending on capital, then this is by no means reactionary, as some claim. This represents a possibility that people in cities will not want to make themselves again dependent on big corporations and the logic of accumulation alone, but will build different urban–rural cities in which the production and reproduction of life is the guiding principle. This is being planned already in Detroit.

NOTES

1. The concept of the 'informal sector' was originally used by J. K. Hart (1973) in his study on 'informal' urban income in Ghana. S. V. Sethuraman used and generalised the term in a study for the ILO. See: E. Maerke, 'A way out of dependency? The uncertain future of the informal sector in developing countries', Heidelberg, 1986.
2. Several NGOs have recognised this ability for innovation of the subsistence orientation in the informal sector of the Third World and try to use it as an escape from the disaster of development aid. A meeting was held in 1995 at the Bad Boll Evangelical Academy with the theme: 'Subsistence Economy, a New/Old Concept in Development Politics'.
3. Personal information from Professor E. Naudascher, Karlsruhe, Germany.
4. In the USA there are an estimated 4,000 smaller and 300 big food co-ops, each having between 5,000 and 10,000 members.
5. Oral communication, Jeanneke van de Ven, April 1997.
6. The 4H garden project is a project of the Department of Agriculture, Wayne County Co-operative Extension Service of Michigan State University.
7. Personal information from Gabriel Chanan, Director of CDF, London.
8. Even in New York – in Brooklyn, on the East River Side and in other parts – there is a movement of Communal Urban Gardens. It is known as Green Finger. These communal gardens in the midst of New York are a place where a neighbourhood meets, analogous to a village square. Neighbourhoods use these gardens to discuss local affairs and celebrate spring and harvest festivals.

6

Defending, Reclaiming and Reinventing the Commons

From fodder to waste:
destruction of the commons and EU agrarian policy

Before discussing the need to reclaim and reinvent the commons in industrialised countries we want to start with two stories, which we hope will contextualise our quest; they will also raise some questions which in our view are necessary if one wants to get clarity about the issue of commons today, namely: Why is this issue raised today? Who destroys the commons? Why have the commons to be reinvented? Can there be something like global commons? What can 'new commons' be in rich industrialised countries?

I, Maria Mies, come from a small village in the hilly area south of Cologne, called Eifel. When I was a child the village had thirty-two peasant households. All were subsistence farmers whose only regular money income came from milk production and the sale of potatoes and sometimes a pig or a calf. The village still had forests, land, brooks, roads as commons, and these commons were maintained through a system of free communal labour, which each household had to contribute.

For instance, when a road had to be constructed or snow had to be cleared off the road, or trees had to be planted in the village forest, each household had to contribute free labour – male and female – to do this necessary communal work. I remember that these community actions were occasions of great fun. On the other hand each household also benefited from these commons. Even today every family still gets a certain amount of free firewood from the village forest. In former times, cows and pigs used to be driven to the village forest for grazing, and the village land was to be used by the poor.

Today only two households are left in this village who are still farming

141

the land. All the others have either given up farming or left the village. The village commons have either been privatised or are being leased out to a few big farmers who buy or lease all the land. The only commons still left is the village forest. But the system of free communal labour has been totally abolished and replaced by wage labour.

These changes are a consequence of EU agrarian policy since the fifties. According to this policy the number of farmers was to be drastically reduced through the modernisation, mechanisation, chemicalisation and capitalisation of agriculture. Europe considers itself an industrialised region, and agriculture is subordinated to industry.

This development model decreed that the subsidies and cheap credits given to farmers were all tied to expansionism, big investments, big machinery and production for the market. Those who could not compete in this field gave up farming, particularly young men who sought wage employment in industry.

Along with this development model came a campaign to 'beautify the villages'. Beautifying meant to make the village look like a suburban area, with parks for children, pavements, well-kept houses whose barns and stables were transformed into flats for tourists, while kitchen gardens were turned into well-trimmed lawns. Due to such 'development' schemes, the village of my mother, Steffeln, now has a debt burden of DM1 million.

On the other hand, since more and more peasants have given up farming, the natural methods of using organic wastes as fodder for pigs and chicken, or as fertiliser, or compost, have also disappeared. Grass growing on the byways, which formerly was used to feed goats and cows, has become 'green waste'. Moreover, the lawns in the new village park and in the private gardens are another new source of 'green waste'. The same is true of the shrubs and trees along the community lanes, which have to be trimmed from time to time.

The amount of waste, particularly organic waste, has increased tremendously. But since the old cycles of production and reproduction have been disrupted, there is nowhere any more, even in the village and its surroundings, where this organic waste can be dumped.

As a way out the district administration has introduced the 'green garbage bin' for 'organic waste'. And this waste is now exported as far as Thuringia where it is composted by an industrial composting firm. The reason for its export to Thuringia – the most easterly part of Germany – is the cheaper wages in the former GDR. Hence, a small rural community that some time ago was still more or less self-sufficient and had a commons regime which kept intact the community, the ecosystem, the local culture and economy now has to export its so-called 'organic waste' to a faraway industry for elimination.

The absurdity of this situation is enhanced by the fact that both the village and the district administration are indebted to such a degree that they cannot afford this garbage tourism, financially speaking. But since the peasants themselves have been declared 'garbage population' by the EU's agrarian policy, the produce of the land that cannot be directly turned into saleable commodities has also to be declared waste and somehow got rid of. But this getting rid of is not only causing further ecological damage – due to long-distance transport – it is also very costly.

While analysing these processes we began to understand that waste, particularly organic waste, could be called 'negative commons'. On the one hand, the old commons regime has been destroyed. The old system of free communal labour has been replaced by private wage labour. Commons and users' rights have been transformed into private property, and individual self-interest as a motive is considered supreme. This has not only changed the ethics of the community but also destroyed the community as such. This is because now people no longer feel responsible for their waste. What is declared waste, and where it is dumped are not their concern. Their only worry is to get rid of the undesired physical remnants of the processes of the production of life. And as this production of life is no longer imbedded in a living interconnected whole, an ecosystem with its organic cycles and symbioses and its continuity with the human community and its culture, but is instead cut off and segregated from other organic beings (plants, animals, microbes) these remnants cannot be valued and understood as part and parcel of this life process. They become waste. They have to disappear. At least they have to be removed from people's sight and smell.

If one looks at waste in modern, industrialised societies, societies based on the institution of private property, individual self-interest and the logic of accumulation, one begins to understand that the tragedy is not the inescapable destiny of the commons, as Garret Hardin suggested, but rather that private property and self-interest cannot solve the problem of waste or of 'negative commons'.

As all common space is already occupied in these societies by private interests, and as the recycling or elimination of waste will be done only if it is profitable to such private interests, there is a frantic search now to export and dump organic or industrial waste, toxic waste particularly, into some other people's 'commons', mostly in the South, which are then called 'free access' areas. Air, water, rainforests and deserts are becoming waste dumps for affluent industrial society.

No reinvention of the commons in the North
without defending the commons in the South

If one looks only at the processes happening today at the local village level in an industrialised society like Germany, one understands only half of the context within which these processes happen. Because what is happening at the village level in Germany is not determined by the village, nor even by the German nation-state or the EU, but is the result of a process of global restructuring of the capitalist world economy. In this global 'free' market system the Ricardian principle of comparative advantages is applied. Therefore it is cheaper to import food items from cheap labour countries of the South than to buy them from small farmers in industrialised society. The institutions that today regulate and promote this system of capitalist global trade and investment are the World Bank, IMF, GATT, WTO, regional trade blocs like the EU, NAFTA and APEC, and the Multilateral Agreement on Investment.

Hence, if we want to understand what is happening to the commons in industrial society or how they could be reinvented, we have to go to the other side of the globe and examine what is happening to the commons there. Because these two processes are causally linked by global 'free trade', though they are apparently separated. They are also separated in the minds of people. But if we want to reinvent the commons we have to realise that the global is in the local and vice versa.

In the discourse on the new 'global commons' the 'global resource managers' (Goldman) of the World Bank and IMF and the transnational corporations (TNCs) often use the idyllic concept of the 'global village' when they want to suggest that there is something like a harmonious 'world community' which only needs some global decision-making elite to manage the 'global commons'. If one goes beyond this rhetoric and looks at reality, however, one realises that the very global institutions that represent the capitalist world-market system use the mechanisms of violent intrusion, enclosure, division, fragmentation, segregation and then hierarchisation and centralisation to get access to the resources that are still controlled and used by local communities as commons.

The destruction, fragmentation and enclosure of local commons and communities in the South are justified in the name of development, progress and efficiency. Thus Daniel Bromley and Michael Cernea of the World Bank see the need 'to improve development efforts to make the commons and the commoners more productive and efficient' (quoted by Goldman 1995: 8).

Here the words 'To make the commons more productive' through 'development' remind us of the World Bank's self-proclaimed aim 'to draw peasants away from subsistence', in order to make them 'more productive' or to 'use women's labour' in the South 'more productively' by making them produce for the world market, not for their own subsistence.

Defending the commons: the case of Papua New Guinea

Our second subsistence story deals with the successful struggle of people in Papua New Guinea to defend their commons. These movements against the Land Mobilisation Programme of communal land have right from the beginning resisted the World Bank/IMF structural adjustment programmes (SAPs) for which registration, privatisation and control of land are some of the key issues.

The structural adjustment programmes have been imposed on Papua New Guinea, as in most other indebted countries of the South, to repay its debt – of 3 billion kina – to the World Bank and other foreign banks (Faraclas 1992b: 3).

What makes the movement here against the neocolonial enclosure of commons so interesting is the clear analysis by the local people of the 'development' policy of the World Bank and IMF and the TNCs. The latter want to get access to the communal land of the clans because they want to start oil palm plantations or to search for minerals, or to get access to tropical timber. On the other hand there are the communities who want to hold on to customary communal rights and use of the land, which is the basis not only of their livelihood but also of their culture and language.

In Papua New Guinea 97 per cent of the land is still traditional commons land. And as Professor Faraclas from the Department of Language and Literature at the University of Papua New Guinea writes, not only has each clan its own communal land, but the four million people speak 869 distinct languages which are linked to the clan or tribal land. 'No indigenous linguistic or ethnic group predominates, either politically or numerically (none makes up more than 7% of the population)' (Faraclas 1992b:1).

Land, language, culture and community are not separate departments but interwoven in such a way that everybody has access to land:

> While 85% of the population live in rural areas and have access to the benefits of this land usage system directly in day to day life, most of the 5% of the population that live in towns and the 10% that live in rapidly growing urban shanty settlements can return at any time to their ancestral areas and use the land. Because of this system, hunger, homelessness and unemployment are unknown, an achievement that should make Papua New Guinea a much more convincing case and model for true developmental success than other countries which, in the name of development, have reduced their populations to landless, homeless, hungry paupers, desperate to sell their bodies and their work at any price'. (Faraclas 1992b: 1)

The resistance to 'land reform' at the dictate of the World Bank is therefore a struggle not only for control over communal land but also for the preservation of languages, cultures and livelihoods. The government tried to sell the 'land reform' to the people as 'land mobilisation' or 'freeing the land' in the name of modernisation and development. The political elite saw a close relationship between its own destiny, the nation-state and development. Thus one commentator in the daily *National* complained:

> Today, as the nation faces a drastic shortage of foreign reserves, land-owners [customary commoners – M.M.] are holding up no less than three multimillion kina [local currency] projects.... In the end it looks like the landowners [the commoners – M.M.] are really the people with power. They give the final green light, a travesty on the meaning of governance. It makes useless the role of the national government. (*National*, 18 April 1995)

What this commentator deplores, namely the impotence of the national government to disempower the local communities, is indeed a sign of the sovereignty of these communities. The communities in Papua New Guinea understand that the modern nation-state and its elected government cannot protect their interests and their livelihood. They hold on to a different concept of democracy, namely people's or communal democracy, or communal rights, based on common ownership of land, language, culture. Community rights are something the Western concept of sovereignty cannot – or rather can no longer – accommodate. Rights are only rights of the individual or of a nation-state, but not of a village, a tribe, the community of peasants, the community of women, etcetera. So long as resources like land, water and biodiversity remain under the control of communities, private property rights – today promoted by GATT/WTO – and the Trade Related Intellectual Property Rights (TRIPs) clause of the WTO cannot easily be put into practice.

Therefore it is also clear that Western-style capitalist entrepreneurship cannot develop if the land remains under communal control of the people; nor can the TNCs have access to it. Another commentator writes:

> In most areas of the country land is communal property. Such a system makes nonsense of the Western private enterprise concept in that individuals will find it difficult to tie up communal land for the long period of time necessary for a plantation or any other enterprise. The pressures from the community would break up the business in any case. (*National*, 17 July 1995)

Financial institutions do not dare to commit money to enterprises on communal land. The local press also makes very clear that it is the World Bank that is behind the land mobilisation or 'freeing of the land' policy of the Papua New Guinean government: 'Being a promoter of free and unhindered success of the free market economy it is only natural that the World Bank should fund this process [of 'land mobilisation'] as part of its commitment to assisting Papua New Guinea' (*National*, 17 July 1995). These sentences are not meant critically. They show, however, how difficult it will be for the World Bank/IMF and the TNCs to continue capital accumulation if local communities continue to hold on to customary commons and resist privatisation and enclosure of commons.

The Prime Minister of Papua New Guinea, Sir Julius Chan, saw himself under pressure from two sides: on the one hand from the World Bank/IMF, the structural adjustment programme and promises of new credits and of foreign investment, on the other from the people who simply refused to implement the Land Mobilisation Act. In despair the prime minister urged the people to obey the law, because 'beggars can't be choosers'. This sentence, however, sparked off a wave of furious protest letters to the press. Here is one example:

WE DON'T WANT TO BE BEGGARS IN RICH COUNTRIES
… The dictionary defines beggar as a person without money and resources. And beg means to ask formally humbly and earnestly. Let me now ask: Why do we beg?

This statement was made as a counter to the people's protest on July 18 led by students and the National Coalition for Socio Economic Justice, comprising NGOs, unions, Melsol and churches against customary land registration and all other aspects of the Structural Adjustment Programme contained in the World Bank/IMF policy matrix. …

We in Papua New Guinea have never been beggars and we do not wish to be one.

For the many thousands of years that our ancestors walked this land, they survived without begging from the outside world. They developed their own system of survival to sustain life. Had they lived by what you suggested, Mr Prime Minister, you and I could have gone down in the book of extinct species of the human race.

If our ancestors have taught us some lessons, they are that we can live without excessive control and manipulation from outside people and international institutions.

The Prime Minister has reduced us to nothing when we know we are blessed abundantly with resources. We are a rich people with what we have.

People who know their true connection to land will understand this.

Take the land and we are true beggars on our own soil. …

The people, NGOs, student unions, churches and concerned Papua New Guineans have been issued a challenge to formulate home grown alternatives. …

Our agenda is simply the survival of our indigenousness and welfare and not be dictated by outsiders … (*National*, 27 July 1995)

The protest movement had been preceded and inspired by an 'awareness training campaign' and 'critical literacy movement' among the people of Papua New Guinea. In this awareness training, people were informed about the implications of the World Bank/IMF structural adjustment on social, economic, cultural and educational life in Papua New Guinea. (*Uni Tavur*, 4 August 1995)

The students' protest movement against the World Bank/IMF structural adjustment programmes and the 'land mobilisation' law was started in July 1995. It was supported by most of the people, by regional governors, trade unions, the churches and even the minister of commerce. Women were active in this movement. They were mostly organised at the parish level. In New Britain, where the clans are still matrilineal, women were called upon never to give up their customary land rights. Here is the appeal of Ms Bata, leader of the East New Britain Women's Council:

> I as the president of the East New Britain Council of Women am telling you women not to allow our precious land rights to be taken away from us by the government's Land Mobilisation Program. We must hold on strongly to our land and protect it by all means from being opened up to exploitation by a few well-to-dos. ... we must keep our land as it is, without registration, so everybody from the richest to the poorest can still have access to the land. (*Post-Courier*, 3 August 1995)

The people in Papua New Guinea defended their communal land rights because they believe in a different concept of development, based on subsistence and autonomy rather than on growth and global trade. They saw clearly that so-called modernisation would turn them into beggars, as had happened to so many former colonies. On 29 July 1995 the movement published the declaration: 'PEOPLE OF PAPUA NEW GUINEA SAY NO TO CUSTOMARY LAND REGISTRATION'. The last sentence of this declaration is: 'The bottom line is you cannot trust the government or the big companies when it comes to customary land. You must control your land yourselves' (*Saturday Independent*, 29 July 1995). As customary land rights were guaranteed by the constitution, the prime minister was in a difficult situation. What escalated the movement was the students' protest marches during which a few cars were burnt and a student was shot by the police. This movement was strongly supported by the people, who praised 'student power'. At the end even a platoon of soldiers marched into Port Moresby to support a student rally. Two women activists spoke at this meeting. One of the leaders of the soldiers said that soldiers, like any other citizens, were co-owners of the communal land. Therefore they would protect, if necessary, these land rights. (*National*, 19 July 1995)

The prime minister had to yield to this massive protest movement. On 19 July he withdrew the Land Mobilisation Act (*National*, 19 July 1995).

The example of Papua New Guinea not only shows clearly who destroys the commons today in the name of modernisation and development, but also that the World Bank and IMF, international capital and even a local government are helpless if communities stick to the principle: YOU MUST CONTROL YOUR LAND YOURSELF.

Is there a connection between these two situations?

If we compare the above two stories, a number of theoretical issues around commons become clearer. We shall state some of them in the form of brief theses:

- Capital has to continue the colonial enclosure of other people's commons if it wants to continue its constant growth or accumulation.
- The fact that small peasants in Germany can be made 'rubbish people' or redundant is causally linked, on the one hand, to their integration into modern, industrial agriculture with heavy external inputs and production for the market, and on the other to imports of raw materials and food items from the cheap labour countries of the colonised South. Thus soya or tapioca for cattle feed exported to Europe from Brazil or Thailand destroys the small farmers' existence in Europe as well as in these countries.
- Whereas people in the South can still see the connection between their sustenance or livelihood and their control over their commons, this insight has almost totally vanished in the North.
- In Europe the enclosure of the commons began in the nineteenth century. Natural resources are mainly either private or state-owned. On the other hand, the people made redundant by this process found alternative livelihoods by migrating to the industrialised cities or to the colonies. As more and more food is imported from the global market into the supermarkets of the North, not only the urban consumers but also rural producers have largely lost the consciousness that their livelihood depends on their relation to the land. They consider money and the market as the sources of their sustenance.
- This has direct implications for resistance against new enclosure movements by capital. In Papua New Guinea there is still a close link between community and commons which is the basis of people's power and sovereignty. In the North, even villages are no longer living communities. Their livelihood and sustenance are no longer guaranteed by their control over land or commons; instead they are affected by the global supermarket and, so far still, by some support from the state. This is the reason why there was hardly any resistance in Germany or elsewhere in Europe against the GATT, the elimination of small peasants and the further enclosure of the

commons. Moreover, so long as the colonial exploitation of the resources of the South goes on under the stewardship of the World Bank and IMF, the WTO and the TNCs, the nation-states in the industrialised world can still afford to feed the victims of their enclosure politics for some time: the peasants made redundant, the jobless, the landless, the homeless. But as recent statistics show, even in these rich countries the welfare state is crumbling and poverty is mounting rapidly.

• In this situation it is indeed time to learn from Papua New Guinea, as Faraclas tells us, how to defend what commons we have that still exist, and also how to re-create new ones. This is a question of survival also for people in industrial society in the North.

New commons and new enclosures

It is usually assumed that the violent processes of enclosure and colonisation of commons, both in the North and the South, belong to the dark, ugly 'prehistory' of modernity. Marx saw in them manifestations of the primitive accumulation of capital, which would disappear with scientific progress and with capitalism as a self-reproducing growth machine.

The fact that we are discussing 'new commons' today shows, as we have already pointed out earlier, that this process of primitive accumulation has never ended but is accompanying capitalist accumulation. This, however, points to a problem inherent in this mode of production: it can enclose, colonise and exploit material and non-material commons, but it cannot re-create them. And yet it needs such areas for the ongoing process of accumulation. What is it to do?

The recent neoliberal phase of globalisation of the capitalist economy has the aim of opening up ever more areas of the world and ever more dimensions of reality, and this also means ever more commons, for enclosure or the process of ongoing primitive accumulation. The 'objects of desire' in this process are not only land, mineral resources and tropical forests, but also the biodiversity of the tropical countries and indigenous people's traditional knowledge of plants, animals, seeds and processes of regeneration. Globalisation of the economy in combination with biotechnology, particularly gene technology, the new 'technology of the future', leads to a new phase of enclosure of commons. Jeremy Rifkin writes about this:

> The granting of patents represents the culmination of a five-hundred year movement to enclose the planetary commons that began inauspiciously on the village green in small rural hamlets scattered throughout England and the European continent. Now even the building blocks of life itself have been enclosed, privatized and reduced to a marketable product. (Rifkin, *Ecologist*, 1992)

The GATT, today guaranteed by the WTO, with its clause on Trade Related Intellectual Property Rights (TRIPs), is a clear case of this neocolonial attempt at enclosure or piracy of indigenous peoples' traditional common knowledge. The patenting of India's neem tree – whose pesticidal qualities have been common traditional knowledge of the Indian people since time immemorial – is one example of this new enclosure of local peoples' common knowledge. As noted in Chapter 2, in 1992 the US citizen Tony Larson, together with the US firm W.R. Grace, were able to get a patent on neem products, although Larson had discovered or developed nothing new. He had simply isolated and preserved the pesticidal substance of neem (azadirachtin). But he privatised and commercialised the traditional knowledge of the Indian people which, so far, had been a commons (Shiva 1995b).

The case of neem shows why international capital has such an interest in getting 'free access' to hitherto non-declared commons. Those who are able to get patents on bio-pesticides like neem products will have a tremendous competitive advantage in the global market. The latest item in the list of areas of reality under threat of enclosure is the Human Genome Project. A UNESCO Ethics Committee, set up to work out an ethical framework for the manipulation of the human genome, declared the human genome as the 'common heritage of mankind' or a 'global commons'.

A close look at the UNESCO document on this issue, however, reveals that the very definition of the human genome as 'global commons' opens it up to 'free access' by commercial and scientific private interests. On the one hand the human genome – in the name of human dignity – is declared inviolable and a global commons. On the other hand, gene technology and commercial interests are allowed access to it.

This kind of double-speak is typical of today's discourse on the commons. Vandana Shiva describes how big pharmaceutical and agro-business corporations are trying to get free access to the Third World's genetic resources. They are putting pressure on the GATT and FAO to 'recognize such resources as a "universal heritage" in order to guarantee them free access to the raw materials. International patent and licensing agreements will increasingly be used to secure monopoly over valuable genetic materials which can be developed into drugs, food and energy sources' (Shiva 1993: 82).

If TNCs want to declare resources that up until now were in the hands of and protected by local communities (peasants, tribal people) as 'universal human heritage' or 'global commons', we can be certain that they want to privatise, commercialise and monopolise these resources. The process by which this happens usually follows the following steps:

- Other people's or communities' commons are declared to be 'global commons' or the 'universal heritage of mankind';
- The TNCs are given free access to these global commons, while at the same

time this theft is legitimised by new laws (patent laws) and by declaring the nation-state to be the guardian of the 'general good';

- Privatisation, commercialisation and monopolisation is legitimised in the name of progress and development.
- The consequence is expropriation and pauperisation of local communities (Mies and Shiva 1993).

The global resource managers (GRMs) of the World Bank and the IMF, whom Goldman identifies as one group of people who have an interest in getting access to commons, all follow the same double-faced philosophy of pretending to protect the commons in order 'to improve development efforts to make the commons and the commoners more productive and efficient' (Goldman 1995: 8). The people of Papua New Guinea have shown that they do not believe in this paradigm of development.

Reinventing the commons in the North

It is against this background of the factual assault on commons of all sorts by worldwide forces keen on capital accumulation that we have to spell out what reinventing the commons could mean for communities in industrialised societies. After what has been said before it should be clear that to reinvent the commons cannot just mean to open up new 'free access' areas for further enclosure, investment and capital accumulation but must mean rather to reclaim material and non-material areas of reality, of life, of nature as the foundations for the production and reproduction of life by local communities. If we do not want to be fooled by the 'enclosure of language' we have to say in clear terms that *there are no global commons. Because commons presuppose a community.* Wherever commons have existed over time they were protected, cared for, used, regulated by a distinct local community of people for whom these commons constituted the basis of their livelihood. The forces today who pretend to be the guardians of the global commons or 'the common good of mankind' are by no means a community but are torn apart by antagonistic interests. They do not depend on a concrete territory or region for their livelihood but on the global market. Their aim is private profit and accumulation.

To *reinvent* the commons within industrialised society, fed by an anonymous world-market system, would mean, first and foremost, to *re-create communities* who would take charge of and feel responsible for concrete eco-regions or areas of life and reality as a basis for their livelihood. We are aware of the difficulty of establishing such communities within atomised industrial society, where the dogma of individual self-interest reigns supreme.

The second point to be clarified is the necessary link between community, commons, culture and subsistence ethics. A commons regime, as long as it functions, is part of a subsistence or 'moral economy' (Mies 1992). It cannot be described and analysed by categories derived from a paradigm of private property, permanent growth and self-interest. In such a moral economy the various dimensions of life processes are not separated from one another as is the case in the compartmentalised, fragmented capitalist world market system.

In such a moral economy also, the boundaries between the human community and nature are not rigid and hard, but permeable. Economics is not separated from ethics, culture and spirituality. Production is not separated from and superimposed on reproduction. None of the dichotomous and hierarchically ordered and antagonistic dualisms can be maintained in a moral economy of which a commons regime is a substantial part.

This is particularly true for the continuity between production and consumption. In a commons regime they are not two separate economic spheres but are linked to each other. Production processes will be oriented towards the satisfaction of needs of concrete local or regional communities and not towards the artificially created demand of an anonymous world market. In such an economy the concept of *waste,* for example, does not really exist. Things that cannot be consumed and things whose waste products cannot be absorbed within such a distinct eco-region cannot be produced. Such a moral economy in a particular region requires, evidently, a community that feels responsible for sustaining the self-regenerative capacities of this region.

In today's capitalist market regime such a sense of responsibility and care for a particular region cannot emerge, because production and consumption are segregated by a worldwide distance. Moreover, the two processes follow a different logic. The producers – the wage workers – have no interest in the use-value of their products as such. Their main interest is their wage. The consumers, on the other hand, do have an interest in the use-value of the commodities they buy. But they do not care where they come from, or where their waste products go to. Their self-interest demands the immediate satisfaction of their individual needs. It does not reach out either to the producers of these commodities or to the ecological consequences of production processes, or to the question of what should happen to the waste products of their consumption process.

The issue of waste points to the need to bring production and consumption together again, as was said before. Only then will a new sense of common responsibility for the continuation of life in a particular region emerge. If people begin to feel responsible for the leftovers or waste products of their life processes again – and this can be done only as a community – the patterns not only of their consumption but also of their production will have to change. In industrialised societies the reinvention of the commons could start with communities taking responsibility for their waste within their own region.

Garbage as commons

After what has been said so far it is obvious that 'reinventing the commons' in local communities in industrialised societies will appear to be an almost impossible task, at least at the present juncture. And yet precisely this is already happening in a number of social experiments in the US and Europe, partly out of necessity (because the welfare state no longer takes care of a growing number of people), partly because people on their own want to try out new forms of producing and living that are not dictated by the logic of private property and accumulation. The creation of communal gardens in the midst of the ruins of de-industrialised cities (described in Chapter 5) could be called a movement towards new commons. Similarly, movements towards building new communities through local and regional economies (described in Chapter 3), new systems of direct exchange of services and goods (like LETS experiments with new forms of money) are all trying to overcome the limitations of a society made up of atomised egotistic individuals, dependent on capital and the state for their survival. But we think we can go a step further in this direction by looking at the contradictions and absurdities of the existing system of garbage disposal as demonstrated in the first story in this chapter.

Let us repeat a common insight: in a constantly growing economy, waste too has to increase, but on a planet of limited size there is no longer enough space on which to dump it. The attempt to turn waste into an economic good only exacerbates the problem. There is no satisfying solution for the problem of garbage disposal within the framework of the capitalist global market. Satisfying the problem would mean not doing harm either to the people or to the ecosphere, either here or somewhere else.

This insight began to dawn on people in Maria Mies's village when the question was discussed of where to establish a composting plant in the district, because exporting organic waste to Thuringia was becoming far too expensive for the district administration. The district authorities tried to solve the problem by engaging a private firm which was to compost the whole organic waste of the district in a modern composting plant. But when the question arose of where to establish the plant, none of the villages was ready to give communal land for this purpose, because people had understood in the meantime that this modern plant would not create more than two or three jobs, but would do harm to the groundwater and would increase the transport of garbage. Moreover, since this company would want to make profits and to expand, green waste from other regions would have to be imported into the district. Most villages refused to have a composting plant in their backyard.

Although this protest was, to begin with, a typical NIMBY (not-in-my-backyard) response, it was not difficult in that situation to remind people that the concept of 'organic waste' is nonsensical in a rural community where there are still some farmers with dung heaps and where there are still gardens. It became immediately evident that the export of organic waste from West German villages to a composting plant in Thuringia in East Germany was an ecological and economic absurdity. In this situation it was not difficult to discuss the possibility of re-establishing a communal form of taking care of organic leftovers by each village community. Such a decentralised solution would not only avoid the need for transportation but also would not damage the ecosystem and would even create work, if accomplished in an ecological manner.[1]

In the concrete case the awareness and the protest did not go beyond the NIMBY level. But what became visible in this case was the prospect of declaring waste, particularly organic waste, a 'negative commons'. This means that a community declares itself responsible for taking care of the left-overs of its life process according to the motto 'We take care of our rubbish ourselves!' (*Wir machen unseren Dreck selber weg!*). If waste is again seen as part and parcel of our life processes, which cannot be dumped 'somewhere', but which has to be reinserted into the regenerative cycles of distinct ecosystems on which communities depend, then also the production processes as well as the circulation of goods will have to change. There will necessarily be an interest in avoiding waste, particularly packing materials and unnecessary advertisements. A new communal responsibility for garbage as 'negative commons' would as a necessary next step lead to new regional economies.

In the present situation in the North, reinventing the commons would imply, first and foremost, as in Papua New Guinea, that people would begin to question the right of local or national governments to privatise common resources, because they would want to get out of their debt trap. Commons and common resources should be preserved as basis for the livelihood, the subsistence, of the poor – particularly at a stage when the welfare state is no longer capable of guaranteeing the well-being of everybody.

Commons, women and nature

A few years ago, we the authors of this book were invited to participate in a workshop with the title 'Reinventing the Commons', organised by the Transnational Institute. We decided to attend as we were convinced that local people have to rediscover and revive their commons. In a way they have to reinvent them, as we have been arguing above at length. However we were surprised when we learned through the introduction by Michael Goldman, reviewing and summarising the literature on the topic, that the essay by Garret Hardin entitled 'The Tragedy of the Commons' (published in December 1968 in *Science*) was considered a key contribution in the Anglo-Saxon world and that the whole debate could basically be structured according to whether a writer's position was *pro* or *contra* Hardin. We were surprised because in the debates on commons in which we have been involved, this author had no importance. Why, we will explain below.

Re-examining 'The Tragedy of the Commons' we learned a lot about the new emerging discourse of the 'global commons'. Hardin, in fact, contributed a good deal to the invention of the 'global commons' by deconstructing (here the term 'deconstruction' applies very well) the real commons of local people in their communities. We furthermore learned that there are two different, opposite concepts of 'reinventing the commons': first ours, which means to defend, to reclaim and to reinvent the commons from below, through grassroots action of local people for local people; and, second, the concept constructed and invented from above, namely the concept of 'global commons', which is being introduced by international agencies and global players, mostly for the benefit of TNCs. This is also a reinvention, however, in a perverted form. That is because it is based on the neglect (or enclosure) of real, historical commons, usurping the term, the idea and, as we will see, people's positive feelings towards the commons in order to serve capital. The way in which Hardin has neglected and slandered the real commons of communities teaches us a lot about the intentions and the ideology of the invention of the 'global commons', to which he has contributed remarkably.

The so-called tragedy of the commons

Hardin's thesis goes as follows: 'From a certain degree of intensity of use onwards, the commons require a morality which cannot be fulfilled by the individual any longer because this morality goes against his self-interest. The solution of this problem can only be a political one' (abstract to the publication of Hardin's text in German, 1973). He illustrates this thesis by an example. 'Picture a pasture open to all ... each herdsman will try to keep as many cattle as possible on the commons. ... As a rational being, each herdsman seeks to maximize his gain.' The result will be overgrazing. 'Freedom in a commons brings ruin to all' (Hardin 1977: 20). Transferring this problem to the level of the whole world, it means that we are too many people for a limited space. The tragedy lies, according to Hardin, in the fact that the personal freedom of the individual leads to the ruin of all individuals together, that is, of all mankind. Therefore we cannot continue 'our present policy of laissez faire in reproduction' (Hardin 1977: 19).

In order to avoid this tragic end of the commons they must be enclosed and privatised. Only by this will it be guaranteed that the single individual assumes responsibility for the correct relation between space and the number of cattle. Instead of being ruined the pasture now will reach its maximum productivity. But every limitation of access to the commons reduces the freedom of the individual. However, 'When men mutually agreed to pass laws against robbing, mankind became more free, not less so' (Hardin 1977: 29). Therefore we have to 'relinquish the freedom to breed' in order to 'avoid the evils of overpopulation'. Hardin does not say what this would concretely mean. But he can assume this attitude as he is a 'genetically trained biologist' and not a UN functionary.

Hardin's key text in the debate on the commons is indeed remarkable. Already his arguments contain in a nutshell all the ideology and justification of globalisation, liberalisation and privatisation. First of all, Hardin refutes the (traditional) moral economy as inadequate for our present times. Instead of this, he believes, politics – that is, a centralised apparatus of power from above – can best solve the problems of this world.

Then he introduces the concept of freedom in the sense of liberalism. Today the main elements of freedom, according to Hardin, cannot be based on the equality of birth and equal rights for all, but only in the limitation given by private property. Survival would not be mutually guaranteed by people organised in local communities. Partitioning the globe under private capital is what would lead to the best organisation of survival for all, namely under the control of capital.

We are surprised by the flatness of the argument. However, what surprises us most are the images Hardin uses for his arguments and moreover that they seem to have been convincing. He compares the world to a pasture and mankind to a herd of cattle – more precisely to a herd of female cattle with their young. The capital owners/managers/politicians, the real 'new lords of the world' (Ramonet 1995) in times of globalisation, are the good herdsman who constructs the fences and the prudent breeder who cares for adequate reproduction.

Domestication of women and enclosure of commons

Why is it so difficult to become aware of the hidden agenda behind the discourse of the global commons? In fact, most of us, when we first approach the idea that water, the atmosphere (ozone layer, climate) or biodiversity are a common heritage of mankind, feel that this is the right way to protect them against destruction. Why can our feelings be so easily cheated? In other words which are the elements of the discourse of the global commons that lead to this mystification? As we will see, the discourse works with all the known elements of the ideology of capitalist patriarchy, namely that nature and the work that exchanges directly with nature – in this case through communal access to nature – are considered improductive and without value.

The way in which commons are actually being invented as a matter of global concern reminds us of another process of enclosure, namely the domestication of women's work in emerging capitalism. In this process, slowly but steadily the economic importance of work in the house, with children, and on the subsistence farm – all mainly done by women – was neglected, until it became socially totally invisible. Now it is no longer considered as work, but only as a mere labour of love. In other words, women's work has been *idealised* and at the same time *de-economised*. A positive feeling, namely the high esteem of work and persons engaged in activities concerning the re-creation of life, has been separated from its concrete, material manifestation. The effect is two-sided. The esteem becomes an inauthentic feeling, not to be taken seriously any longer, a sentimental affair. Economy, on the other side, becomes something done without love, that is, without positive feelings towards other economic actors, plants, animals or the objects of work.

Once women's subsistence work was no longer considered to be work, it was legitimate to appropriate it without remuneration, a fact that did not even appear to be exploitation. We have called this process 'Hausfrauisierung', housewifeisation or domestication, not only of women's work but of women themselves (Bennholdt-Thomsen 1988b). From the beginning of the Modern Era onwards, that is, since the long sixteenth century and through the modern witch-hunt, the social category 'housewife' has become reality for women. Parallel to this, the social category 'proletarian' has taken shape for men. Women, of course, become proletarianised as well, but with the difference that socially they are categorised as housewives anyhow. This is a stigma by means of which women become a lower caste. Lower, because what they are supposedly destined for by birth has no (economic) value. This explains why women as wage workers get less pay than men (today they still receive everywhere on an average only half to two thirds of men's wages). This continues to be the effect of idealising women's subsistence work as pure love (see Chapter 2).

Something very similar happens to the commons with the advent of the modern era. They are no longer considered part of a certain type of economy, socially and customarily organised; they slowly but steadily disappear as a necessary part of how local people produce their living. The commons formed part of moral economies within which everybody belonging to the community had customary rights and could find the means to produce his or her survival. Today this type of economy simply does not exist within the narrow range of categories in affluent, culturally ignorant societies.[2] The social and at the same time economic aspect of commons has become invisible. Commons, on the contrary, become highly idealised, and everybody feels entitled to 'protect' them, that is, to manipulate them according to what is said to be 'everybody's' interests. By means of this process commons are being idealised, apparently de-economised and then expropriated from those who used to rely on them for their living.

The positive feeling towards the commons, namely that they grant survival, is separated from the concrete material need, the moral is separated from the economy. Still the moral feeling survives, but somehow hanging in the air. Therefore it can easily be manipulated as everybody's right to have access to the commons, whether he or she belongs to the community that reproduces the commons or not. As the commons are no longer considered part of the

[margin note: WHEN TO CARE FOR ♀ & THEIR WORK]

economy, the fact is ignored that they are not pure nature or 'wilderness' but have materially to be reproduced. This fact becomes more obvious in the case of 'negative reproduction', that is, destruction. People in the North tend to forget that they destroy their commons, socially and materially. Nevertheless they feel the moral right to demand that the Amazon rainforest should be 'protected' for them because it purifies their global atmosphere. (The way in which positive feelings like mother love or identification with one's own native area [*Heimat*] can be perverted and manipulated, once abstracted from the concrete personal and economic, local context, can be seen in the case of the Third Reich.) *eek.*

Domestication and enclosure of nature

The ways in which women's subsistence work and the contribution of the commons to the concrete survival of local people are both made invisible through the idealising of them, are not only similar but have common roots. The background is the modern world-view that separates nature from the economy. According to this world-view, any mode or way of production that is based on exchange between the human being and nature is made invisible as an economic fact and is considered a natural process itself. Nature and the new relation of humans to nature are idealised, the relation not being seen any longer as something necessary. This unnecessary, hence uneconomic, idealised relationship makes 'free access areas' out of the commons and gives free access to the appropriation of women's work without remuneration. In a way, women are treated like commons[3] and commons are treated like women,[4] and the link is the modern notion of nature.

[margin note: TECH A.I.]

In modern society, nature is recognised only as a resource, which must be exploited in order to *make* nature productive, in order to create. Now, only what has been artificially produced, that is, man-made things, have economic, that is life-(re)producing value. Natural fertility is despised and nature should be violated, as Bacon said, so that she gives away her secrets, out of which scientists design natural laws, the basis for mass production. Before the modern era, nature had been identified as Mother Nature or Mother Earth and venerated. With the shift towards a mechanical world-view with its exclusive high esteem of artificial production, the mother principle loses its sacred aspect at the symbolic level, and at the real level women are confronted with an inferior social position (see Merchant 1980; Fox Keller 1985). Also, communities could be egalitarian only under the rules of 'natural law', which means that the egalitarian human existence was based on the fact of having been equally born of a mother. Therefore the natural law as such is intrinsically mother law, says Bloch (1961). It is no surprise, then, that the reduction of nature to a mere resource destroys the community and the commons, its material base, at the same time as it devalues mothers.

[margin note: POWER OF ♀ & THEIR CHOICE OVER their own REPRODUCTIVE POWERS — PROLIFE = anti Nature]

History against 'tragedy'

When we reviewed Garret Hardin's 'The Tragedy of the Commons' (1968) after having read Michael Goldman's literature review on the commons (1995), it was the first time that Veronika Bennholdt-Thomsen took notice of the essay. Hardin's text had not come her way till then, despite the fact that she has been working on commons for about twenty-five years. Her field of research was the *comunidad indígena*, the native Mexican community, namely questions of communal land ownership, of the socio-cultural cohesion of the *comunidad* and of the ritual-religious world-view reproducing the community (Bennholdt-Thomsen 1976). Those who were engaged in the debate about (native) peasant communities in the early seventies discussed whether these communities would be able to continue to exist or would have to disappear. This was the famous *campesinistas – descampesinistas* discourse. We call it 'discourse', using the Foucaultian term (Foucault 1976), because the *descampesinistas* wanted the community to disappear and therefore they continually talked as if it had disappeared already. They followed a socialist political project. According to them, organic solidarity such as the solidarity practised within native peasant communities was inferior to the mechanical solidarity of the working class, and was furthermore hindering the politically correct consciousness of the working class from developing (see Feder 1977/78).

What these so-called progressives were doing was justifying a process that was happening in Mexico anyhow, with or without their approval. The locally based communities were being expropriated and destroyed by the state, which replaced them by larger, state-run property and production regimes (*ejidos*), which were collective or cooperative enterprises, seemingly organised according to communal principles. The philosophy behind this policy was, the larger and the more mechanised, the better for everybody. This is the normal argument for industrialisation and maximisation. Concrete local reciprocity is destroyed in the name of efficiency and in the name of the benefits for the generality through the returns from an anonymous, abstract and competitive market.

From this *campesinistas – descampesinistas* discussion it was in fact possible to understand what a community is and what commons are, in historical terms and in terms of the mechanisms of their social reproduction. One can learn to distinguish between a community based on reciprocity, that is, relying on the commoners, and so called communal regimes imposed from above. Collectivisation and the different cooperative steps towards collective enterprise are nothing else but a means of state control over former peasants in order to industrialise agriculture. This has nothing to do with a communal regime. In reality by means of this policy peasants are forced into a rural proletariat. The mechanisms perhaps are even more coercive under socialist politics, but with the positive aspect that employment is guaranteed. Capitalist cooperatives expropriate peasants in a less immediately violent way, but the majority have to give up in the end anyhow. Therefore the opposition between a cooperative and a private regime turns out to be a minor one, or not even to exist. Similarly the difference between real capitalism and real socialism in reality did not exist or was only minor.

By means of this discussion one could learn to demystify the talk about the benefits for everybody emanating from always greater so-called collective entities with centralising rules of economic organisation and property. Based also on this experience we came to the conclusion: no commons without community, and no community without reciprocity.

Cultural ignorance

Here we come back to Hardin's text. It was published in 1968, and he wrote it more or less at the same time as Mexican, Latin American and Middle European researchers in Peasant Studies were involved in the debate summarised above.[5] It is obvious that Hardin has no idea about the whole debate. This may have several reasons. First, it seems, he is not informed because he is not an expert in agrarian or peasant questions. However, the question of the commons is first of all a question of an agrarian land property regime. Second, he did not inform himself about real commons before writing the article, because he was not interested in historic facts about the commons, or in the history of the scientific and political discussion about them. Third, Hardin does not even write an article about the commons, despite the title. He in reality writes about what he calls the 'population problem', which he does not really specify either, though he at least mentions some other authors on the topic. In conclusion, Hardin simply gives his opinion about what he considers are the problems, even such a severe problem as a 'tragedy', without asking for historical facts or for the contribution of experts in the field. This, of course can be done: everybody can write an essay on whatever question. The interesting thing is its effect. And that is what is most striking: Hardin's ahistoric utterance of an opinion that is not even based on expertise on his topic becomes the centre of an experts' debate about the commons. His thoughts must have echoed a widely held opinion. Or to put it in other words, he obviously spells out a very popular ideology.

In reality, Hardin's essay is neither on the commons nor on population growth. Rather, it is a justification of overconsumption in the North, respectively by the rich and the middle classes of both the North and the South. He writes, implicitly, a justification of the economy of maximisation, especially of the attitude of those who benefit from this type of economy at the expense of the majority of people. He does so by turning the truth upside down. He says that poor people are destroying 'our' – that is, rich people's – water, air, space. Therefore population growth should be stopped. His argument is an attack on the sovereign control of other people over their bodies, their cultures and types of economies, their types of social structure, their resources, their water, their air, their space.

Hardin writes a justification for the type of economy of his own society, more specifically for his class or caste, without saying so, simply by asking, What do we have to do in order that things can go on as before, presupposing that this way of living is the best for everybody? We call this methodology 'cultural ignorance'. It consists in simply projecting one single type of existence on to all mankind, in generalising and universalising it as *that of the human being in essence.* However this abstract human being can easily be identified: it is male, white, over eighteen years old, lives and works in an industrialised surrounding and thinks accordingly; it is a yuppy. Hence cultural ignorance applies not only to others but to one's own society as well, because this way of thinking does not know its own culture either. A basic methodological principle therefore says that I can know about my own situation only by reflecting it in the other. This is at the same time a precondition for overcoming racism.

The logic of economic rationality:
'Economy gives life, while mothers and commons destroy it'

Hardin's essay has been widely criticised, but it nevertheless became, with all the pros and cons, a key article. Our thesis on why this happened points to the singular conglomerate of socially accepted and traditionally inherited positive feelings and values that he presents, combining this presentation with the shameless deconstruction of inherent moral principles, so that the reader at the end feels justified in overthrowing these archaic sentiments and being unscrupulously modern.

The subject matter of Hardin's essay is the repudiation of natural fertility or the mother principle, not only by de-economising or neglecting the economic quality of the exchange and cooperation between human beings and nature, but by categorising natural fertility as destructive. Until Hardin and mostly still today the economic character of the human–nature process has been veiled and hidden. For example women's subsistence work has been made economically invisible. But this happened at least through idealising it, the semblance of high esteem being conserved. Hardin, however, takes the next step and openly declares it not only economically irrelevant but destructive. He takes a 180-degree turn from the world-view that respects mother earth. Now only artificial, man-made production secures life, that is, is fertile; giving birth, according to him, threatens life.

Hardin reaches this conclusion – without anybody being upset – by ignoring that women give birth to children. Giving birth and caring for children according to his approach (which is a widespread discourse), is not a human activity, but pure nature. His concept of population growth is a straight Malthusian one. According to this, people multiply like plants unless they are hindered from doing so. Social determinants and women's conscious decisions are neglected. Here the attitude of the witch-hunters is adopted, who through brutal violence destroyed women's possibility to decide upon procreation.

The same principle is applied by Hardin in his view of the commons. As giving birth and the role of the mother are dehumanised, equally the commons and the community are excluded from conscious human reproduction and maintenance. Hardin cannot imagine a responsible social caring for commons, and the natural surroundings in general, because he himself does not function in that way. For him, only one type of rationality exists, namely economic rationality – which destroys the environment, as he explicitly admits. However, for him, it is not economic rationality that has to be changed; rather, people, societies, cultures that do not act according to economic rationality should disappear.

In Hardin's essay the commons are no longer idealised as something in which everybody, everywhere is equally participating irrespective of concrete material relationships, that is, he de-economises the commons. Such an idealisation, in fact, would still have been a semblance of the feeling that Mother Earth is nurturing us all, though a sentimental one, because separated from the context. Hardin goes a step further. For him, what cannot be privately owned is absurd, because it cannot be productively used in an economically rational way. Therefore, according to Hardin, the commons suffer from an in-built contradiction. They do not offer abundance and liberty, but inevitably lead to the failure of any real economic enterprise. In this version it is not private property that is an enclosure but the commons. Those who possess private property are properly economically acting human beings, the rest are 'surplus' population.

Reinventing the commons: the subsistence perspective

In our view commons cannot exist without a community, but equally the community cannot exist without economy, in the sense of *oikonomia*, that is, the reproduction of human beings within the social and the natural household. Hence, reinventing the commons is linked to the reinvention of the communal or commons-linked economy.

What does such an economy look like? We think that this reinvention of a communal economy has to be a *process*. To this process belongs the following:

- the defending and reclaiming of public space. Opposition to further privatisation of common resources and spaces, both in the North and the South. In the North reinventing the commons could well start with responsibility for what we have described as 'negative commons', for example, waste.
- regionalisation and localisation against the trend towards globalisation. This means production, exchange and consumption within the region, so that an ecological regional reproduction takes place. Only in such regions can people form communities and feel responsible for the region.

- decentralisation   *NO DIGGITY*
- reciprocity as against mechanical mass solidarity. Mechanical solidarity, we argue, means only that everybody should have an equal share of the booty from the plunder of the environment. This is usually called social justice. This aspect of the process reflects our critique of the socialist belief in technological progress, which provides an apologia for industry and proletarianisation, with the consequence of ecological destruction and women's subordination.
- the policy from below instead of the policy from above. This concept means policy as a living process of the people in local communities, including reciprocity. We do not believe in global solutions, nor in the global politics of a new megastate, sometimes referred to as 'global governance'. These global solutions only serve as a legitimation of a capitalist and imperial power. In the case of women, global politics serve to establish a discourse of all women being equal, so that they can be treated and controlled equally, according to the norm of the white, urban woman of the North under a patriarchal regime. That exactly is the case today and how this discourse functions can be seen very well in global population policy, acting in the way Hardin had envisioned.

YES - manifold ways of realising a community and a multiplicity of communities.

NOTES

1. In the meantime the district administration has given up its plan of finding a site for its composting plant. Instead it asks people to make compost out of their organic waste in their own gardens. This change of policy is due partly to the fact that the administration is hugely indebted and partly to the resistance and intervention of the people.

2. Instead of speaking of 'Eurocentrism' we prefer to call the phenomenon 'cultural ignorance', because the fact of ignoring the functioning of other cultures has the effect also that one's own culture cannot be understood.

3. After a film in which a Turkish actress performed the role of a Turkish woman having a German lover had been shown on German TV, the actress received many threatening letters from Turkish immigrant men living in Germany. The letters claimed that a Turkish woman should be available to Turkish men only. This idea is strengthened by the fact that significantly more Turkish immigrant men are married to German women than the other way round. The same ideology is inherent in a well-known German expression: 'The Germans and their women'.

4. When a woman is not accompanied by a man, she is much more at risk of becoming a victim of male violence than when she has a (private) 'owner'. This is what happens now to the commons. As they are not privately owned, it is considered that if they do not belong to anybody and can be appropriated by everybody.

5. The debate was not only a Latin American one. Literally everybody engaged in questions of peasant communities and commons had automatically to deal with the debate about what commons are, about the different types of commons, and about whether cooperatives/collectives maintain communal principles or not (see *Journal of Peasant Studies*, Frank Cass and Co. Ltd., London, from Vol. 1, 1973, onwards; see also Wolf 1966; Shanin 1971; Bennholdt-Thomsen 1982).

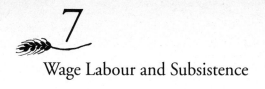

7
Wage Labour and Subsistence

The following subsistence story is based on research by Corinna Milborn, who in 1996 worked for several months with resistance communities in two areas of Guatemala (Milborn 1997a and 1997b).

There is life before and after wage labour:
The resistance communities of Guatemala

The *comunidades de población en resistencia* (CPRs), that is, 'communities of people in resistance', are a response by the Mayas to the genocidal scorched-earth policy of Guatemalan military governments. The first CPR organisational structures were created in the years of the worst repression, 1980 to 1982, when many people were already in flight. Today there are resistance communities in three relatively inaccessible areas of the country: the Sierra, the Ixcán (both in the Quiché district), and in the Petén. In the Sierra, the CPRs encompass a total of forty villages, which mostly belong to the Maya groups and languages of the Ixil and Quiché. In the CPRs of the Ixcán, there are families representing all twenty-two peoples of Guatemala. This 'ethnic mixing' has broken the centuries-long isolation of the country's rural communities, arousing and strengthening the awareness of a common Mayan identity. The CPRs, then, are not a small, isolated attempt at organisation but a fully fledged resistance movement.

Since the peace agreement was finally signed in December 1996, the CPRs have been able to hope that they will no longer be banished and persecuted. With the CPRs the Mayas have rebuilt a peasant subsistence economy, in which the weekly regional market plays a major role as a site of exchange and communication. For the people in the CPRs, it is part of their resistance that they do not perform any (migrant) paid labour. This fills

---

165

them with pride and restores the self-esteem that was so brutally damaged.

For centuries the indigenous population of Guatemala was driven into forced labour by the Spanish colonial rulers. Wage labour for big land-owners, especially in the coastal plantations, was and is a direct continua-tion of those imposed constraints. Around the middle of the twentieth century, nearly the whole population of the highlands began to migrate to the coasts for several months of each year. They were forced into this because national politics, which was in the service of mestizo and white landowners and foreign agri-TNCs – Guatemala is in large part a banana republic – robbed the villages of their common lands. Moreover, the peasants have been pressured to give up maize and beans and to grow cash crops for export, so that their subsistence basis has become ever smaller. (The mechanisms were and are similar to those described in Chapter 2 for the neighbouring Mexican state of Chiapas.) The Mayan peasants are also often duped, made drunk and driven into debt, then forced to perform migrant labour in a situation of debt bondage.

Resistance has grown ever since the 1970s: the communities link up with one another and organise their subsistence on a cooperative basis (especially in the newly settled areas of Ixcán). In the 1970s guerrilla warfare was supported by the villagers. When the 'war on subsistence' (to quote Illich) did not prove successful enough, the military resorted to genocide. Whole areas of land in the Guatemalan highlands were depopulated. Tens of thousands fled or were murdered. Then the refugees began to reorganise in the forests and hills. In order to survive, they first had to make sure they could feed themselves. And this is how the new subsistence economy of the resistance communities came into being.

The CPRs consciously fall back on forms of production, culture and organisation that were unconsciously employed in the time before forced wage labour and persecution.

- The land is common property; work is collectively organised in accor-dance with the *reciprocity principle*. Non-agricultural labour is included in this system; those who hold some office are temporarily released from farm work and materially supported, without this leading to a hierarchy. Surpluses are collectively consumed at festivals of merit.
- The belief system (comprising various religions and sects) consciously links up with the Mayan cultural tradition, and this makes it easier to reconcile any differences between the various Mayan groups and languages.

- Political decisions are taken according to the *consensus principle*, so that everyone can take an active part in opinion formation. Once a year an *asamblea general* is elected, each village contributing one old woman and one old man, one woman and one man of middle age, and two young people. The *asamblea general* also reaches its decisions by consensus, and a referendum is held on every question of importance. There is a local and a regional structure for decisions involving short-term issues. There is no court, and any disputes that cannot be settled by discussion are resolved by the council of elders. The CPRs explicitly refuse to aim for higher, supraregional institutions of power.

- Healers and teachers practise in the midst of people from the same background as themselves; if they know something, they are expected to pass it on. Thus, in the CPRs' fifteen years of existence, the rate of illiteracy has fallen to 20 per cent of the membership, whereas in Guatemala's other indigenous communities the figure is between 80 and 90 per cent.

What is non-wage-labour in an overindustrialised country today?

'The way into a pure society of wage and salary earners is a dead end for employment policy.' These are the words not of a 'people's economy' theorist representing the eco-village movement or a rural commune, but of Edmund Stoiber, the Christian Social Union (CSU) prime minister of Bavaria and a leading advocate of the so-called 'business location' policy (*Frankfurter Rundschau*, 11 March 1996).[1] This policy means that social, fiscal and infrastructural conditions are created so that national and international capital will choose Germany as the business location for its investments. But what kind of employment other than for wage and salary earners is supposed to result from these investment incentives?

Is Herr Stoiber, in fact, bidding farewell to the goal of full employment that has been promised by the Christian Democrats and their CSU partners in Bavaria? Obviously he is speaking not of the regular staff of big companies but of labour they do not need. Today in the former West Germany, only two thirds of all employees have a full-time contract for an indefinite period. Twenty years ago, the figure was four fifths. In terms of the ideology of the business locationists, who maintain that state support for big companies and banks will sooner or later be to everyone's benefit, Stoiber's statement is either remarkably honest or remarkably callous. In any event, even from the business locationists' point of view, it implies that the dissociation between growth in capital and growth in employment is now an immutable fact.

What form of non-wage labour and non-pay can the Bavarian prime minister have in mind? Stoiber made the above statement at the opening of a crafts fair in Munich in 1996. Perhaps he is of the view that independent crafts can survive alongside large-scale industrial production. But it is doubtful whether there are any self-supporting crafts left at all. Electronically controlled production has long since been applied to all the typical craft products (in carpentry or tailoring, for example), and this has in turn forced a process of concentration.[2] Former craft businesses have disappeared or become small industrial enterprises.

The question also arises of how small-scale industry is supposed to sell its goods when the doors are being thrown wide open to cheap world-market products. And how should small service businesses offer independent employment at a time when large-scale organisation has conquered not only the retail trade (supermarkets) and catering (snack-bar and restaurant chains), but also building maintenance work (from cleaning through security to external painting)? Stoiber cannot have been thinking of those sectors either.

Rather, in the age of globalisation that is upon us at the end of the twentieth century, self-made employment can be found in what is called in the Third World the 'informal sector'. This stretches from shoe polishers through therapists and hotdog stall-owners to software specialists working from home and unemployed sociologists writing magazine articles – most of them with a precarious income and little or no social security and sickness cover. First World conservative theorists and politicians like Stoiber naturally have a much more positive image of self-made employment. In their eyes, every self-employed person is a small entrepreneur or capitalist who, if only they work hard enough, can rise like Rockefeller from shoeshine boy to industrial magnate, or like Bill Gates from hacker to software billionaire. The fact that state support for big capital does not create any jobs is thus not a contradiction but part of the very concept.

Also part of the concept is a promise that the whole economy will blossom as a result. In international development politics, this is conceived as the 'trickle-down effect' – a trickling down from company profits to popular living standards. But in reality, the small-time 'self-employed persons' who are held up as the workers of the future are subject to the highly subsidised and politically generated market power of the really big fish. It is these latter who are able to use the labour of 'self-employed persons' for short periods of time, without providing any social protection.

Hence the constant rise in the number of insecure '610 deutschmark' jobs – a category which includes the so-called 'new self-employed', estimated by Uwe Jean Hauser at more than half a million people in Germany. 'Among these are lorry drivers whose former employer has sold them their vehicle complete with all its legal obligations, and who now drive it on their own account.' Journeymen bakers and abattoir workers are also 'employed' in this way by their former bosses (*Die Zeit*, 14 February 1997). Any business risk is loaded on to the shoulders of the self-employed, but the profits flow to the banks and companies that have the infrastructure and the organisation in their hands.

The capacity of political action to defend the labour norms of the social state has been considerably restricted. At the end of the twentieth century, the economic dominance of the big corporations and financial institutions has become so overwhelming that the state itself can be pressed into serving their interests. This did not come about only with the advent of neoliberal policies; it is a consistent and necessary result of a social-cultural tendency whose course was set decades ago, especially with the post-1945 Marshall Plan and the establishment of an international growth policy centred on the World Bank and the IMF. More important still, a culture of consent to the mechanisms of accumulation took shape in that period, so that we must speak not only of a maximisation economy but of a maximisation society.

The fixation on wage labour

Today no one believes that the type of situation once considered normal – that is, the skilled worker with security of employment – will be available to every member of the working population. For a long time it was assumed that, at least in the industrial societies of the West, every dependent labour relationship could be brought in line with this ideal type: in other words, that well-paid, secure jobs for all were part of the nature and capacity of the existing economic system. It seemed to depend only on the trade unions and government policy how quickly and by which route (through redistribution and transfer payments, for example) the wage-labour way of life could be made universal.

The later sobering-up should lead to a different vision. The fact that this new vision has not emerged is a consequence of internalisation of the idealised wage-labour discourse – which is to say that the impossibility of conceiving any other labour relationship has deep roots in the culture.

Thanks to the widespread disorientation, Herr Stoiber could drop his already-quoted remark without unleashing a wave of indignation that he and his political friends should cynically prescribe bitter pills against the outbreak of unemployment sickness, while making common cause with what lay behind it. No doubt Stoiber was quite right to say that 'a pure society of wage and salary-earners is a dead end for employment policy', even if this had no other function than to make gaps in the dead end appear to be not such a difficult path after all. We cannot really expect the CSU prime minister of Bavaria, however, to say that *we should be turning our back on the dead end of the maximisation economy, and releasing from its clutches the working conditions that have been repeatedly degraded by the political power of the profit and interest mechanisms.* In the end, however many allowances we are prepared to make, Stoiber believes that the dominance of the relationship between capital and wage-labour is indispensable to the paradise of progress. And his Marxist counterparts on the Left think the same, with almost greater ardour.

The socialist faith in technology, and in the centralisation and concentration of production, has always gone together with a conviction that wage labour (and especially the wage labourer) serves the only purpose that is at once historically possible, morally right and socially necessary. Even the long dominance of the skilled worker in images of wage labour can be traced to socialist ways of thinking. Nevertheless, the socialist countries (in which capital appeared from the outset as state capital) never represented an alternative but only one variant of capitalism, as Wallerstein was arguing long before the collapse of actually existing socialism (Wallerstein 1983: 93). To this day, however, neither the Left nor the Right has really grasped this fact, and certainly neither has thought it through. If they had, they would have raised the question that has been absent from debates on the current crisis of the world economy: namely, does globally triumphant monopoly capitalism have to face the same limits that applied to socialism? This does indeed seem to be the case. The limits are being reached, because the maximisation society does not concern itself either with reproduction of the (natural or planetary) environment or with reproduction of living labour power.

The ideology of the wage-labour regime

Each of the two capitalist systems was so fixated on wage labour that it became synonymous with work as such. It could thus be said of a housewife with three or four children, 'She doesn't work.' There was no concept of work that applied to other than paid labour. In the Third World, the conflation of the economy with the capital/wage-labour relationship has led to the bunching together of all other activity under the category 'informal sector', even though it is this latter that constitutes the situation of life, and therefore the real economy, for the overwhelming majority of the population.

In Germany as elsewhere in the world, where most work situations cannot be subsumed under the category of wage labour and do not approximate to the traditional, euphemistic conception of wage labour, it has to be asked what is meant by the concept of a 'normal work situation' that plays such a dominant role in debates about the future of work. What the concept does do is evoke a positive link between wage labour and capital and strengthen the belief that 'when the economy is in good shape, things go well for all of us'.

As the fiction spread in society that a certain ideal type of wage labour can be made universal, the wage-labour *regime* (which is not at all the same thing) actually became universal without encountering any opposition. In a wage-labour regime, certain relationships of economic and political power have been established as a result of which the overwhelming majority of people depend existentially on wage labour for their living but in reality cannot rely on it. We are now gradually becoming aware of this trap. The reason why it is so difficult to find a way out of the impasse is that socialist as well as bourgeois theory believes in the further development of technology or the productive forces tied to the capital/wage-labour relation, and cannot therefore conceive of any other work regime. The subsistence approach does not share this fixation. We know from experience of reactions to this approach, on both the right and the left of the spectrum, what a breach of taboos is involved in a theory whose focus is other than wage labour.

The public discussion of solutions to unemployment oscillates between demands for more of the Keynesian welfare state and demands for more of the neoliberal, global market economy with a 'slimmed down' state. (Let us repeat here that the neoliberal free market economy is anything but 'neo', 'liberal' or 'free'. It consists in massive national and international support for finance capital, the TNCs and the rich – the real winners from economic warfare.) Both demands stick fast to the wage-labour regime, the neoliberal version (despite its romanticisation of self-employment) even more strongly than the Keynesian one. For neoliberal theory and politics have the wage-labour regime as their underlying postulate. For them, there is no need for further thought: all workers have to depend upon capital for their existence.

Robert Kurz thinks that we should break free of this dilemma.

> Would it not be clever to present the militant neoliberals with a surprising answer. You are right, we could say, personal initiative and decentralized organization are superior to the dinosaurs of statism, as David is to Goliath. But who is to tell us that the alternative must be commercial? (Kurz 1991)

He sees the first steps in this direction in the non-profit organisations (NPOs) and non-governmental organisations (NGOs): that is, in the initiatives of a newly emerging third, or autonomous, sector. 'They create public kitchens, lay out gardens, build water pipes, dispose of rubbish, look after street-children, make housing available, organize their own school lessons, etc.' But Kurz, too, is neither able nor willing to see off the fetishisation of the productive forces and technological growth. And so his vision is like a cross between Orwell's *1984* and Robinson Crusoe's island: 'Perhaps the future belongs to a "micro-electronic natural economy" organized on a collective basis.'

The fixation on men

What cultural obstacles prevent us from regaining control over our own subsistence? What is the reason our social image of work is limited to dependent labour? How has it been able to lodge itself as the unquestioned precondition of social progress, despite the broad discussion of social justice over the past two hundred years? How is it that a labour relationship that presupposes hierarchy (that is, a context of subordination and superordination) has not been exposed as such in democratic societies? The answer is simply that the relationship is itself an integral part of hierarchy, and that power interests and repressive mechanisms come together in the wage-labour situation.

The fixation on wage labour is the very instrument of modern patriarchal ideology. The concept is already male-centred in its exclusion, indeed negation, of female elements. The model of wage labour is industrial male labour, not the work of mothers and women in providing for the immediate needs of everyday life, especially of children and old people. It is hardly surprising, then, that equality for women in wage labour (equal pay, equal jobs and equal promotion) means that they must increasingly adopt ways of living that have been shaped by men.

On the other hand, the capital/wage-labour relation establishes the patriarchal relationship between the sexes as a state of society. The idea of economic growth (increased production and profit maximisation), market conquest and competition is bound up with this relation of production and moulds an image of the economy as a male enterprise. In this way, the concept of the economy is reduced to commodity production, as the concept of work is reduced to wage labour. The peaceful and preserving side, without which even 'killer capitalism' cannot keep going, is imagined as a female natural backdrop. Only this bifurcation of values enables the misanthropic and anti-social version of economics to gain acceptance and to be legitimated as socially necessary. Women – or rather, the female–maternal side of human existence – are thus excluded from the relations of production as an external pendant.

The skilled worker, the prime image of a wage labourer, is conceived of as being male. At the same time, the skilled worker or 'normal earner' is supposed to be the family 'breadwinner', whose wage feeds and supports the housewife. Yet the wage labourer cannot be conceived of without the housewife, either materially or actually – not actually, because his commodity, labour power, first has to be produced, and that does not happen in the realm of commodity production. His labour power has also to be reproduced. And despite all the fast food on offer, or the leisure breaks obtainable as service commodities, a living person is also needed to introduce the qualities of a housewife. This constellation can also be found in same-sex arrangements (Christa Müller 1994).

Nor can the wage labourer be conceived of without the housewife in non-material aspects of his existence, for her subordination was and still is the 'compensation' for his dependence within the wage-labour relationship. The fixation on wage labour for the man also fixes the demand for housewife's services. This explains the whole complicity with the capitalists displayed by trade unions and individual men, who until the 1970s did nothing against gender-based wage groups and therefore against wage inequality for comparable jobs. As part of the same syndrome, the unions tried in the end to protect 'normal' male wage earners through a reduction in working time, instead of standing up for better social protection of female part-time work. This omission has since caught up with them in the shape of the 'flexibilisation' of labour, as already in 1983 we predicted it would during the discussion on the thirty-five-hour week. Finally, we should not forget the real-life satire of 1993, when the DGB (German trade union federation) chairman could overturn the May Day slogan 'Women First!' simply by refusing to speak about the topic.

The main way in which women themselves contribute to the fixation on wage labour is by thinking that their only prospect in life and at work is to be either a housewife or a wage labourer. Many imagine themselves to be feminist and anti-patriarchal when they dismiss a housewife's existence as hell and a wage labourer's as a heaven of independence. What a misapprehension!

In Chapter 2 we showed that housewife-like conditions of wage labour are spreading in the contemporary world. Their typical expression is the labour of young women in factories in the Export Processing Zones, on the global conveyor belt as it were. In the North, too, housewife-like labour has been growing as a result of the demolition of job security and the neoliberal attack on the welfare state. Flexibilisation is now also affecting men, and in fine patriarchal style women are driven down into still worse jobs.

The fixation of most people on wage labour, which means that they are unable to conceive of other, non-hierarchical work situations, is a gender-specific mechanism of domination. One consequence is that the hierarchy of capital and wage labour is being consolidated and intensified at the present historical moment.

Do we live from wage labour?

The social mode of interchange with nature is closely bound up with the mode of labour. Indeed, we could say that the mode of labour not only marks but is the way in which a society relates to nature. In today's world, environment and labour power are both subject to the diktat of maximisation. In short, this simply means that the goal of economic activity is not to assure the reproduction (or 'sustainability') of the environment or labour power, but rather to get as much as possible out of both. We tend to understand this in relation to nature, but less so in relation to labour power.

Now, the point of the wage is never to reproduce living labour power, but only to reproduce the commodity labour power. This becomes especially apparent in times of capitalist rationalisation. For society as a whole this makes no sense, because enough labour power is available already, but for capital it means a saving on an expensive input. The saving bears particularly upon every aspect of labour power that goes beyond its status as a commodity: that is, upon everything in it that is bound up with the human life-cycle. Ageing people who might fall sick are dismissed before they reach pensionable age. Women who might become pregnant are not employed in the first place. Those who come closest to the pure commodity labour power are adult males and young women who will later leave to start a family. The work situations that come closest to the pure commodity relationship are those in which the employer can hire and fire at will and flexibly define the hours of work and leisure. This is the true face of the new self-employment, for which the 'business locationists' want us to develop a taste. It is the basis of the much-vaunted 'jobs miracle' in the United States.

According to the democratic ideology of social partnership, the state's task is to ensure that not only the commodity labour power but also living labour power are paid. But in the present context of neoliberal globalisation, the state with its focus on 'business location' explicitly divests itself of this regulatory function. We thus become aware of something that for a long time did not constitute a problem, or was at least one which we could live with. Part of the wage-labour mystification was a belief that people could reproduce their existence through wage labour, and that the state or labour struggles or capital would make sure that everything turned out all right in the end. In the capital/wage-labour relationship, however, labour power is only a source from which value is created. As the labour theory of value rightly states, the only value-creating power is living labour power.[3] In the process of value creation, however, its living quality is used up without being replaced.

Life reproduces itself not in the exchange with capital but in the exchange with nature. But our modern ideological apparatus, indeed our modern culture, is designed to erase this banal yet fundamental point from our consciousness. Human beings and nature – and that means also the economy and nature, society and nature – are seen as separate from each other. Thus, living labour power can be treated in the capital/wage-labour relation as a natural resource whose reproduction remains a matter for nature. Marx: 'The capitalist may safely leave this [reproduction of the working class] to the worker's drives for self-preservation and propagation' (1976: 718; cf. Neusüss 1985).

In the characteristic world-view of modernity, the aspect of human beings as natural creatures is left to natural drives. It is the woman's job, however, to ensure that this reproduction takes place through the operation of her instincts. The true modern 'man', *homo oeconomicus*, is thought of as male and rational.

The naturalisation of labour power

In ... ions of the South, where local forms of production have assured ... fectly well for thousands of years, hunger is on the increase. In the ... North, amid the overabundance of commodities, women find ... s and less capable of bringing up children in a climate of care and respect. The reason for this should be sought in the loss of the so-called 'natural' reproduction funds of agriculture, housewife-mothers (who still make something out of nothing), common land and colonies. This loss has two aspects. First, disregard for the fact that economic activity involves an exchange between external and human nature leads to destruction of the natural-material foundations. Second, people are increasingly cut off from direct access, independent of capital, to the natural conditions of reproduction. They are more and more 'enclosed' and privatised. This is graphically illustrated in the practices of seed and gene patenting, which is now being applied more and more to human reproduction itself. Pregnancy and birth are almost completely medicalised – that is, capitalised. In the technology of reproduction, all that women still supply are certain 'components'.

So are we now witnessing what Rosa Luxemburg predicted as long ago as 1913? To the extent that natural economy has vanished, is capital necessarily incapable of realising profits any longer? Is capitalism itself – aka the industrial growth economy – breaking down? As we argued in Chapter 1, Rosa Luxemburg had too narrow a concept of the accumulation fund of natural economy. But in building upon her analysis, we have seen that there are areas within capitalist society that are being constantly renaturalised by various capitalist mechanisms.

One of these mechanisms is the sexism that again and again drives women into the position of housewives, as happened on a massive scale after the absorption of East Germany into the Federal Republic. Another mechanism is the generation through war of conditions akin to natural economy, as happened in Germany in the aftermath of the Second World War. And there are also the structural adjustment programmes imposed by the IMF and the World Bank upon countries of the South with a high level of debt. The discontinuation of policies to even out social differences means that a majority of the population must either tighten their belts still further or work even more intensively to buy their means of subsistence.

This is quite simply a mechanism of devalorisation that affects whole national economies (Mexico's, for example, in 1994–95), as well as the labour power of individuals. The Third World is not alone in suffering from it, but it has been hit especially hard. More characteristic of the capitalist mode of production are the periodic, cyclical devalorisations of capital, as in the world economic crisis of 1929, or the recurrent devalorisation of labour power, as in the current neoliberal and 'business locationist' environment. In this way, subsistence production expands as a share of living labour power, or its repro-duction, is strongly naturalised.

In contrast to an organisation of society along the lines of genuinely natural economy, naturalisation constantly creates more wretched life situations that are deprived of any cultural or social context. We can see what this means from the slums, homeless refuges and asylum-seekers' camps. We can also assume, along with Rosa Luxemburg, that as the industrial capital/wage-labour relation spreads both internally and externally around the world, the waves of devalorisation will follow one another at ever shorter distances – or devalorisation will take on a permanent form, through such processes as the division of the workforce between an ever-shrinking 'core' and an overworked mass of casual or 'self-employed' jobbers, as has already happened in the United States. We stand on the threshold of a new caste society. The course of history is not an evolutionary striving for linear progress but a cyclical, wave-like movement.

No capitalism without subordination in both centre and periphery

The mechanism of naturalisation and devalorisation of labour power functions as a means of solving the crisis of capital only so long as living labour power, living people, remain in the clutches of capital and the regime of wage labour prevails. In the centres of the world capitalist system, this power is guaranteed by the fact that subordination is rounded off in people's heads. Much as feudal rule was secured and legitimated through religious faith, the domination of capital is legitimated through faith in technology and the productive forces, and through the religion of progress. If divine right did not suffice as an ideological mechanism of subordination, then feudal rulers turned to the same use of force that had established their power in the first place. The same happens in the case of capitalist rule. The state, which is supposed to be withdrawing as a regulatory power in accordance with the doctrine of neo-liberalism, is in reality strengthening its monopoly of legal, police and military force as the underpinning of capitalist rule and the regime of wage labour. We can feel this in Germany with the new laws on foreigners, the 'Great Bugging Operation', legislation on nuclear power and conservation, and so on. 'Informal' violence is also on the increase, especially on the part of men.

Recently, with the emergence of global capitalism, this policing/military function has been assumed not only by the nation-state but also by the supranational state whose institutions were established one after another in the postwar period: the UN, IMF, World Bank, NATO, G-7, GATT/WTO. In September 1990, in the build-up to the Gulf War, President Bush called this a 'new world order', in which 'peace and security, freedom and the rule of law' would prevail. 'The New World Order is completely real,' says Noam Chomsky.

> Its basic elements were already distinguishable twenty years ago ... when economic power was distributed within the Western camp. The USA remained the dominant military power, but its economic superiority has vanished.... With the collapse of the Soviet tyranny, the US enjoys greater freedom to deploy force than it has ever done before.... In the New World Order, parts of the Third World will still sometimes have to be controlled

by force … the USA will stick with its historic task … while others pay the bill.

But 'of course, force is only the last resort. It is more cost-effective to use the IMF than the Marines or the CIA' (Chomsky 1991: 69ff.).

In the Third World, as the example of Guatemala shows, the regime of wage labour is not implanted in people's minds in quite the same way as in the First World. Fewer people there support the religion of progress and its ostensibly civilising process. In the periphery, state violence is brutally deployed against heretics: that is, against those who still (or again) keep their subsistence production outside the control of capital. It is not a question of early-capitalist methods with still-feudal characteristics, as some writers once maintained with regard to big landowners, but of an ultra-modern policy serving global capital, which in Guatemala, as in many other Third World countries, is directly represented in the shape of US agri-business. As Corinna Milborn correctly points out, the task of the government in Guatemala has been and still is to maintain an economic model based on agricultural exports. To this end, the indigenous workforce is supposed to reproduce itself as extensively as possible on a subsistence basis, but in such a way that it is always available as migrant labour. True economic independence would not be tolerated.

In the Ixcán, where resistance communities were formed in the primal forest, in 1982 the military carried out a massacre of people involved in the subsistence-oriented 'Ixcán Grande' cooperative. On 14 March, while a Sunday market was taking place, soldiers surrounded Cuarto Pueblo ('fourth village'), the cooperative's trading centre. They killed everyone and razed the village to the ground. Only two young men survived to bear witness. Berthold Unfried, who wrote a report on the events, explained the mass murder as follows.

> This subsistence-oriented agriculture is an obstacle to social differentiation, nor does it generate any big surpluses. The land belongs to the cooperative, cannot be sold and therefore cannot be accumulated. No one is supposed to have more than one plot, but no one is supposed to be landless. (*Neue Zürcher Zeitung*, 3 January 1997)

Similar events to those in Guatemala are now taking place before the eyes of the international public in Irian Jaya, the western part of New Guinea occupied by Indonesia. For the last twenty years, the New Orleans-based mining corporation Freeport has held exploration rights for the gold and copper located there. The Indonesian government let it have one hundred square kilometres of ancestral common lands of the Amungme and Komoro peoples. There, villages were 'resettled' – or, in other words, their inhabitants were driven out by the military. Freeport's hired thugs in uniform ensure that (wage) labour continues smoothly in and around the mining area. Anyone disturbing operations is harassed, kidnapped, tortured, killed. Huge excavators are destroying the land, and mining operations pollute the rivers, the air and the soil (Jürgen Dauth, *Frankfurter Rundschau*, 25 November 1996). A short time ago, the press carried a picture of those driven off the land. Some years ago, they would have smiled out at us with colourfully painted faces and an array of feathers and mussel shells. But now this was a photo of hungry, emaciated people, looking like inmates of a concentration camp.

People living in the heartlands of world capitalism must pose the question of their complicity in such events. Again and again, the rule of capital proves it to be a totalitarian system which has lost none of its totalitarian character through globalisation. The regime of wage labour is here a crucial instrument of power. Control over subsistence is part of this regime, and the various forms of wage contract and sales contracts for goods or services guarantee a tight grip on subsistence.

The policy of the World Bank, which is supposed to 'draw peasants from subsistence to commercial agriculture', continues to have this function. In terms of legitimation, this political maxim has been used as if villagers would otherwise remain in autarky and avoid all market dealings. Only development aid, it is implied, can 'free' them from such a primitive and static existence. Similarly, 'hunger relief' can come into operation once farmers have been taken out of their subsistence regime and, lacking the necessary income to buy food, have started to go hungry (see Chapter 3). 'Hunger relief' is there not to promote independent subsistence but to maintain dependence, even to increase it by destroying local markets.

Liberation from the wage-labour regime

It is necessary for us in the heartlands of the First World to shed our faith in progress, development and the idea that wage labour guarantees life – as well as the idea that we could get a still bigger share of the cake. We must relearn how to be full, and regain the pride and self-esteem that comes from not living by anyone's favour. Only by such an attitude associated with the subsistence orientation will we cease being complicit with the murders in Guatemala, Irian Jaya, Nigeria and the many other war showplaces of global capital. By such an attitude, we will also cease to be the victims which, though willing, we still are. A turn towards subsistence is the opportunity offered us by the economic crisis. The subsistence orientation is free of violence. It means that, whenever we make decisions, large or small, we ask ourselves whether we are gaining more subsistence-freedom or merely letting ourselves in for more unfree money, more unfree consumption, and more complicity in wrongdoing.

To act otherwise is easily possible, as soon as we change our outlook and realise that it is ultimately ourselves who produce our own and our children's lives. For in reality, human beings do not reproduce themselves 'naturally' or automatically, but only through work and food, through care, love and tenderness. Precisely because living labour power is not a natural resource, precisely because it is not the 'inauthentic' element serving only as the precondition of 'authentic' production, we do not refer to this process as 'reproduction'. Instead, by speaking of subsistence production, we stress the creative aspect together with the necessity of proceeding as we do. For the universal spread of the wage-labour regime, and the conversion of all things and services into commodities (Wallerstein 1983) entail that subsistence production has less and less room for manoeuvre. What we argue is that, instead of continuing to bind ourselves to capital and vainly hoping for good wage labour to come along, we should take the means and the conditions of subsistence back into our own hands.

In individual chapters, we have given numerous examples of initiatives and situations that are making this kind of subsistence politics a reality. Many of these examples are taken from the Third World – which is hardly surprising, because most people there have not been corrupted by colonialism as we in the North have been, but are the ones who have suffered from the process of colonisation. We also find there – for example, in the CPRs of Guatemala – an awareness and a clarity that still await their counterpart in the North. This is why we think it an important 'subsistence operation' to decolonise the hearts and minds of people in the heartlands of the capitalist world system, clearing away, among other things, the fixation on wage dependency. This chapter has been mainly concerned with this demystification. For concrete examples of how a reorientation away from wage labour might look in the North, we refer the reader to other chapters.

Concluding remarks: a cow for Fritjof Bergmann

In conclusion, we should like to mention a new departure from the traditional concept of wage labour that has been much discussed in Germany. 'New Work' is a practical initiative in urban self-help, self-organisation and self-provision which first appeared in the United States. The idea came from Fritjof Bergmann, a philosophy professor of Austrian origin who teaches at Ann Arbor; he first tried out his model in Detroit and Flint.

Bergmann begins with a redefinition of the concept of work. He wants to do away with work in the sense of an alienated job to earn one's daily bread, and to associate it once again with the concept of a *vocation*. Everyone ought to do the work they feel a vocation to do. Work that cripples people should be done by machines. Everyone should work to provide for themselves, by making use of modern computer technology.

With much less time spent on work, it would still be possible for individuals to produce eighty per cent of the things necessary for life. Everyone should thus regain access to their buried creativity, to writing, art, invention. In Bergmann's view, people should rely less on the state (including the welfare state) and more on their own capacities, for the state is anyway becoming less, and the corporations more, powerful all the time. To be sure, Bergmann sees his concept of 'New Work' as not so much an anti-capitalist strategy as a way of overcoming the disorientation that large-scale unemployment causes in politics and the economy. Further automation will in any case, he believes, mean that in the future no more than one tenth of today's paid industrial labour will remain.

In a magazine interview, Bergmann spoke of 'a series of companies' in Detroit 'where 'New Work' projects are under way in conjunction with progressive businessmen. People do regular work for two days a week, devote two days to high-tech self-providing, and for two more do what they always really wanted to do' (*Kölner Volksblatt*, 18 June 1997).

Although he speaks of self-providing, Bergmann does not follow a subsistence approach. When he was asked, 'Do you want to turn people into peasants and self-providers again?' he shot back, 'Of course not.' He has also repeatedly emphasised that all his proposals for the production of clothing, food and accommodation should be carried out through people's own work with 'high tech' machinery. It is not a love for everyday necessity that is godparent to these ideas, but rather the classical patriarchal desire to transcend the realm of necessity. Only there is the freedom of creativity supposed to begin. What is our view of this evidently ineradicable male fixation on technology, especially on computer technology?

- It contaminates the environment to a high degree (Freiburg Ecological Institute).
- It is a technology designed for military purposes, and we doubt whether it can ever free itself from this original logic (Weizenbaum, personal communication; Chapter 2).
- Who produces it and for whom (Chapter 2)?
- We do not believe in the possibility of decentralised application of microprocessors; their production and sales are highly monopolistic; their use always depends upon centralised supply (of energy, cables, etcetera – George Orwell sends his regards!).
- There is any amount of evidence that it does not make subsistence work any easier.
- So who is supposed to use it? Who does the work of providing on a daily basis? Or are there no children to be cared for in this model?
- It is not necessary. There are other subsistence technologies, tried and tested for hundreds or thousands of years, which are adapted to the environment, to community structures and cultural specificities.

The subsistence perspective is deliberately concerned 'to link up with what exists, to strengthen and expand practical resistance, and not to invent some

new utopia' (*Informationsblatt* of the ITPS). In Bergmann's and other technologically fixated blueprints, we can find no point of contact with the real
female–maternal, agrarian subsistence practice. Bergmann wants to have
nothing to do either with the land – vegetables will be grown in 'easily loadable
biotonnes, with special substrata that assist rapid growth' – or with people who
live on and from the land. He does not include the Third World in his
thinking. *Netherlands*

Where are the products and high-tech machinery for Detroit's 'self-
provision' supposed to come from? How and under what conditions are they
to be produced and sent to Detroit? Billions of people around the world
produce their subsistence without the 'inputs' that people in the North,
especially men, think necessary for them to engage in any kind of subsistence
work. Would work for the men of the North otherwise be too dirty and too
menial? What are the gender and skin colour of the people who remove the
garbage from the Detroit 'New Work' projects?

In our introduction, we evoked the wisdom and expertise in subsistence
matters of the women in Maishahati in Bangladesh. With this in mind, let us
sum up our reservations about the 'New Work' model with the slogan: A cow
for Fritjof Bergmann!

NOTES

1. 'Business location' is the literal translation of *Standortpolitik*, a concept used frequently
   by the German business community and politicians to express the supposed need to
   keep German capital within the country and to attract foreign investment.
2. Computer-controlled production of doors, windows and furniture takes place not only
   of standard products but even of items of varying measurements. By the same principle,
   standard items of clothing can be ordered from the factory to individual measurements
   and with a range of optional touches.
3. Or as Marx put it: 'Labour-power exists only as a capacity of the living individual'
   [1976: 274].

BEGIN ESSAY w/ DEFINING FEMINISM → into
eco feminism & cause for equality of
all's mature — ecology & social
nature are feminist issues.

8

Women's Liberation and Subsistence

'What has this all got to do with feminism?'

In May 1997 I, Maria Mies, held a seminar on the theme 'Ecofeminism: The Need for a New Vision'. I pointed out that politicians, trade union leaders and economists do not offer any other medicine for healing the present crisis than the old one which caused this crisis in the first place, namely: more economic growth, ever-newer labour saving technologies, globalisation, deregulation (liberalisation) and privatisation. After this analysis I presented a few theses about the necessity to create an economy based on fundamentally different principles than the one we know, an economy that does not need to exploit colonies, or women, or other classes and people, or nature, in order to achieve a never-ending process of expanded capital accumulation. In the discussion that followed some women asked, 'Okay, this all sounds plausible, but what has it all got to do with feminism?'

I was astonished. I had thought my presentation had been on feminism and more specifically on ecofeminism. How come that this had not come across clearly? 'What do you mean by feminism?' I asked, but there was no reply. Then we tried to clarify whether the subsistence approach in its critique of global capitalist patriarchy and its alternative economic and societal vision was feminist.

This anecdote shows that many women – and men – have a very narrow understanding of feminism today. From the sixties till the early eighties when we developed our theoretical framework, most feminists still knew that issues like the exploitation of the Third World, ecological issues, militarism and peace, and the economy were feminist issues. In fact, we considered all issues feminist issues. Feminism was seen as the movement that started with the 'woman question'. But it was clear that in order to solve that question the 'whole' had to be revolutionised.

This broad and holistic understanding of feminism and its goals has meanwhile been largely replaced by a much narrower and much more 'idealist' understanding. Most modern feminists do not want to be bothered by the economic basis, or 'material base' of our societies, to use a Marxian concept. This they consider to be the responsibility of the state or of large corporations. Feminism has been narrowed down mainly to equity politics and cultural feminism, to mean a change in one's sexual orientation, in linguistic and social behaviour. Whereas the slogan 'the personal is political' once meant that the personal, the nearest, was the starting point of feminist analysis, and was connected with the general and farthest issue in time and space, this slogan today often refers only to individualistic and egocentric concerns.

We frequently experience this narrow understanding of politics when we talk of successful women's resistance in the South. Many Western women then comment, 'Yes, this all sounds quite interesting, but what does it mean for me, here in Europe, in our country? My life is totally different from theirs. Such stories don't help me'. Many modern feminists' thoughts and empathy no longer reach beyond the narrow borders of Western industrialised society.

What has gone wrong with the women's movement which started with the slogan of international sisterhood and a holistic understanding of politics? The fact that younger women no longer understand that an analysis of the globalised, capitalist–patriarchal world economy is relevant for feminists cannot be explained simply by a generation gap, or by a moral or intellectual weakness, or by the argument that the world has become 'so complex'. We have to find better explanations for this changed mood, for this depoliticisa-tion of the women's movement, as some call it. Why this limited perspective and the inability to understand what is going on and act accordingly? Can it be that this change of mood has something to do with the contempt for subsistence?

We shall try to answer these questions by focusing on three streams of thought that have played an important role in feminist movements since the mid-eighties:

1. the discourse on identity and difference
2. the discourse on women's participation in power-structures
3. the postmodern feminist discourse

We want to know whether these discourses have contributed to the change in the orientation of the new women's movement, to its depoliticisation, to the abandonment of the concept of international sisterhood, to splits, confusion and the lack of vision.

Equality, identity and difference in gender relations
or: Has the women's movement liberated women?

We want to remind our readers that concepts like 'equality' or 'equal opportunities' did not play a prominent role in the early years of the new women's
movement. In the seventies 'women's liberation', 'freedom from exploitation
and oppression, from sexism and violence', 'fighting capitalist patriarchy' were
the key concepts and goals of the new feminist movement. This movement
drew its inspiration and strength from its rejection of the whole system of
dominance, not from a struggle for equal rights with men *within* this system.

In October 1989 a women's studies conference took place at Frankfurt
University which had the title 'Difference and Equality'. Here the process of
change in orientation which meanwhile was occurring in the feminist
movement in many industrialised countries could be felt. Although we –
Veronika Bennholdt-Thomsen, Maria Mies and Claudia von Werlhof – had
also started our explorations of the subsistence perspective by first looking at
the 'difference' between men and women, we did not use this concept in our
analyses. We rather spoke of 'liberation' from exploitation and oppression. We
saw that women's 'difference' was not a handicap in the struggle towards this
goal but rather their strength. Women were not only passive victims in a
patriarchal division of labour imposed on them from outside; they also
subjectively and stubbornly insisted on the positive character of their work for
the creation and maintenance of life, even though this work was devalued by
capital. From this perspective we developed our *subsistence approach*: subsistence meaning the production and reproduction of life directly, not mediated
by commodity production. Thus a subsistence orientation is different from a
growth-oriented economy as well as from the equal opportunities policy of
Liberals, Social Democrats and Greens, and also from the postmodern
discourse on difference and identity. At the Frankfurt conference, a positive
concept of 'difference' was still used, in the sense of women being proud of
their difference from men, insisting on a female perspective, thus uniting
women instead of dividing them into innumerable different identities. This
positive concept was represented by the Italian group Libreria delle donne di
Milano, who reclaim the 'symbolic order of the mother' (Cavarero 1987/1990;
Muraro 1993). But another use of the concept of 'difference' was already
gaining ground. The postmoderns continue to discover ever more differences
between people, supposedly as barriers between them, but they never talk of
exploitation and oppression.

Money, equality and freedom: from women's lib to equality politics

Today, for the majority of feminists and non-feminists, equality with men is
the goal of the women's movement. This is particularly so for those women

who, after twenty years of the movement, have achieved some public visibility. This goal did not exist in the beginning of the movement when we began to struggle for liberation from patriarchy, from humiliation and contempt for women, simply because they are women. Today it is timely to ask how far this movement has indeed liberated women. This question has not totally disappeared behind the discourse on equality and difference. But it seems the women's movement has not gone far enough to liberate women. Why is that so? Let us look at women's own orientation to find the reasons.

Although women wanted to break away from patriarchal structures, many aspired in reality to find a niche in this rigid but secure framework. They hoped that Father State would welcome them to his house and guarantee them a better place there. They wanted to move up from the status of a slave to that of a mistress in that house. They wanted to share the privileges with the men in this master's house. But they did not realise that this is never possible for *all*. The masters never allow this. Some might, of course, become female 'Uncle Toms', helping to carry the system along yet somehow remembering that they once wanted more than just that. The figures on women's low incomes every-where, on female poverty, particularly the poverty of single mothers, statistics on the continually low political participation of women, are evidence enough of the fact that all did not go well for women in their master's house.

On the other hand, women in the affluent countries of the North may experience doubts because, after all, financially their living standard is still better than that of most women in the world. And yet are they happy? Could it be possible, they may think, that the realisation of a happy life for women is not as dependent on money as they had thought? Also, if women in the affluent countries look at women from the former GDR, whose situation in the process of transition to a capitalist economy has become comparatively much worse than that of men, they may begin to question whether the market economy can bring equality for women. Yet it is this system from which many women expect equal opportunities and participation with men. They demand to get 'Out of the Margin' – and 'Into the Mainstream'. 'Mainstreaming' became a popular programme of many women's non-governmental organisations (NGOs) in the early nineties. This strategy promises women everything: money, *and* freedom *and* equality. But it mystifies the fact that within capitalist patriarchy only a minority of women will be able to achieve these goals.

In the beginning the new women's movement did, indeed, liberate women. Many women experienced a wonderful feeling of freedom. The discovery of their commonality gave women a strength they had not known before. They stormed ahead; nobody seemed to be able to stop them. They learned to love women just because they were women. This was a great liberation. The times seemed to be over when women jealously had to distance themselves from other women, because they might belong to another, lower class, or simply because they were 'women', members of the 'second sex' (Beauvoir 1974).

For many, however, this newly discovered commonality, the empowering new sisterhood, did not encompass the whole spectrum of female existence worldwide. In spite of its intentions towards international sisterhood the movement *de facto* was not able to transcend barriers of class and race easily. In the USA black women and migrant women rebelled against the dominance of white middle-class feminists. Similarly in the UK, women from Ireland, Asia, Africa, the Caribbean and other British ex-colonies began to use the concept of 'black women' for all those women who did not belong to the white, middle-class majority. Instead of fighting together to overthrow capitalist patriarchy as a system the struggle against racism among feminists became an important concern of the women's movement in North America and Europe. This campaign, which started in the USA, highlighted the fact that in spite of various government programmes to overcome racial discrimination, racism still played a dominant role in everyday life and behaviour even among feminists. In continental Europe this campaign focused mainly on discrimination against women from minority groups, particularly migrant women. We consider that the question of racism, between women too, is an important topic, with which we dealt earlier (Mies 1986b/99; cf. Mamozai 1982); however, this campaign against racism was geared deliberately to destroy the concept of an international sisterhood. More important than the commonalities embracing all women now were their *differences*: differences of class, race, culture, ethnicity, religion, sexual orientation, age, etcetera. More and more differences were discovered and began to separate one set of women from another.

The campaign against racism was important because it destroyed a naïve notion of women's solidarity based simply on our difference from men. But the concept of 'discrimination' used in this campaign produced a shift in orientation of the whole movement. The fight against discrimination means that women in general and women of minority groups in particular should be given equal opportunities with men in general and with women of the majority society in particular. In short, anti-discrimination programmes do not aim at the abolition of capitalist patriarchy but at giving women an equal share within that system. We shall come back to the question of why this shift occurred in the USA and the UK around the early eighties.

In Germany this shift was less inspired by the anti-racism campaign, although this also played a role, than by the success of the Green Party and its entry into parliament in 1983. This success marked a general shift in policy from a more fundamental opposition to an ecologically and socially destructive system to '*Realpolitik*', that is, to trying to get a share of power in that system. From this time onwards the goal of the women's movement was re-defined to mean only equal rights with men.

Those who did not follow this new line were more and more marginalised. Their position was no longer discussed. Gradually, without much discussion, a new majority opinion emerged. A landmark in this process of shifting the orientation of the women's movement was the congress entitled 'Future of Women's Work' held in Bielefeld in 1983. We had organised the congress to counter a congress on the 'Future of Work' which had been organised a year before by the German Greens. At this earlier congress, the end of burdensome wage labour as a result of the computer 'revolution' was proclaimed. This future was hailed as the beginning of a period where autonomous work could easily be combined with heteronomous work in a working week of twenty to thirty hours, what Gorz called a 'paradise' (1983). For years we had talked of women's unpaid housework as a reason for low pay and the lack of insurance and job security in women's wage labour. Now, when men discovered this 'autonomous own work' they ignored first its gender aspect and second the fact that this work is not just fun. They ignored totally that women's working week is already reduced by part-time jobs. In our congress we wanted to show that for women the Gorzian paradise meant just more and more badly paid work. We asked the women to look at their own personal experience and to assess what women contribute to a life-sustaining economy. We wanted to show that women do much more than just 'reproduce' labour power for capital. From this assessment we hoped that women would feel encouraged to create women's networks and leagues as a basis for an alternative economy. But we had to learn that the mood had changed. Most women were no longer keen to try out an alternative women's economy. They wanted to participate in the mainstream economy, they wanted to share political and economic power with men, they wanted jobs and positions in the existing political structures.

Women began to fight for equality. Because they *had* to fight. Equality was not given to them. Their aim was equality in wages, in positions, in working hours, in money, in privileges. In earlier years a sense of sisterhood, nearness, love, friendship, had united women and created a new valuation of women as women. Autonomous self-organisation, diversity, solidarity had given them an enormous strength. But now they abandoned this power for the sake of getting a secure place in capitalist patriarchal men's society. Commonality was transformed into uniformity, a typical phenomenon in hierarchies. Equality among diverse women, the living, uncontrolled equality in a living whole, was changed into standardised equity, measured by money.

Many women were of the opinion that it was their 'human' right to share money and power equally with men. They wanted respect and recognition. Therefore they wanted to be equal not with men 'below' them – for instance, peasant men in the colonies or poor men in white society – but with privileged white men 'above'. But 'human right' is natural right, is the birthright of every child born in this world. In its consequence this birthright would mean that we women would neither beg nor fight for a share of the privileges of a small male elite, but would delegitimise their 'rule of right', showing it for what it is: a 'rule of might'. The discourse on equality among women of the North, by its focus on the privileges of white men, has blinded them to the fact that *vis-à-vis* women and men of the South they, too, are privileged. This may be the reason why many shy away from working out a concept of a better society.

Money, freedom and security

Modern economies, be they capitalist or socialist, Islamic or Christian have been constructed on the backs of women. Their foundation is the devaluation of nature, which for its part is closely connected with the devaluation of and contempt for women. The history of the destruction of nature goes hand in hand with the history of women's oppression. This is because femaleness is more than only a symbolic metaphor for natural, life-giving growth. Its valuation is a principle that characterises and structures the social organisation, and the interconnectedness of humans with the surrounding nature and the economy. But the modern economy is based on superiority of the artificially produced commodity over anything organically grown. Contempt for women is not just a negligible side effect of modern economy; rather, it is at the core of the contradiction that decides over the existence or non-existence of male and capital dominance. The modern economy, based on commodity production, on money and high-tech devices, has to eliminate all reminiscences of another economy. This is because what is artificially produced eventually cannot compete with what exists by itself.

After all, women's capacity to give birth to children cannot be separated from women, in spite of all the intellectual acrobatics of postmodern feminists. Yet because anything that exists by its own natural capacity is being turned into raw material or a resource in the modern economy, women begin to look at themselves in the same way and exchange their own potency for money. The latest inventions of biotechnology are doing exactly this: substituting women's autonomous potency by commodifying the 'production' of human life. Many women have resisted this blatant robbery. They object to the separation of the interconnectedness of nature and culture, nature and women, women's potency to give birth and their power. But other women accuse them of biologism or today of essentialism. True biologism, however, means reducing woman to the capacity to give birth only, as if that was her whole nature. This way women's bodies are robbed of their human, cultural, spiritual dimensions. They really become raw material, to be fragmented, manipulated, and commodified. The process by which modern science dissected, despiritualised, reified, killed nature is now repeated with regard to women. Yet many women expect their freedom and security not from a change of social relations but from this science and technology. Technology is expected to solve the problems of unwanted fertility and unwanted sterility. But women's strength and freedom lie in their wholeness, in the identification with their corporality. Only as whole beings can they develop self-reliance and self-respect. Many women, however, do not trust their own strength. They rely instead on the security provided by technology and money. They do not have any other concept of wealth, freedom and security than the one provided by money. But in view of the fact that all natural sources of wealth and security are rapidly being destroyed, we should realise that money also eventually will not be able to buy security and freedom. Therefore it is time to search for another concept of security and freedom.

In addition to being based on the wholeness and self-reliance of persons, on the interdependence of people and their mutuality and responsibility as the bases for security, in a subsistence perspective such a concept will no longer be looked down upon as backward and will not be abandoned for the security provided by anonymous money and the state. Because this freedom and security are myths. Women are forced by these money relations to subordinate and sell themselves piece by piece to capitalist patriarchy. Yet, they will not get big money and they will not get the big jobs. Instead they will lose their own power.

The struggle for power

The 'mother question'

In addition to the shift from 'liberation' to 'equity politics', the main focus for the reorientation of the women's movement and its integration into mainstream economics and politics was the expectation that women would also participate in the existing power structures. Internationally the concept of 'empowerment' was created to express this new orientation. In Germany it found its manifestation in the controversy that arose around the so-called 'mother question'. As similar controversies could be observed in other countries at that time – around 1985 – it may be useful to discuss the relationship between the power issue and the 'mother question' in Germany.

Many feminists had joined the Green Party in Germany. As soon as the party was able to enter parliament these women demanded that 50 per cent of all seats in all party bodies should be reserved for women. The party agreed to this demand and many young women were quickly able to get political jobs and positions. But in the course of time it became obvious that mothers with small children were not able to attend all party meetings in the evenings or during weekend seminars. And there was no other alternative that allowed them to combine political work with mother's work. Whereas men and women without children could devote all their time to the new political project, the old/new mother question had not played a role in the ecological concerns of the Greens.

In 1987 some Green women published a 'Mothers' Manifesto' in which they expressed all their frustration and complaints. They were not very critical of the dominant economy, but they demanded that the work and organisation of the party should be altered in such a way that mothers with small children could participate in politics and could get the same positions as men – or women without children, whom they called 'career women'. Why should women forgo children if they wanted to be politically active?

This 'Mothers' Manifesto' raised a true storm of indignation among men and women. It was answered by another group of women who accused the manifesto women of following reactionary positions, of glorifying motherhood and childbearing (a strategy propagated by the Christian Democrats who wanted to get cheap part-time workers), of idealising a 'mother instinct', and of trying to get women back to *Kinder, Küche, Kirche* ('children, kitchen, church'). Were they not aware of the fact that they only served patriarchy and capital with their manifesto?

The controversy was not restricted to the women in the Green Party; it split the whole German women's movement into two antagonistic camps. Although nothing in the 'Mothers' Manifesto' could be interpreted as reactionary or rightist, and although the so-called career women were not all careerist, what this controversy brought to the surface was a deep emotional problem of many women in the women's movement, not only in Germany but also in other countries, namely an outspoken or latent hostility against mothers: against their own mothers and against mothers in general. This highly emotional need to distance themselves from mothers cannot be understood only as a reaction to the erstwhile Nazi propaganda about motherhood (Mies, in Mies and Shiva 1993: 132–63). We think it contains a lot of contempt not only for one's own mother but also for one's own female body and its potential to bear children. Obviously, many women in the Western women's movements were and are still caught up in the dilemma of being born a woman and aspiring to a male or rather patriarchal concept of emancipation in a capitalist society. The female body is still seen as an obstacle. Contempt for this body is one of the reasons why the original power of the women's movement lost its momentum.

In Germany, women and girls have a particular problem which is not found in other countries: namely the accusation that those who talk about mothers and motherhood in a positive way are ideologically close to the Nazis. The fact that the National Socialists misused motherhood for their propaganda is now used against these women and men as a kind of thought taboo to prevent a new, unprejudiced valuation of mother's work in our society. Together with mother craft, other artisanal crafts and the whole subsistence orientation are also looked down upon with suspicion and seen as close to reactionary or rightist tendencies. In Germany the discourse on the need to arrive at a self-reliant economy, an economy not based on the exploitation and destruction of our natural surroundings, an economy based on regional production and consumption, and on one's own labour, is often discredited as being reactionary. Yet all these polarising polemics about Right or Left, bourgeois or socialist, reactionary or progressive, have one thing in common, namely that the decisive question of modernity is avoided. This question concerns the anti-life, anti-women, anti-nature character of the modern concept of progress. Most people simply want a larger share of the loot made possible by modern technology in combination with capitalist patriarchy. They no longer want to fight against a system that is based on looting.

How do women use power when they get it?

When we talk of the subsistence perspective we often hear it said that this may be possible for a few privileged outsiders who want to opt out of the system, but that it is not a viable solution for the majority of women. They, it is said, have to fight for participation in the political power structures.

Our position has never been that a subsistence perspective is tantamount to a radical rejection of any participation in the existing political structures. It first of all means a different perspective, a different orientation. But if such an orientation is not there, one has to ask how women use power, once they have managed to get some of it into their hands. Does it really make a difference if women occupy the seats of power?

Whereas the controversy on equality and difference is carried out on the level of discourse, the power question is a matter of real politics, of *Realpolitik*. As noted before, in Germany the struggle for women's political participation gained momentum after the entry of the Green Party into the parliament in 1983. The Greens were the party that had profited most from the new women's movement. Many feminists had joined the party who put pressure on the men to change the male–female ratio in the party and in all party bodies to 50 per cent. During meetings women were given preferential treatment with regard to speaking time. Initially the party supported and financed many feminist projects and conferences. When the Green Party had achieved the status of a 'normal party' it could, like the other parliamentary parties, establish a foundation to further its goals. Feminists inside and outside the party convinced the party leadership that a separate 'women's foundation' (Frauen-anstiftung) was necessary. This foundation was created and sponsored a large number of women's meetings and initiatives in Germany and particularly in the South. It cannot be denied that women were able to grab a big piece of power in and through the Green Party.

The example of the Greens had an effect also on the other parties. If they did not want to lose many of their female voters to the Greens they too had to introduce a 'women's quota'. The first to follow the Greens were the Social Democrats who introduced a women's quota of 40 per cent; the Party of

Democratic Socialism (PDS) followed with 50 per cent, and finally also the conservative Christian Democrats began discussing a women's quota. This policy of fixing a certain percentage for women's political participation was successful in so far as it drastically changed the proportion of men to women in the German parliament. Whereas between 1949 and 1987 the proportion of women in the Bundestag had never been more than 10 per cent, from 1989 onwards this proportion rose. In 1996 it was 26.4 per cent (Pfarr 1996). The arguments by which this women's quota politics was justified are similar to those that advocate women's access to the economic mainstream, and are as follows. More women must first share political power. Then by this quantitative change a qualitative change will occur. When women participate in the power structure they will use their power for a more women-friendly, children-friendly, nature-friendly policy. But the first step should be to get more women into the seats of political power.

This strategy appears convincing at first sight, but if we look at its results we have to question some of its premisses. A mere change of the quantitative gender composition of parliaments without a fundamental change of patri-archal structures and policies will not lead to the results the feminists had expected. It is not enough just to have more women in the seats of power. These women must at least follow some sort of feminist or eco-feminist agenda if this power is not to be misused for the maintenance of the existing system.

But let us ask what this struggle for women's political power has achieved so far. As an example we want to analyse the processes that occurred in the Green Party in Germany. This is a party that, more than any other, made feminist demands its own from the beginning. Women still play an important role in that party. After the 1998 election the Greens, for the first time, won enough seats to form a coalition government with the Social Democrats. Of the three ministers of the Greens in the government only one is a woman. During the struggle for electoral success and political power the Green Party had already abandoned or weakened a number of its more radical goals, particularly with regard to ecological or feminist issues (Sarkar 1999). The women who had enough patience, ambition and stamina to make it to the seats of power were not the ones who wanted a systemic change.

Even before these elections certain changes had occurred in the Green Party which amounted to a dismantling of earlier feminist achievements and a change in feminist orientation. The *Frauenanstiftung* was wound up and in its place a new institute was created as a think-tank for policy advice for the party. This institute was not advocated by the men in the party, but by women who wanted to break the link between the Green Party and the movements out of which it grew, particularly the German women's movement. In a 1995 workshop where this new feminist institute was advocated, the new pragmatic line was spelled out: there should again be a clear separation between theory and praxis, between social and political science and politics. A new professionalism should replace the link between movement and research. Politics and research as two separate spaces should no longer be connected as early feminists had demanded, because the two spheres needed different competences and qualifications. The private and the political should be separated again (Holland-Cuntz 1995: 27). One of the female members of the party leadership, Krista Sager, even said, 'We need a critical revision and further elaboration of the concept "feminism". For young women this concept is old-fashioned' (Sager 1995: 39). Meanwhile the new institute has been founded in Berlin. It still has the name Feminist Institute. But its opening ceremony was a funeral for the German feminist movement rather than an assertion of women's power. Ingrid Kurz-Scherf, a professor at Bielefeld University and a Social Democrat, stated that the new men in the Red–Green coalition – Joschka Fischer, Jürgen Trittin, Gerhard Schröder and Oskar Lafontaine – 'do not want any women's politics' (*Frankfurter Rundschau* 2 November 1998).

The process that took place in the German Green Party with regard to the question: How do women use power once they get some? – may not be generalisable. But it can teach us that it is not only men who undermine women's movements but also women. Feminists themselves may betray the early goals of their movement because they want to move up within the existing structures and share power with men. There seems to be a link between the 'murder of the origins', as Suzanne Blaise called this behaviour (1986), and the possibility of gaining power within the system. For the Green feminists the road to power meant that they had to forget, as soon as possible, the connection between the women's movement, Women's Studies and politics. They had to denounce the radical principles of this movement, its new concepts of science and politics, as non-scientific and emotional: good enough for mobilising people, but not for 'real', 'professional' politics and scholarship.

These feminists also have to forget that the success of the Green Party was to a large extent due to the mobilisation of women in the ecology, peace and women's movements. Instead of remembering this they follow any new *Zeitgeist* or new fashion of 'young women' who no longer want to know what feminism is. If gaining power is the only concern of such feminists it is not surprising that they distance themselves from the earlier, radical beginnings of the movement. They want to stick to power, they want to remain in the men's house. They want to participate in men's power games which they now call 'professional *Realpolitik*'.

There is nothing very new about this transformation. It is not unique to women, but has happened often in history. The drama of transforming rebellion into acceptance of and integration into the existing system of dominance follows the same stages: first, a great rebellion of all the oppressed and humiliated against tyranny; second, the struggle for and conquest of the

er, the 'men's house', or participation in the power games; third,
...alisation, professionalisation, transformation of the new power into
...ce, usually following the tradition of the erstwhile 'fathers' and rulers;
..., distantiation of the new power elite from its own radical beginnings
and the radical 'mothers', 'sisters' and 'comrades', and from the radical principles
and discourses; fifth, recognition of the new power elite as the legitimate 'sons',
'daughters', 'heirs' of the earlier rulers. There is nothing to be surprised at when
women do the same as patriarchal men have done since time immemorial. But
we can learn from such processes that to be a woman is not yet tantamount to
a political programme. It is not sufficient to struggle for 50 per cent
participation of women in a political and economic system that, as a whole, is
based on oppression and exploitation. Unless women produce a vision of
another economy and society this sharing of power is of no avail. Women are
not automatically the better gender.

Feminist postmodernism:
the ideology of oblivion and demater-ialisation

The tendency of groups to forget or 'kill' their origins is by no means an
isolated case, specific to Germany. We find the same in the USA and in the
UK, from where under the banner of postmodernism this tendency spread
throughout the whole world. Postmodern feminism has become the dominant
theoretical stream in most Women's Studies departments, particularly in the
Anglo-Saxon world. Feminist scholars who do not follow this stream
experience problems in finding a position in Women's Studies programmes.

The discourses on identity and difference, on gender and power are heavily
influenced by postmodern thinking. Postmodernism is not only the 'newest'
in feminist theory but it is used to legitimise political about-turns like the one
described above. At the same time it helps the process of forgetting the
beginnings of the women's movement, because its ideology is based, as Füssel
remarks, on five 'strategies of oblivion', namely:

1. Everything is only surface and appearance. Reality is like an onion,
   consisting of peel after peel of appearances. There is no essence under these
   appearances.
2. Everything is of the same value. Everything is questionable. Hence everything is basically valueless and arbitrary. Due to this indifference there is
   no reason why one should choose one option and not any other.
3. There is no relationship between input and output in the production
   process. What counts is the result in the form of money. It is forgotten who
   is at the helm of this process and in whose interest it is maintained.
4. Class differences are forgotten. They are substituted for by consumerism
   which homogenises masses and elites within a globalised culture. Following

the market, 'tradition' or 'ethnicity', or 'modernity' may be propagated.

5. Nobody takes a position on anything. There is only a plurality of different opinions, one of which is as valid as any other. They are private and without consequences. 'The main thing is that conflict is avoided. The confrontation of contradictions is replaced by the side by side arrangement of differences.' There is no unifying vision and strategy (Füssel 1993: 53ff.).

The concept 'postmodern' was coined by the French philosopher Jean Francois Lyotard in his book *La condition postmoderne* (1979). In this book Lyotard presents a thorough critique of 'modernity', the concept by which he and all his followers characterise the period of the Enlightenment, beginning with the eighteenth century and, supposedly, coming to an end in our days. Above all, postmodernists question the Enlightenment concept of rationality, namely that human beings are responsible subjects guided by reason, and that they are also subjects of their history. At the same time the postmodernists do not accept that there is a material or 'essential' reality of the world, a 'real' history that is not just a linguistic construct or narrative. For postmodernists there is no given reality which can be understood. Reality is what time-bound, context-bound and space-bound discourses have constructed. According to postmodernism there cannot be a universal grand theory valid for all people from all cultures, for all times.

We have asked why feminists, particularly in North America, were attracted by the ideas of these (male) French philosophers. Why did they adopt the postmodern ideas of Lyotard, Derrida, and particularly Foucault as their theoretical framework for the explanation of women's oppression?

From the outside there seem to be certain similarities in the feminist and the postmodern critiques. Both criticise the dominant concept of rationality. But both come to this critique from different practices. The French philosophers came to their theoretical position from their critique of Marx and Freud. The feminists, at least in the seventies, came to their critique from their experiences in the women's movement, from their objection to patriarchal violence, to militarism, to nuclear and gene technology, in short, from their rejection of Cartesian hubris, an epistemological paradigm which was based on dominance of men over nature and over women (Merchant 1980; Fox-Keller 1985; Chodorow 1978; Gilligan 1982).

In the United States, however, this connection between the women's movement, its various campaigns and feminist philosophising was soon forgotten. This happened, it seems, around the eighties, when Women's Studies departments were established as a regular feature at most US universities. The institutionalising of women's studies not only went along with the separation between the movement and women's research but also with a shift from the earlier feminist theorising to postmodern philosophising. Nancy Fraser and Linda J. Nicholson write about this shift:

Since around 1980, many feminist scholars have come to abandon the project of grand social theory. They have stopped looking for *the* causes of sexism and have turned to more concrete enquiry with more limited aims. One reason for this shift is the growing legitimacy of feminist scholarship. The institutionalisation of women's studies in the United States has meant a dramatic increase in the size of the community of feminist inquirers, a much greater division of scholarly labour, and a large and growing fund of concrete information. As a result, feminist scholars have come to regard their enterprise more collectively, more like a puzzle whose various pieces are being filled in by many different people than like a construction to be completed by a single theoretical stroke. In short, feminist scholarship has attained its maturity. (Fraser and Nicholson 1990: 31–2)

It is interesting that Fraser and Nicholson in the United States, like Holland-Cuntz in Germany, characterise feminist scholarship as 'mature' only after it has been accepted by mainstream academia, institutionalised, with full-fledged departments, professorships and budgets, and after it has been 'purified' of its radical 'universalist', 'essentialist' beginnings. The effect of this theoretical shift is not only that postmodernists are no longer able to recognise links and commonalities in the plurality of people, cultures and issues, they also do not know what is important and what is not. Political activity is reduced to 'political correctness', a mere verbal enumeration of 'gender', 'race', 'culture', 'sexual orientation', 'ethnicity'. Most postmodernist feminists are afraid of taking sides. They are afraid of 'essentialising' any social category, be it 'woman' or 'mother' or any other. In particular the discourse on gender, as part of postmodern feminism has contributed to the depoliticisation of the women's movement.

Essentialism – the new original sin

In spite of all their differences and their rejection of any 'grand theory', postmodern feminists unanimously reject one theoretical sin: essentialism. Much of the theoretical writing of postmodern feminists consists of tracing this sin in the works of other feminists. But they are also very careful in their own texts not to step into the trap of essentialism.

What is essentialism? If you ask postmodernist feminists they usually denounce something that earlier feminists had called 'biological determinism'. This is the idea that the anatomy of men and women is the cause of patriarchal gender relations and not social, politico-economic, cultural or historical relations. For postmodernists, categories like gender, class, race, etcetera are just differences. The criticism of essentialism means that such differences should not be considered as universally valid or quasi-nature-ordained. There is no 'male' or 'female' essence, only different constructions of maleness and female-ness, dependent on time, culture, history, space, class, race, sexual orientation.

According to postmodern feminists, essentialism is not only restricted to the biological differences between the genders; there can also be cultural or social essentialism in so far as certain localised and time-bound experiences are universalised in a metanarrative. Fraser and Nicholson criticise Chodorow's analysis of 'mothering' as essentialist, because it

> ... stipulates that this basically unitary activity gives rise to two distinct sorts of deep selves, one relatively common across cultures to women, the other relatively common across cultures to men....
>
> From a postmodern perspective, all of these assumptions are problematic because they are essentialist. (Fraser and Nicholson 1990: 30)

Our problem with the postmodern criticism of essentialism is not that it rejects biological determinism which legitimises dominance relations as nature-ordained. This we have done from the beginning of the movement (Mies 1978). But postmodern feminists seem to be throwing the baby out with the bathwater. In their anxiety to avoid essentialism and any universalistic 'grand narrative' they step into several traps. First, they practically deny that there is any material and historical reality to the categories 'women', 'men', 'mothers', etcetera. Thus there are only individual differences, which then, however, are seen as the only feature of human societies. On the basis of such individual and increasingly individualistic differences it is difficult to perceive any commonalities among people and to develop a notion of solidarity. Moreover, the radical constructivism that considers maleness and femaleness as *only* the result of cultural manipulations not only repeats the old Enlightenment dualistic and hierarchical division between nature and culture but also continues with the old valuation of this division: culture, anything made by humans, is superior to anything given by nature. This split is most acutely felt in our female bodies. According to postmodern feminists, women can never live in peace in and with their bodies. They are either cyborgs (Haraway 1991) or they are animals. This dualistic view has been particularly promoted by the Anglo-Saxon discourse on gender, in which a split was introduced between 'sex' as supposedly only biological and 'gender' as supposedly cultural (Rubin 1975).

One of the most negative results of this postmodern feminism is that on the basis of this ideology struggles for women's liberation – or for the liberation of any other oppressed group or class – become virtually impossible. First, there are only differences, and these are not seen as enriching diversity, but as competing or antagonistic interests. There is no commonality, no common cause, no common ethics, no common vision. In order to become politically active, however, a somewhat larger perspective than one's own experience is necessary.

On the other hand, if women want to become politically active, they must at least have a sense of reality of themselves, they must be able to consider themselves as subjects and their cause as real, important and part of a long-term perspective. Otherwise they will not have the necessary motivation and strength even to start getting involved in political action. This means they have to consider some issues as *essentially* important.

Such essentialism, however, is not allowed by postmodern feminism. This dilemma has also been observed by some of the spokeswomen of post-modernism. Judith Butler, referring to Julia Kristeva's analysis that 'women' actually do not exist, asks how such persons, who do not exist, can still be politically active. Her solution is interesting. She proposes to use the category 'woman' as a political instrument, but without granting it some ontological integrity. Butler quotes Spivak who argues that feminists should construct an operational essentialism, a false 'ontology of Woman' as a universal category in order to be able to start their political programme (Butler 1990: 325).

This means, if women want to act politically they have to erect the pretence that the category 'woman' has any universal, ontological essence. If they want to theorise, however, they have to avoid such essentialism by all means. This schizophrenic situation of postmodernist feminist thought is precisely the result of the new idealism that postmodernism represents. Somer Brodribb was one of the first to criticise this new idealism in feminist theorising. She points out that this new Platonism is based on the elimination of *matter* and *history* in postmodern, poststructuralist and existentialist theory and its replacement by discourses and narratives or language games which, for their part, can be traced to the 'murder' of the mother, matricide, as the beginning of human life. In her book *Nothing Mat(t)ers: A Feminist Critique of Postmodernism* (1992) Brodribb reminds us of the common Latin root of *mater* (mother) and *materia* (matter). She shows that the male cultural heroes of postmodernism – Nietzsche, Lyotard, Lacan, Derrida, Foucault – could not really accept that we are all born by women and that we die like other organic creatures. She identifies the 'murder of the beginning' (Blaise 1988; Kristeva 1989), the factual or symbolic killings of mother or woman, as the main impetus of postmodern philosophy. Without this murder of mat(t)er, without this de-materialising, obscuring and devaluing of our beginnings, our *arché* in this world, it would not have been possible to establish man as the creator of culture, of technology, of the symbolic order, and eventually of life. It would not have been possible to separate culture from mat(t)er and to subordinate the latter to the former and women to men. Postmodern men and women who want to move up into the symbolic order of capitalist patriarchy have first to forget that they are of 'woman born' (Rich 1977; von Werlhof 1996). Only after this can they conceive of themselves and of other humans as 'self-constructed', as cyborgs or hybrids between organic 'systems' and machines (Haraway 1990).

This postmodern murder of mat(t)er has produced a new idealism which not only reduces all reality to a 'text' but also eliminates our sense of history –

our sense both of our individual history and also of our social history. More-over, it condemns to oblivion the awareness of the link that binds us to other organic creatures on this planet. The awareness that in spite of all technological manipulation nature is first something *given*, and not constructed, disappears.

We do not understand why women, particularly in the centres of industrial capitalism, embrace this new idealism and even propagate it in the name of women's emancipation. As we saw, this happens not only in gender studies but also in politics. How was it possible that feminists forgot their roots in the women's movement and the centrality of 'body politics'? How could they forget the link between the women's movement and women's studies, between practice and theory? (Mies 1978). Why did they no longer understand that their enemies were not 'mothers' but global capitalist patriarchy? Why did they – again – believe that technology/science could 'emancipate' them from their real and symbolic mothers, from Mother Earth, and their organic bodies? This emancipation means, as Renate Klein put it, that they can eventually 'float bodyless in cyberspace' (Klein 1996: 376f.). Only in 'virtual reality' can they feel free and equal. Postmodern feminists' criticism of 'essentialism', for example of ecofeminism, has its roots in this denial of our own origins as 'of woman born', of real mothers and the symbolic order of mothers and of the female body. For women this denial is self-destructive. Gene and reproductive technologies are then the only means to 'emancipate' women from the 'wilderness' of their female body. Barbara Duden, in her criticism of Judith Butler, calls this postmodern, dematerialised woman the 'woman without abdomen' (Duden 1993: 36).

The denial of material individual and social histories goes hand in hand with the hope that it will give women, at last, access to the technocratically and patriarchally defined realm of the men. This realm is seen as the 'realm of freedom' and of culture. The old dream of all oppressed people, to move up into the house of their masters – instead of breaking down this house – is also many women's dream. In politics as well as in women's studies *some* women have indeed been able to move up in that house. But they were accepted by the 'Male-Stream' (O'Brien 1989) only after their denial of the origins, the separation from the women's movement and a re-academisation of Women's Studies had taken place (Mies 1996b).

In the Anglo-Saxon countries this re-academisation of Women's Studies was promoted largely by the discourse on gender. This gender discourse, though started earlier, culminated with postmodernism and the institutionalisation of Gender Studies depar tments in the universities. The effect of the shift from 'Women's Studies' to 'Gender Studies' was not simply to eliminate essential-ism and biological determinism but rather to make Women's Studies respect-able for the academic male-stream. With the disappearance of the category 'woman' from the academic discourse, other 'radical' concepts such as patriarchy, capitalism, exploitation, and oppression also disappeared. To talk of gender was decent, and it threatened no one. Gender neatly divided sexuality – supposedly linked to our organic female body – from the abstract and supposedly higher spheres of culture, society and history. We have already pointed out (in 1986) that human sexuality is not only an anatomical but also a social and historical category. To divide the two opens up this most intimate sphere of human experience to the technocratic and commercial manipulations of the one pole (sex) and to the romanticising and idealising of the other pole (gender) (Mies 1986b/99).

Gender discourse did not reach Germany until around 1990. But then a similar process of killing of origins happened. The beginnings of German Women's Studies in the late seventies were ignored or ridiculed. Whereas translations of American feminist writings were hailed as the origins of Women's Studies, the relationship between the German women's movement and Women's Studies was totally obscured (Bublitz 1992). And history was turned upside down: the women's movement was now said to have emerged out of Women's Studies. In the established German Women's Studies departments, meanwhile, it came to be considered progressive to talk of 'Gender-Studien' instead of using the German translation: *Geschlechterstudien.*

Yet the killing of origins is not only a problem of 'forgetting' certain writings. It has hit a number of internationally known German feminist scholars who are among the pioneers of German Women's Studies and who were not able to find positions in German universities. Among these are Luise Pusch, Senta Trömel-Plötz, Heide Göttner-Abendroth, Veronika Bennholdt-Thomsen and Claudia von Werlhof (von Werlhof 1996).

This process of eliminating the 'mothers' and of killing the origins seems to follow the stages that Catherine Keller has identified as the secret of establishing patriarchal dominance. For her the patriarchal 'myth of origin' is the Sumerian myth of Marduk and Tiamat. Marduk, the warrior son, has to kill his mother Tiamat, the ruler of the seas and of 'chaos'. Then he has to cut her body into pieces and to distribute them throughout the land. These places, where pieces of Tiamat were buried, then become centres of the new patriarchal civilisation (Keller 1986).

This schema of murdering the mothers is used not only by men time and again if they want to establish themselves as the origin of things but also by women. Matricide – the destruction of the origins and of female genealogies, the deconstruction and reconstruction of women's history into new narratives – is today a matter of a few hours' work at a word processor. Postmodern idealism legitimises this matricide, because there is no reality anyway any more.

We are surprised, however, that postmodern feminists ignore one important postulate of constructivism. This is the postulate to contextualise one's narratives, to ask in which historical moments which discourses are initiated by which actors and in whose interests. Had the postmodernist feminists asked these questions they would have discovered that the rise of postmodernism as the dominant theory in the universities, particularly in Women's Studies departments, coincided with the rise of neoliberal economic politics in the USA and UK in the eighties – Reagonomics and Thatcherism – and later, after the breakdown of socialism, in the whole world. Obviously, they do not realise that there is an exact fit between postmodern idealism, its attack on essentialism and on 'grand narratives', its neoliberal pluralism and political indifference, and neo-conservatism. These postmodern feminist scholars were and are not a threat to patriarchal capitalism. Indeed, words like 'patriarchy' or 'capitalism' do not appear in the postmodern discourse. Postmodernist ideology has effectively depoliticised large masses of people, particularly young people, so that they are not even aware of the connection between economy, politics and ideology: much less do they feel concerned about the growing inequality and social and ecological devastation produced by neoliberal economic policy. Seyla Benhabib rightly warns that the political alternatives that follow from Lyotard's philosophy, namely neoliberal pluralism and contextual pragmatism, will not be able to counter the onslaught of neoliberal politics and, as its results, growing inequality and ecological destruction. Postmodernism instead is 'motivated by a desire to depoliticize philosophy' (Benhabib 1990: 124).

Since women worldwide are the main victims of neoliberal policy it is a tragedy that Western feminists are among the torch-bearers of an ideology according to which 'anything goes and nothing mat(t)ers' (Brodribb 1992).

Women's liberation and subsistence

We have elaborated on our criticisms of the discourses on difference and identity, of pragmatic power politics, and of feminist postmodernist thought because we are of the opinion that these tendencies hinder the process of women's liberation from patriarchal relations. They not only depoliticise women but also destroy the basis for international solidarity among women and among men. We do not intend simply to sit back and watch this self-destruction and degeneration of the women's movement. We know that it is one of the main forces today that can expose and counter the blatant brutality of an economic system that sacrifices everything on earth to its greed for ever more money. Therefore we cannot afford to remain indifferent. This ideology may be seductive in a situation when, after the collapse of socialism, capitalism appears as the only possible alternative. As we noted in the Introduction, many people, particularly young people in the North, suffer from what has been called the TINA syndrome (There Is No Alternative). Pessimism, apathy and hopelessness seem to be the dominant mood. But we know that pessimism and hopelessness are luxuries which can only be afforded by those who are still able to share the loot of the whole world. The poor in the South are not pessimistic. They have no use for postmodern political indifference. Their vision of defending and re-creating their subsistence is not only necessary for their survival, it is also more realistic and down-to-earth, more far-sighted, more holistic, more creative and more human and ecologically sound, than post-modern idealism. This vision is not based on the capitalist concept of scarcity and hence on the necessity of constant competition. A new agricultural movement in Bangladesh has proclaimed 'Ananda' as the aim of their turning away from modern industrial agriculture in order to recover the richness of their own subsistence economy. *Ananda* means 'happiness for all'. This happiness is not an ascetic and poor life at the margins of existence, but a full life. This movement was sparked off by women who were fed up that the Green Revolution had not only destroyed their land and its biological diversity but had also resulted in unprecedented violence against women and reduced them to an endangered species (Akhter 1998). For such women the discussions among feminists in the North about whether women 'exist' or whether they are just virtual realities are just cynical and ridiculous.

As we said in the Introduction, our teachers and guides are women such as these in Bangladesh. It is from the perspective of the majority of the women in the world that we have developed our subsistence approach. It is well known that the model of a good life as demonstrated in the industrialised countries is neither economically or ecologically sustainable nor generalisable. Only a minority of men and women may benefit, for some time, from the loot of such a system. Hence, equality for all is not possible, even through catch-up develop-ment (Mies and Shiva 1993).

A vision of women's liberation that is valid for only a minority of women in the world is no vision at all. A vision of liberation has to be valid and realisable for all women. This means that we have to look for an economy which is no longer based on patriarchy, colonialism, and exploitation of nature. We call such an economy a subsistence economy. It must be valid in the South as well as in the North, because otherwise it is neither morally acceptable nor ecologically and economically sustainable.

We want to close this chapter with some theses, which we propose against the present dominant discourses among middle-class feminists:

1. The main problems of women world-wide are not difference and/or identity but exploitation, oppression, violence and colonialism. Our differ-ences, or rather our diversities, are our strength, our richness and our beauty. But capitalist patriarchy, which cannot tolerate equal valuation of all, has managed ideologically to transform diversities into antagonisms. Hence, every 'other' becomes an enemy, a competitor within a world of scarcity. We want to create a world in which biological and cultural diver-sity is maintained and celebrated.

2. We remain here below, on this earth, connected to all other creatures on this planet. We do not expect freedom, wealth, happiness and a 'good life' to come from some kind of transcendence , beyond the realm of necessity, be it the transcendence of religion, of money or of postmodern virtual reality. We continue to celebrate mat(t)er as the basis of life. We reject the dualism that divides matter from spirit, devalues matter and idealises spirit.

3. Our empowerment is based not on technocratic dominance over other creatures or other human beings, nor on participation in the capitalist and patriarchal power structures, but on self-reliance and autonomy, mutuality, self-organisation, self-provisioning, local and global networks, and subsistence relations instead of profit relations.

4. We know that we are historical beings. We know that without the knowledge of and the respect for female genealogies, both individual and social, women will not be able to overcome patriarchy. We want to reclaim and reconnect ourselves with our mothers. We want to reclaim and reconnect ourselves with our daughters.

5. We also want to reclaim and connect ourselves to our sons. We will not accept that our sons have no other perspective than that offered by macho, militarist global capitalism.

Our vision for women is closely related to their work and life. Its context is their everyday life and activity and the production of life, also in a symbolic sense. The satisfaction of our basic needs is both goal and path, not only in the South but also in the North. And this includes our needs for beauty, leisure, respect, dignity, in short a 'good life' for women. Instead of plundering nature this vision further comprises production in cooperation with nature. This implies knowledge of our surrounding local landscape and its natural conditions. Autonomous control over our work and products is a central topic in this vision, because we want to be proud of our products. Apart from enjoying them ourselves we want to offer them with generosity to others. Our wealth consists in our equality in diversity by which we are able to resist the coerced, housewifeised, McDonaldised, homogenised global culture. Under such conditions there is no need to deny or to idealise or to control our female body. This body is our source of strength, of wisdom and knowledge, and of vitality. With our bodies, our landscape, our strength, our work, our communities, we can remain rooted within ourselves.

For us the perspective of a subsistence-oriented women's liberation consists in recognising and respecting limits. Such limits will no longer be frontiers when we give up the patriarchal fantasies of omnipotence, and when in its place we respect our own strength, the identity with ourselves that allows us equally to celebrate our own value and that of others.

For us, differences have never been obstacles to solidarity and sisterhood. Our experience has been that we women could launch many international,

national and local political actions and campaigns not *in spite of*, but rather *because of* our diversities, be they based in culture, religion, class, caste, race, education, sexual orientation or other differences. Meanwhile many international feminist networks have been built up which for many women are sources of direct support and solidarity, of strength and sisterhood, and of political and spiritual inspiration and joy. These networks are not just symbolically important: they have intervened effectively on various occasions, and not only at UN women's conferences. These international networks don't need a central committee, or a party, or a formal hierarchy, or a rigid organisation. They usually originate from resistance and dissidence against certain manifestations of capitalist patriarchy and from common reflection on their causes. In these international networks feminists in the North have been greatly inspired by feminists in the South.

A recent example of such new international feminist communality was the Women's Day on Food organised on 15 November 1996 during the FAO World Food Summit in Rome. It was jointly prepared by women of the South and the North. For a whole day five hundred women from all over the world discussed the implications for women of the new globalised agricultural and food policy based on neoliberal free trade principles. Although these women had not known each other before, they reached consensus that 'food security must remain in the hands of women' and that local and regional self-sufficiency must replace the globalised food industry of the TNCs.

Vandana Shiva and others initiated a new international women's network at this Women's Day on Food: the Diverse Women for Diversity (DWD) network. This network comprises women from the South and North whose main concern is the protection and celebration of biological and cultural diversity and to protest against the homogenising and destructive tendencies of global capitalism. At the Fourth UN Conference on Biodiversity, held in Bratislava in 1998, the manifesto of this network was read to the delegates of governments. It expresses most clearly the new common concerns of women worldwide who do not want to accept the dominant economy as something without an alternative and thus become accomplices in this system.

Diverse women for diversity

Statement by Diverse Women for Diversity to the Plenary of the Fourth Conference of the Parties to the Convention on Biological Diversity, 4 May 1998

We are women from diverse regions and diverse movements committed to the continuation of the rich and abundant life on Earth. We come from different backgrounds, in full recognition of our history, and we believe there are and should be limits to human use and appropriation of the Earth and its diverse living beings. We take responsibility for our use of the things of this Earth and demand that all others of our species do the same.

We are moral human beings. We know that we occupy a given time and given space and are responsible for how we live in that time and the condition in which we leave that space for the future. We do not accept distrust, greed, violence, and fear as ways of relating to each other or to other beings. We reject such ways of relating, whether they take the form of negative personal actions, unacceptable products, or structural alliances among transnational corporations and national governments that trade weapons, risk wars, and form free trade treaties and other devices that roll back hard-won social and environmental protections, appropriate and monopolise the living diversity of our planet, and threaten our democracies, our farms, our livelihoods, our cultures, and our communities.

We support Article 8j of this Convention because we recognise that communities have boundaries and rights. And we insist that the sovereignty of communities with respect to their knowledge and resources take precedence over the freedom of outsiders to access and appropriate that knowledge and those resources. We assert that we and our communities will make the decisions that affect our lives, our livelihoods, our lands, and the community of species with which we share our space.

We recognise the wisdom that joins precaution to the search for knowledge. We see that precaution is needed to prevent harm to all that we love and value and steward and seek to understand and we know that whoever arrogantly discards the precautionary principle puts at risk the very basis of our lives.

We seek a world of good health and nutritious, safe, and affordable food for all. We reject the patenting of life in any form and we avoid those technologies and products that threaten the food security, health and well-being of any living being.

We recognise and celebrate the diversity and interrelatedness of species, cultures, and ways of knowing. We reject that which does not sustain the diversity of life and culture and so we reject the World Bank, the International Monetary Fund, the World Trade Organisation, the Multilateral

Agreement on Investment, and other such agreements and collusions. And we support the Convention on Biological Diversity, this important little treaty that creates tiny spaces for people to act and beckons us all to take a small step in a new direction and move towards mutual respect and joint well-being.

Secretariat of Diverse Women for Diversity
c/o Research Foundation for Science,
Technology and Ecology (Vandana Shiva)
A-60 Hauz Khas
New Delhi – 110016 India
Tel: 91-11-6968077, Fax: 91-11-6856795
Listserve of Diverse Women for Diversity c/o The Edmonds Institute
20310-92nd Avenue West
Edmonds, Washington 98020 USA
Tel: 425-775-5383 Fax: 425-670-8410
(Please mark the fax 'for Beth Burrows'.)

Subsistence and Politics

Taro field politics or men's house politics?

The woman peace and environmental activist Zohl dé Ishtar of Sydney, Australia, wrote a book about the resistance of the women of the Pacific: *Daughters of the Pacific* (1994). She participated in the action of Greenpeace against French nuclear tests in the Pacific. Before this she sailed the Pacific for a year and recorded women's stories about their experience with Western colonialism and militarism and their resistance to it.

The importance of control over their own communal land is stressed in almost all the reports and stories of the women, particularly in the places and islands where matriarchal traditions still prevail and the clan land is still inherited matrilineally. Almost all the indigenous peoples of the Pacific own communal land which connects them into a community. The Maori of New Zealand say, 'The land belongs to the people, and the people belong to the land. Land and people form a unit.' This world-view is most clearly expressed in the Maori term, *te whenua*. It means both 'land' and 'afterbirth'. Your land is where your afterbirth was buried. Thus you are existentially connected with it and with your ancestors. In the name of the island of Belau, 'belau' means both the land and the people who were born there. Maori women see many similarities between themselves and other indigenous peoples, for instance the natives of North America.

The statements of the women of the Belau island group, which was once a German colony and is now controlled by the USA as a strategic military zone, are particularly interesting. A massive movement sprang up against the occupation and militarisation, particularly against US nuclear politics. It was mainly supported by women. Belau was the first country on earth to declare itself nuclear-free. A leader of the movement, Gabriela Ngirmang, writes thus:

The main point of the disagreement (with the USA) is the land. This is a very sensitive issue here, because we have private land and clan land. The compact with the USA declares, that the government has to make land available within 60 days if required by the USA. But the government has no right to do this. It doesn't own the land, it belongs to the clans. This compact is going to cause a lot of problems between the clans people'. (Zohl dé Ishtar 1994: 47)

The clans in Belau are organised on matrilineal principles. Therefore the women carry most weight, not the elected government, which consists only of men. Women who work in the taro fields and produce the daily bread hold the power in their hands. They designate one of their sons, not the husband, to represent them as clan speaker in public affairs. He has to justify to the women the decisions made by the men, and the women are able at any time to overthrow the decisions made by the men. They don't discuss this in special meetings, but in the taro fields where they are by themselves. There all news, all reports, all political issues great and small are discussed and pondered. Men don't come to the taro fields. They 'hang out', have no power, says Bernie Keldermans, one of the women of Belau. Another, Cita Morei, describes the political, psychological and philosophical importance of women's work in the taro fields with these words:

The women were left alone. They were left alone in the taro patches doing their own thing. So these foreigners they thought they had influenced Belauan politics, but then they have not because they have not influenced the people who elect those men, to talk and talk. That was a flaw in the outsiders' views. They left the women alone, to do what we did. Women went on and on and on, untouched by foreign administration, greed and all that penetrates the men's psyches.

The taro patch is a place to tell women what is happening with the compact. When you tell them they will tell others. Taro-patch politics is very influential. It is sort of a sacred place in a way, you're thinking about the land. You are thinking, 'this is what I value'. You are not thinking of politics or of money. You are thinking about what it is to be Belauan. And that is played out in the taro patch. You get to think about what are *our* priorities, what are *our* needs, what are *our* weaknesses. When we want to keep coming to the taro patches then we have to look after Belau. We got to keep on going. Taro-patch politics. Men, they think about politics, they think about money. But women have been strong, because of the taro. (Zohl dé Ishtar 1994: 57).

Politicisation of subsistence?

A few years ago a left-wing group in Wuppertal organised a workshop where the politicisation of subsistence was to be the main issue. Invited were representatives of projects and initiatives that in the opinion of the organisers pursued a subsistence approach. The 'mothers' of this approach – Veronika Bennholdt-Thomsen, Maria Mies and Claudia von Werlhof – had also been invited. The group was eager to demonstrate that it considered the subsistence approach important and correct as a theoretical basis for social change but that it was, unfortunately, still too apolitical. The group considered it their duty to further develop this approach in its political dimensions.

We were unable to demonstrate convincingly that our thoughts were based on a different understanding of politics. The group accepted, however, Claudia von Werlhof's statement 'No Subsistence without Dissidence', as pointing in the correct direction. The criticism of our alleged political deficiency was elaborated and defined by Christoph Spehr in his 1996 book: *Die Ökofalle* (The Eco Trap). Here, in summary, are Spehr's most important criticisms.

1. The subsistence approach is not attractive. Subsistence projects are too small, demand too much work, are impotent against the dominant system.
2. 'Subsistence niches' help the state to lower the cost of the social system and of ecological repairs.
3. Subsistence is not defined. Who has the power to define it?
4. The women theorists of subsistence tend to romanticise and maintain an 'allergic distance' to the question of power and organisation. They remain stuck in individual actions.
5. As the past history of the accumulation logic is based on violence and not on ideological manipulation, it cannot be erased simply by convincing everybody of a different concept of the good life.

We have discussed some of these arguments in earlier chapters. Here, we want to concentrate on the aspect that allegedly is missing, namely the political aspect. Offhand, we are inclined to answer Christoph Spehr with, 'If you ask the wrong questions, you get the wrong answer or no answer.' Wrong doesn't mean that these question are wrong in themselves, but that the underlying thought horizon is not suitable for understanding the subsistence perspective. On the one hand, the position of the questioner is wrong because it is not authentic. He asks from the position of a left avant-garde, in other words from above and from outside and from the assumed strategical power of the mass line. On the other hand, the method of questioning is also wrong because it is non-productive. It is the style of so-called rational discourse, where argument is exchanged with argument in the hope that in the end new insights will be reached. Even though we know this paradigm and don't want to dismiss it totally we know from experience that such discourses don't convince anybody of the necessity or even the attractiveness of subsistence. Conviction grows out of relevance and partisanship and not out of an indifferent rational discourse.

Our concept of politics is obviously different from that of Spehr. We won't give a new definition in order to elucidate it, but instead tell the story of the women of Belau and how they understand politics. This is the concept of politics that we consider right and appropriate for the subsistence perspective: taro field politics instead of men's house politics. We want to reply to the objections from this perspective.

Re 1

Unsurprisingly, the subsistence approach remains unattractive for all those whose thought and experience horizon is limited by the dominant paradigm. This limitation of thought makes it almost impossible for intellectuals socialised in Western thought to understand under politics anything but what the old Greeks understood – an elitist male activity separated from the household, the *oikos* and daily concerns; the occupation of 'free men' with the business of the *polis*. We all have known for a long time that women, slaves, foreigners and colonised people had no access to these politics in the Athenian men's house, the so-called cradle of democracy. It was not the *demos* at all, the common folk, that gathered there, but a class of men who had relegated the care for subsistence on to the women and slaves. So long as this structure exists the men's house, particularly for those who have access to it or hope to gain such access in the future, is certainly more attractive than the *oikos* or the taro field.

 None of our arguments and no propaganda campaign can, under the conditions of people's identification with this structure, make subsistence attractive to the people. But the reverse does not succeed, either, namely that with further equal rights legislation more women would be accepted into the men's house and more men would work in the taro field. The structure itself is the problem, the separation of daily life from politics, and the hierarchisation between politics and everyday life.

Re 2, 3, 4, 5

Without doubt, subsistence niches, such as eco-projects, eco-villages, food co-ops, barter circles and other initiatives, help the system to reduce social costs. But does everything that reduces costs for the state have to be bad for those involved and for the advance of a subsistence perspective? Also, this objection comes in our opinion from a narrow black-and-white way of thinking. Perhaps these subsistence niches are workshops where we can learn to break down the enclosures. Perhaps we all, women and men, can stop fantasising ourselves into a position of subservience. As long as we persist in this attitude of subservience, neither freedom nor autonomy will be the way or the aim, but only what we believe we can demand from the state.

Whenever we say anything like this, we hear the reply, 'These are all only small scale experiments.' In Spehr's words, we have an allergy to the question of power and organisation. If we understand this correctly, he means power in the old sense of big, organised masses, following the example of trade unions, political parties, churches and other large institutions through which politics can be changed. And, if possible, all at once. He considers all other attempts as 'individualistic' or 'partial' and therefore too 'small' and impotent.

Christel Neusüss has compared this leader–masses model with a dredger and a dredger-driver: the dredger represents the masses, the driver the party, the political avant-garde under whose direction the dredger pushes the enemy aside (Neusüss, 1985: 160). It is true that Spehr does not refer to the old Communist or Social Democratic dredger model. Nevertheless, we have the suspicion that he and his friends still adhere to this concept of revolution and that they comprehend power as the usual political power – as domination *over*.

Power and domination are not taboo for us. We have frequently and in many different ways talked about violence, power and domination. However, we no longer believe that in order to gain power we must or can fight like with like. With this we have reached the question of violence.

We all know that in the men's house politics, power and domination come 'in the last analysis' out of the barrels of guns. This is also true, as we have always stressed, for the economy, and its dominant logic of accumulation. Time and again we have made it clear that violence, particularly against women, is an intrinsic part of this economic system. But this doesn't mean, as Spehr and his friends insinuate, that such a system can only be overthrown by force, and that such a domination cannot be destroyed by convincing everybody of an alternative path to a 'good life'. According to Spehr, persuasion is naïve. For millennia the model has been violent revolutions (and wars) in the patriarchal men's houses and it is still so today. And what has it accomplished? How has it formed men's and women's psyches? This model of violence and counterviolence has by now created a male identity that sees its ideal in a Kalashnikov-waving Rambo figure. One of the biggest problems of our time is the Ramboisation of our young men.

Globalisation has robbed men of the basis for meaningful, and at the same time physically demanding, work. The new technologies produce simultaneously fantasies of super-potency and violence of which women and children and 'others' become increasingly the victims. The armaments industry adds its efforts to militarise and Rambo-ise young men, and the media encourage this weapon-laden, ultimately infantile male image. No women's movement, however brave, nor the best-thought-out peaceful approach by women alone, can stop the Ramboisation of male children and juveniles. A men's movement is required that opposes the generalised brutalisation and demands a thorough demilitarisation. So here again subsistence politics does not mean that women mimic the Rambos, and try to enter the fighting forces, as happened during the Gulf War in the United States. On the contrary, it means that men share the subsistence work of women. This initiative ought to come from men, not from women (Mies 1994).

We learn, if we let ourselves be inspired by the politics of the taro fields, that the women in the taro field have a different concept of power from that of the men, 'who only talk and talk'. The power of women grows out of their control over subsistence and the means of subsistence, particularly the land. They defended this collective power against their husbands, against the colonial masters and against the US military.

And the men know that they depend on their mothers and sisters. They don't have a 'colony' outside which they can exploit. They therefore ultimately accept, in their men's house, the decisions of their women, in spite of the fact that the USA has tried to bribe them – the newly elected politicians. The solidarity between women and men in Belau has obviously not yet been totally destroyed. We noted the following additional aspects of taro field politics:

- politics is not separated from everyday life, from subsistence. You make politics while you work. Women do not require a special space, a special time, or special payment. Taro work is simultaneously political work and subsistence work.

- Politics does not function through delegations, elections and parties. Everybody is directly involved, everybody can talk and act directly. Everybody is empowered.

- Politics is not only concerned with the small daily problems. In the taro field, questions of history, of the ancestors, of the meaning of life are interwoven with current affairs. Thus taro field politics is not provincial, but it is concerned with the whole 'system'.

- What is important and what to do is evident to all, especially since there is no power to define what could be important to all. That, of course, is the end of all avant-garde dreams.

- The women work by consensus. But here consensus is something different from our concept. It is reached through informal talk among the women which is combined with the subsistence work. It doesn't need to be formalised.

- Special media and channels of information are therefore not needed to disseminate taro field opinions. They spread from the closest to the most distant by a system of interwoven friendships, family and clan relations.

- Taro politics is understood as a process, analogous to the process of seeding, weeding, and harvesting. It does not develop from sudden interventions, wars, or revolutions. Politics, focused on the requirements of local communities, on a 'moral economy', on the protection of the environment and the care for the future, has to have a long-term perspective. It cannot be determined by short-term profit interests or the scramble for power.

- Taro field power is everywhere, compared to the isolated power of the men in the men's house. It passes from mother to daughter; therefore it is hard to control.

At this point, Spehr and people of similiar opinion would interject, 'That is romanticisation of pre- or anti-industrial societies, the hierarchical structure of which is denied or lyrically covered up. This cannot be applied to society today' (Spehr 1996: 197). With regard to the argument of 'romanticisation' we would like to say that it is implicitly derived from the image of a lineal historic process in which Western industrial society is seen as the pinnacle and the inescapable image of the future for all 'pre-industrial'societies. As we stated in Chapter 3, exactly this is the true fairytale romanticisation of modernity. In this interpretation is also manifested what Veronika Bennholdt-Thomsen has called the 'cultural ignorance' of most Westerners.

By no means do we deny the fact that in societies like Papua New Guinea and Belau (why are they called pre-modern and pre-industrial?), domination and violence also existed, against women too. That, however, does not explain the ability of women in Papua New Guinea – in spite of colonialism, missionary activities and global capitalist policies – to mobilise soldiers against the elected government. Or why the women of Belau succeed in their taro fields in keeping US nuclear and military politics within its limits. True, we don't have such taro fields here (any more), but neither do we recount the story of the women of Belau because we consider it a model that can be replicated here point by point. We are concerned with something else: to inspire ourselves and others – who impotently and hopelessly face the 'black holes' which the dominant system has opened before us – to the realisation that Papua New Guinea or Belau or many other subsistence societies are the norm according to which the majority of people have lived for millennia and that industrial society is very young, very marginal, and cannot be generalised. It is a destructive deviation from this historically normal mode. We want to overcome the tunnel vision, the ignorance, the narrowness, the blockage of thought of our metropolitan arrogance. For that it is helpful to hear how people elsewhere understand and make politics. A friend once expressed the incarceration of our thoughts in the following image: we are like battery chickens – if they were suddenly let loose on a green meadow, they wouldn't know how to eat grass.

No subsistence without resistance!
No resistance without subsistence!

We have shown in previous chapters that people in the North, as well as in the South, have started to oppose globalisation with their own projects and diverse creative designs. Many still hesitate to see in these approaches something like politics from below, taro field politics. Others find the subsistence approach plausible and correct in its criticism as well as in its perspective of the future, but they cannot imagine how something like it could be realised here and now. 'How do we get from here to there?' We cannot answer this question with a fully developed strategy. But a simple listing of the most important principles of subsistence would not be sufficient either. We can again try to reply with two stories which show how people 'got from here to there'. These stories also come from the South where the confrontation between the subsistence interests of the people and the neoliberal enclosure policies of capital is far more brutal and direct than in the North. These stories show mainly that the struggle for the maintenance or recapture of subsistence is at the same time a struggle for different politics and for a different *concept* of politics.

The struggle for the recovery and reclaiming of autonomous subsistence is the absolute opposite of what since the end of the Second World War has been called 'development'. Now, fifty years later, it has become evident to many of the 'underdeveloped' that so-called development is nothing but another form of colonialism and imperialism. According to Terisa Turner and others, the old class analysis no longer helps us to understand the struggle in defence of subsistence. She and her colleagues demand instead a 'gendered class analysis'.

If such an analysis was carried out on concrete resistance movements, for example those against further privatisation and enclosure, not only would the connection between the exploitation of women by their own men, the state and international capital become obvious; also in these struggles the exploitation conditions as well as politics would be creatively changed and transformed (Turner and Benjamin, 1995). How dynamic processes such as a 'gendered class struggle' can be accomplished is described by Turner and others in the following example from Kenya. What follows summarises their story.

The women of Maragua

Maragua is situated eighty miles northwest of Nairobi, in the centre of a coffee-growing area. The men are the owners of the generally small, 1 to 5 hectare farms. Their wives are by law and in fact landless, but they had in Kenya the traditional right to work the land of their husbands and to control the product of their work. The women traditionally performed the work collectively. When export production was introduced, the women refused to work individually in the export production of their husbands because the proceeds of this work only benefited their husbands. Only the successfully housewifeised women worked individually in the cashcrop fields of their husbands and had no control over the proceeds of their labour.

Until 1975 coffee growing produced a good income for the small peasants, and more foreign currency for the state then ever before. That the economic miracle of Kenya didn't continue is partially a result of the refusal of the women to cooperate in this new gender and production relationship which is so important for export production. They insisted on their subsistence production through self-organised communal women's work. In addition, the world coffee price declined in the late seventies, the price for African coffee dropping by 70 per cent between 1980 and 1990. For the women this price collapse meant that they received even less of the proceeds of their work in the coffee fields from their husbands, even though they and their children performed the bulk of the work done there. The men spent their time in the bars in town, drank up the income, and didn't want to acknowledge that the coffee had been picked by their wives and children.

The women were tired of their husbands behaving like great landlords, even as absentee landlords. Several said, 'I won't pick coffee any more.' The men threatened to throw the women out of their houses and complained to government officials. These tried to mediate between the angry women and their husbands. They supported the women because they knew how important their work was for export production. The government officials tried to save both, marriages and coffee production. It didn't help. Coffee production dropped until 1986. That brought the World Bank and the IMF into action. They were worried about the interest payments that should primarily have come from the incomes from coffee exports.

The IMF prescribed for Kenya its famous–infamous structural adjustment programme (SAP) and provided funds for increased coffee production. The government gave higher coffee prices to the men and encouraged them to force their wives back to picking coffee. In the course of the SAP and the giving of new credits, expenditure on health, education and social programmes was reduced – all programmes that are especially important for women. International development experts tried to persuade the women to resume their unpaid work in their husbands' fields. Before and after the Third UN Women's Conference in 1985 in Nairobi, 'Women and Development' projects were top of the heap. Even the World Bank advocated 'Investment in Women'.

But this new advancement of a 'women's policy' was unable to break the resistance of the women. In Maragua, women simply started to plant beans between the coffee bushes. This was, of course, forbidden, but they did it and fed themselves and their children better. When the women of Maragua realised that neither their husbands nor the government officials were willing or able to satisfy their requirements for subsistence food and a secure cash income they advanced to direct action. In Maragua and elsewhere, women pulled up the coffee bushes and used them as firewood. Damage to a coffee bush was punishable by seven years in jail. The women didn't care and said, 'Let the police come and bring us money for our work in the coffee plantation.' The movement soon became unstoppable. This type of resistance for the recapturing of subsistence was repeated at different intensities everywhere in East Africa.

The struggle of the women was directed against at least three levels of women's exploitation: that by their own husbands, that by the state, and that by international capital, for instance the chemical industry, the international coffee trade and the World Bank. Women won this struggle because they simultaneously created a new subsistence base. They could no longer be blackmailed by the new and old exploitative and oppressive structures. The regaining of their subsistence base, land, freed them from control by their husbands. They broke the circle of chronic indebtedness which tied them to the state, and they established their own regional market with home-grown fruits and vegetables. They also freed themselves from the international coffee corporations and with that from control by transnational capital. By the end of the eighties, the men also had realised that it was better to produce fruit for the local market, and they joined the struggle of the women.

The direct action taken by the women of Kenya to recapture their autonomous subsistence was not only an economic action in the narrow sense of the word, but also had immediate political consequences. Small women traders in the town of Sagana refused to sell their coffee to the government agencies. The women contributed materially to the formation of a political opposition, and to the fact that the one-party government finally allowed opposition parties. The men realised that the resistance of the women represented an economic base and an organised militancy that enabled them to keep their land despite the neoliberal policy of enclosures which the government was trying to impose. The women reinstated control by producers over the land and over the type of production (Brownhill, Kaara and Turner 1997a: 42).

With regard to the question, 'How do we get from here to there?' the resistance of the Kenyan women teaches us the following:

1. Women began their resistance by developing an independent subsistence production within the exploitative, export-oriented production. They did not fight for wages for their work, but brought the essential resources – land, water, etcetera – under their control. They accomplished this in silent, direct and collective action, and not after they had got themselves strategically organised in order then to be able to act 'politically'. They acted on a different level of politics than their husbands and the state. They created a subsistence society by creating regional markets.

2. Women struggled simultaneously against all powers that exploited them: husbands, state and transnational capital. These powers were closely interwoven with each other. The government badly needed the husbands as agents in the mobilisation of women as an unpaid work-

> force. International capital and its institutions, the head of global patriarchy, controlled and manipulated them both by forced export production and through the debt trap.
> 3. They didn't try to rise in the dominant system as 'housewifeised' individuals, but adhered to their traditional, collective women's structures. They re-created and expanded these structures, again outside the government-regulated market, into a flourishing regional and local production and marketing system.
> 4. Since they had, in this manner, created their own, independent local and regional subsistence base and had withdrawn their labour power from their husbands, the state and the TNCs, only two options were left to the men: either to support the women and to recognise their authority, or to oppose them and attack them violently together with the government and capital (Brownhill, Kaara and Turner 1997a and 1997b).

The Seed Satyagraha of the Indian farmers

As mentioned earlier, since the early nineties Indian farmers have been fighting against the GATT, especially against article 27 on Trade Related Intellectual Property Rights (TRIPs). According to those rules, Indian patent law would have to be adapted to that of the USA. This would mean for the Indian peasants that they would lose control of the production, modification and sale of their own seed corn. Multinational seed companies, such as Cargill Seeds India, backed by biotechnology and GATT, are trying to monopolise seed production in their hands. After TRIPs, Cargill can modify and then own patents on all Indian seeds. This means that peasants are no longer allowed to save and reproduce their own seed and sell it. All seed would have to be purchased from Cargill anew each year.

The South Indian farmers' organisation Karnataka Rajya Ryota Sangha (KRRS) is fighting against this expropriation of farmers' seed corn, their knowledge, and their food sovereignty. Following the example of Gandhi, they started a Seed Satyagraha[1] which commenced on 29 December 1992 by storming the regional office of the food and seed multinational Cargill Seeds-India Pvt. Ltd. in Bangalore. They threw Cargill's papers in the streets and burnt them. The flyer produced after the action reads thus: 'The KRRS activists demand the maintenance of the Indian patent law of 1970 which forbids the patenting of agricultural, horticultural, and fish-farming methods, and which forbids the multinational companies any intrusion into the Indian seeds domain.' Some 500,000 peasants demonstrated in March 1993 in Delhi against the new bio-colonialism. They demanded the right to feed their people and self-reliance in respect to food, and urged the TNCs to leave the country.

'We are going to expel all multinational seed companies, which exploit our country,' said Dr Nanjundaswamy, the leader of the movement. Other multinationals, such as Kentucky Fried Chicken in Karnataka, were also asked by KRRS to cease their operations. Dr Nanjundaswamy called this the second Quit India movement against imperialism. (The first was led by Gandhi against British imperialism in 1942.) The Seed Satyagraha of the Indian farmers was directed, like the action of the women of Kenya, simultaneously against all actors and agencies that were trying to force neoliberal global enclosure policies upon them: their own government, the TNCs and GATT/ WTO. Instead, they demanded that the Indian government should get out of the GATT, that 'self-sufficiency' should become once again the aim of food policy, and that they the farmers, should themselves have the right to feed the people of India (*BIJA* 15/16, 1996).

A different concept of the economy leads to different concepts of politics

It is evident that movements with the aim of regional and local self-sufficiency will end up in conflict with the dominant global free market policies. They will have to develop different political concepts too. The South Indian peasants, like the women in Kenya, didn't waste much time in sending petitions to their respective governments but resorted immediately to direct action. A number of resistance movements, 'people's movements', have occurred in India in the last few years which acted similiarly. All these movements were sparked off in response to local problems caused by neoliberal globalisation, and all of them arrived at new concepts of what politics should be. In the dossier that the Research Foundation for Science, Technology and Ecology presented to the UN Special Assembly in Rio plus 5 (23–27 June 1997), the authors reported that the following citizen movements against globalisation in India had been successful:

1. The action of the National Fishworkers Federation against foreign trawlers which fished the coastal waters empty. Their licences were revoked by the Supreme Court.
2. The action against the multinational shrimp farms, which were salinating the land and the groundwater and destroying the mangrove forests. The Supreme Court of India forbade industrial shrimp farming on India's coasts.
3. Actions against slaughterhouses that process beef for export. The Supreme Court ordered a reduction in the number of slaughterhouses.
4. The action against Du Pont which wanted to produce toxic substances in Goa. Du Pont had to leave Goa.
5. Actions against the import of toxic waste. The Supreme Court forbade the import of toxic waste into India.

The authors of the dossier ask the decisive political question, 'Who is to have control in conflicts over resources: local communities or transnational corporations and their henchmen, the national governments? The people's movements of recent years declare that:

> People's movements are demanding that power should not be concentrated in the institutions of the centralised nation states but should be distributed throughout society and should be dispersed through a multiplicity of institutions, with more power at the local level, controlled by local communities and their institutions. (Shiva, Jafri and Bedi 1997: 82)

The 'Peoples' Agenda' demands localisation instead of globalisation, in the economy as well as in politics. The politics of localisation in India is based on Gandhi's principle of 'self-rule', *swaraj* – which has its most important seat in the village, the local community, from which, according to Gandhi, all power flows. Decentralisation and localisation are the answer of the Indian people's movements to globalisation and free trade. 'If globalisation is the corporate-driven agenda for corporate control, localisation is the countervailing citizens' agenda for protecting the environment and people's survival and people's livelihood' (Shiva, Jafri and Bedi 1997: 83). Women and men have to assume responsibility for this protection, since national governments no longer protect citizen's elementary rights. Citizens create a new policy, a new protectionism – that of the local community – against the protectionism of the corporations by the state. Their protectionism is based on a different concept of democracy: it is pluralistic, direct or 'people's democracy'. The philosophy of this pluralistic, direct democracy of local communities acknowledges that different communities have different interests which they should be able to express through self-rule and self-determination. Within communities democratic pluralism will also have to abolish colonial and dominance structures based on caste and gender.

> In systems characterised by patriarchal domination of women, urban areas dominating over rural areas, colonisers dominating over indigenous people, democratic pluralism necessarily requires an inclusion of communities who have been excluded. This would necessarily transform both the communities characterised by internal inequalities as well as governance structures within countries' (Shiva, Jafri and Bedi 1997: 85).

If the political structure of a country, for instance, India, were to consist of a multitude of such self-governing, more or less autonomous communities and regions, the prospect of maintaining a pyramidal iceberg structure, in which the visible peak is supported by ever larger, invisible layers of exploited and excluded people, would not exist. On the contrary, life would be organised, as Gandhi saw it, in 'oceanic, concentric circles', the centre of which is the individual; the might of the most peripheral circle, that of the nation-state, would serve all these individuals in communities.

When we seek a political answer to the globalisation of the capitalist economy, it becomes evident that we in the industrialised North can adopt much of what the Indian people's movements see as a political perspective for the future: decentralisation of power, localisation and regionalisation, self-rule (autonomy) of local communities, democratic pluralism and direct democracy, local and regional control of resources, protection of the environment, and protection of the livelihood and the basic conditions of existence of the people.

What our Indian friends say about the role of national governments in respect of the multinationals and capital applies even more to our own situation. In the framework of the global market, of GATT, the WTO, MAI and regional trade blocks such as the EU and NAFTA, national governments are no longer capable of protecting the vital basic needs and basic rights of their citizens. This becomes dramatically clear in the example of gene-manipulated food and the BSE scandal in Europe. Inside the EU, citizens have lost their sovereignty over food. They neither know nor determine what they eat. When the EU Commission declares that beef is BSE-free and can be sold again everywhere in the EU, nobody is able to monitor the truth of this declaration. Approximately 80 per cent of German consumers are against gene-manipulated food; nevertheless it is being produced, and mostly sold without labelling. Consumers have no choice. In a situation where we are practically made into 'coerced consumers', a local economy and direct democracy are ways to regain basic democratic freedom rights, like food sovereignty. The undermining of basic democratic rights is even more pronounced on the global level. This became dramatically evident in the OECD negotiations about the Multilateral Agreement on Investment, the MAI. Had it not been for a vigilant citizens' movement worldwide, this agreement in favour of the TNCs would have been signed without people knowing about it (Clarke and Barlow 1997; Mies and von Werlhof 1998).

The experience with the MAI is also a warning to those who believe that 'global governance' will have to follow the globalisation of the economy. We oppose 'global governance' not only because it will not work, as one can see in the example of the UN, but mainly because we know that it would be nothing but a kind of totalitarian regime by 'global players', the gigantic TNCs, and that everybody would be made into impotent, ignorant, remote-controlled coerced consumers of global politics. It would be the end of everything we understand as democracy, liberty and self-determination.

In contrast, subsistence politics represents the concrete political and economical empowerment of the individuals in specific places and in their communities. Their life should not be determined by some abstract, remote, political supreme power. They ought to shape it themselves, out of their own strength, together with equals.

If we try to achieve subsistence instead of global governance, this does not mean that we advocate some kind of mere parochial politics. We are of the opinion that true internationalism, not based upon exploitation, becomes possible only when subsistence communities in the South as well as in the

North determine also their subsistence politics. Only then can international solidarity again be a meeting and exchange between equals, free of all paternalism. Only then can the diversity of cultures, societies, and ethnic groups be conceived of as true richness, as a source of power and not as a threat.

The successful worldwide campaign against the MAI is the most recent example of how local initiatives and communities can form global alliances against all-powerful corporate policies. In this campaign there was no central leadership, no hierarchy, hardly any money. Its success lay in the creative worldwide networking of committed citizens.

What can subsistence politics mean here and now?

Subsistence politics is not a model but a process. For that reason, we are unable to give point-by-point directives on how it can be put into practice. The path is the end! The most important step is the first step. We would like, however, to stress the following important political aims, partly already mentioned in previous chapters, for those who ask for relevant middle-range political goals.

- It is absolutely necessary that urban consumers defend the small peasant agriculture more strongly by promoting direct marketing, producer–consumer co-ops, local weekly markets, purchasing of goods produced in the region, and preparedness to pay an honest price for good food.
- It is absolutely necessary that far more people than up until now openly oppose genetic manipulation in agriculture, the patenting of life in all its forms, and the ongoing enclosure process of global food politics. The control of our food is a basic right which is destroyed by food TNCs, by the WTO, the MAI, NAFTA, the EU, MERCOSUR and other regional trade blocs. We citizens have to oppose this destruction of our basic right to food sovereignty and, at the same time, act through the politics of the shopping basket. This means that we should boycott, as far as possible, big food TNCs.
- It is absolutely necessary that the issue of work is no longer left to the politicians, to corporate bosses or to the labour unions who are unable to think beyond the wage-labour regime. Non-wage labourers, beginning with housewives, have to gain public recognition. We need a different, comprehensive concept of work. Non-wage workers must make themselves heard.
- It is important to dissolve the hegemony of the wage-labour regime. This does not mean the end of wage-labour as such, but the end of its dominance. Practically speaking, instead of continuing with the destruction of peasant agriculture and small artisans and especially the destruction of supplementary income from subsistence farms, combinations of subsistence and wage-labour should be further developed as, for instance, that of the Yabo farmers in Tokyo (see Chapter 5).

- It is necessary that we stop the policy of enclosure (privatisation) of public space. Citizens have to assert their collective rights in these public spaces and resources and must defend them. Beyond that they could create new commons by demanding land owned by cities or state, in order to make them into new commons: communalisation of land instead of privatisation or state ownership! We have to stop the export of our garbage. Nothing should be produced regionally whose waste cannot be disposed of regionally.

- It is absolutely necessary that *men* stop the increasing 'Ramboisation' of young men. This they can do by participating together with the young men in unpaid subsistence work. Men and women have to demand prohibition of the production and sale of military toys and of the representation and propagation of violence in the media and in public. Solidarity between men and women can only redevelop if men cancel the 'male deal' with capital and the state, listen to the women and accept their concept of politics. This was the demand of women at the Women's Day on Food held in Rome in 1996.

- Instead of expecting that governments and/or UN conferences will solve the problems of environmental destruction, poverty and wars through 'global governance', we should familiarise ourselves with existing international networks of popular movements (peasant movements, women's movements, indigenous peoples' movements, etcetera), link up with them, popularise them, learn from each other and organise a People's Agenda.[2] We can start immediately to tell each other encouraging subsistence stories.

- It is necessary to start with the work to make cities arable. This movement could be combined with the reclaiming of the commons, the creation of new communities and neighbourhoods and the establishing of a different concept of work and the solving of ecological and social problems in the cities. We can start immediately and everywhere, both in the North and the South, in the cities and in the country, as our final subsistence stories tell us.

The first women's potato field in Cologne

When we – Ulla, Margit, and Inge – stand today in front of our potato field, full of admiration for the luxuriant potato plants, supporting the tall peas with a few small twigs and cutting back the pumpkin in its rapid growth, we can hardly believe that this was an unkempt wilderness only four months ago. We got the idea and the strength to transform this wilderness into ecologically useful land from the lecture series of Maria Mies called 'Women and the World Economy'.

On the last day of the seminar she told us about, among other things, some subsistence projects. We were particularly inspired by a project that is being put into practice in the middle of Tokyo. We were convinced that we would be able to realise such a project in Cologne also because here also there was enough unused land. We sat together having a coffee after the seminar and, inspired by the idea, thought of how we could bring the project of the first women's potato field in Cologne into existence. When we asked ourselves where to obtain the land, Margit remembered that behind her allotment garden there was uncultivated land which was rented by the allotment garden association. Only a week later we met again to inspect our 'new land'. Looking at the land, covered by enormous blackberry bushes, we almost lost our confidence. But we didn't let ourselves be discouraged; we realised quickly that together we could make good progress clearing the land. Whenever a really thick root resisted the efforts of one woman, three of us managed easily. We worked twice a week, and after four weeks we had cleared the land and planted the first potatoes.

People around us on the whole reacted positively to our work. Unexpected confirmation and help came from the originally sceptical allotment garden neighbours. They offered their help with the clearing and the purchase of seed potatoes and lettuce, cabbage, and turnip plants. Many a useful gardening tip was exchanged across the fence. They were also surprised that the children's beds were looked after with enthusiasm by our children. Every child used the chance to care for a bed. The early positive experiences gave us the energy and courage to enlarge our project. On a still-to-be-found piece of land, we want to give kindergarten and elementary school children the chance to experience gardening and nature. We also want to socially reintegrate long-term unemployed women by letting them work in such communal city gardens.

The following story about a new peasants' movement was reported by Farida Akhter from Bangladesh. It summarises most clearly what a new subsistence economics and politics could be and how it could integrate the local and the global, the material and the symbolic.

Nayakrishi Andolon: a peasants' movement for food security and happy life in Bangladesh[3]

Farmers of Bangladesh are organised against '*beesh*'. The word literally denotes poison in Bangla and that is how pesticides and harmful chemicals are normally termed by the farmers of Bangladesh. The women farmers started to organise themselves to save from poisons their *deha*, that is their Body, with a capital B. There is no separation, no real difference, between the female body in the shape of a woman and the spatial extension of the universe, the *Prakriti* – the Body of all bodies. Thus the Nayakrishi Andolon (New Agricultural Movement) started as a women's movement in order to defend the Body and to celebrate the joyful originary posture of Prakriti in her profound act of creation. It has rapidly extended to a unique practice of agriculture through mixed cropping, crop rotation and other subtle arts and methods producing *Ananda*.[4] *Ananda* is of course food and other agricultural products depending on what you mean by 'food' or 'product'. The Nayakrishi Andolon is definitely a movement for ecological food production and economically viable activity for the farming community of Bangladesh. But it is above all a creative, joyful activity to celebrate life and relations between human beings and the rest of nature. Ask a farmer belonging to the movement why she practises Nayakrishi. In almost all cases she will reply, 'I want to be happy and enjoy my life. That's all!' You will not hear any fancy ecological rhetoric, or any teleological projection of a future claiming liberational promises. The farmers, particularly the farming women, want happiness right here, in this real world, and right now.

In 1998, more than 25,000 farming households in Bangladesh practised Nayakrishi. The movement has proved that small farmers owning less than 5 acres of land can manage, regenerate and produce amazingly diverse crops: timber, fuelwood, medicinal plants, fish, livestock and other products. It is clear that biodiversity is directly related to the existence of the farming community to whom agriculture is a way of life, not simply a sector of production for investment and profit. The transformation of agriculture can follow two different paths.

The *beesh* was introduced in the mid-sixties as a component of the High Yielding Varieties (HYV) technology of the Green Revolution. The farmers were given fertiliser free of cost. They were also given all sorts of incentives, such as credit and free training, to take pesticides and fertiliser from the government Agricultural Department. With the fertiliser they were given paddy seeds developed in the laboratory and known as the HYV variety. In addition they were given pumps to extract ground water for irrigation. Monoculture of HYV seeds narrowed the genetic base of agricultural practice. Previously, at least 15,000 varieties of rice had existed, but Bangladeshi farmers ended up with only eight to twelve HYV varieties. The extraction of ground water has resulted in a major crisis in the water supply because of its very high arsenic content in many areas. The overall result of the Green Revolution has been disastrous.

The fertility of the soil started to decline after initial years of increased productivity. Men in the families did not need women any more for seed preservation, germination and post-harvest activities. Women's value within the agrarian economy declined and the new technology drastically disempowered them without any positive transformation of the old patriarchal world. Seeds are available in packets, rice husking is done in the rice mills – so why do you need women except for the production of children? They are simply valueless. Violence against women rose to a peak, causing increasing rates of suicide in areas of intensive agriculture that used chemicals, poisons and pumps. Women who wanted to kill themselves used the same *beesh* which was used to kill pests. Pesticide was available in each farming household.

The rise of the global market has exacerbated the plight of women. They are now available as cheap labour for export-oriented industries. They are constructing roads in the rural areas by working in the Food for Work programme. They are targeted for the dumping of contraceptives considered unsafe in the West and for the testing of new drugs. Their reproductive functions are controlled for population control, and young girls and small children are trafficked out of the country to be sold in the sex, slave and organ trades.

Women are angry. They say: So-called modern agriculture has destroyed our lives, our society, our culture, our land, our soil, and the life forms around us which sustained us. The male farmers for two generations became greedy, but now they are ashamed of their foolishness. They miscalculated the benefit – misunderstood the message. The loss of the huge variety of paddy crops, fish, vegetables and fruits is a tragedy for the country. For the new generation of children, there are merely the stories of the grandmothers: 'We had this, we had those ...'

But the farmers in Bangladesh are not the sort to just mourn their loss. The history of the peasant movement is very strong in this region. '*Mora tulbo na dhan porer golay, morbo no ar khudar jalai*' (We will not allow our produce to end up in the stores of the exploiters. We will resist. We will not accept death from hunger.) This is an old song from the Tebhaga movement of the 1950s, the well-known peasant insurgency that demanded rights and justice for the food producers. The spirit is still there.

Now, in an area like Tangail, Nayakrishi farmers cultivate at least 110 different varieties of rice. In some villages farmers do not require ground water any more. Surface water sources are used sustainably. The seed network between farmers of different areas is collecting and conserving seeds of local varieties, and where possible a centre for Community Seed Wealth is instituted. The farmers are becoming aware of the policy of privatisation of seed and genetic resources in the name of 'patenting', and resistance to biopiracy is being built up.

Apart from its broader cultural and political implications, the Nayakrishi Andolon is based on the following simple principles:
• absolutely no use of pesticides; the integrity of life is respected

- no use of chemical fertilisers, or a gradual decrease in their application
- the use of mixed cropping and multicropping, agro-forestry and other familiar methods to retain and enhance soil fertility
- the practice of agro-forestry and integration of the growing of fuelwood, fruit and various multi-purpose trees along with rice and vegetables
- the practice of calculating the total yield of a farming household and the material gains of the community as a whole through the maintenance of fields and the enhancement of biodiversity
- livestock, poultry and semi-domesticated birds and animals are considered an integral component of the farming household. Farming households are not seen as either 'farm' or 'factory' in terms of the industrial paradigm
- priority is given to local varieties of livestock, poultry and fish. Local varieties are almost always economically advantageous and ecologically suitable
- Seeds and genetic resources are conserved at the household and community level. The farmers must be in control of the seeds. The privatisation of genetic resources and the patenting of life forms are not acceptable.

Nayakrishi Andolon's practical attempts to develop the art of living a happy life and its immediate task of ensuring food security activities for the conservation and enhancement of biodiversity and genetic resources are of fundamental importance.

Nayakrishi Andolon aims to bring the primary food producers, such as farmers and fishermen, to the centre in the discussion and resolution of the question of food security. It emphasises the centrality of the role of women.

Nayakrishi Andolon also insists that food and food production must be seen in the context of diverse cultural systems and in their relation to the rich cultural practices of the community. Food items are not simply commodities or consumer goods.

Nayakrishi Andolon farmers have rejected patenting of life forms. They become surprised when they hear that companies are trying to patent seeds. They laugh and then get angry: 'We will not let them do it.' They call them '*chor-dakat*', meaning thieves and armed robbers. 'The *chor* or *dakat* has no right to claim any right over our natural resources.'

NOTES

1. *Satyagraha* means 'truth'. Gandhi chose this term to name his non-violent campaign against British colonial rule.
2. One such network is 'People's Planning for the Twenty-first Century' in Asia.
3. *Source:* Farida Akhter, UBINIG, Dhaka 1998. The text has been slightly shortened.
4. *Ananda*, a Sanskrit term, means 'happiness', even 'bliss'. For this farmers' movement all happiness begins with food or the agricultural product. It comprises both the material and the symbolic dimensions of 'food' in a non-dualistic sense.

References

A.G. Bielefelder Entwicklungssoziologen (ed.) (1979) *Subsistenzproduktion und Akkumulation*, Saarbrücken.

Akemine Tetsuo (1997) 'Subsistence Agriculture in Tokyo' in: Pestemer, Richard (ed.) *Landwirtschaftliche Selbstversorgung als Überlebensstrategie in der Metropole Tokio: Texte zur Vortragsreihe von Akemine Tetsuo in Deutschland.*

Akhter, Farida (1998) *Naya Krishi Andolon: A Peasants' Movement for Food Security and Happy Life in Bangladesh*, Dhaka, UBINIG.

Althabe, G. (1972) *Les fleurs du Congo*, Paris, Maspero.

Altvater, Elmar and Mahnkopf, Birgit (1996) 'Die globale Ökonomie am Ende des 20. Jahrhunderts', in: *Widerspruch*, Vol. 16, Part 31.

Amadiume, Ifi (1987) *Male Daughters, Female Husbands. Gender and Sex in an African Society*, London, Zed Books.

Arbeitskreis Zukunft der Frauenarbeit (ed.) (1985) *Dokumentation des Kongresses 'Zukunft der Frauenarbeit'*, Proceedings of the conference held at the Universität Bielefeld, 4 June 1983. Bielefeld.

Bagby, Rachel L. (1990) 'Daughters of Growing Things', in: J. Diamond, and Gloria Feman-Orenstein (eds), *Reweaving the World: The Emergence of Ecofeminism*, San Francisco, Sierra Club Books.

Bartra, Roger (1974) *Estructura agraria y clases sociales en México*, Mexico City.

Bartra, Roger (1976) 'Y si los campesinos se extinguen … (Reflexiones sobre la coyuntura política de 1976 en México)', *Historia y sociedad*, No. 8, pp. 71–83, Mexico.

Beauvoir, Simone de (1974) *The Second Sex*, Vintage Books.

Becker, Ruth (1988) 'Befreiung durch Konsumverzicht – konsequent zu Ende gedacht. Provokantes zu einem ökofeministischen circulus vitiosus', *Beiträge zur feministischen Theorie und Praxis*, 21/22.

Bell, Diane and Klein, Renate (1996) *Radically Speaking: Feminism Reclaimed*, Melbourne.

Benhabib, Seyla (1990) 'Epistemologies for Postmodernism: A Rejoinder to Jean François Lyotard', in Linda J. Nicholson (ed.), *Feminism/Postmodernism*, New York and London, Routledge.

Bennholdt-Thomsen, Veronika (1976) 'Zur Bestimmung des Indio', *Indiana*, supplementary issue No. 6, Berlin.

Bennholdt-Thomsen, Veronika (1979) 'Marginalität in Lateinamerika. Eine Theoriekritik', in Bennholdt-Thomsen *et al.* (eds), *Lateinamerika, Analysen und Berichte*, No. 3, Berlin (published in Spanish as 'Marginalidad en América Latina. Una crítica de la teoría', *Revista Mexicana de Sociología*, Vol. XLIII, No. 4, 1981: 1505–46).

Bennholdt-Thomsen, Veronika (1980) 'Towards a Class Analysis of Agrarian Sectors: Mexico', *Latin American Perspectives*, Vol. 7, No. 4, pp. 100–14.

Bennholdt-Thomsen, Veronika (1981) 'Subsistence Production and Extended Reproduction', in Kate Young *et al.* (eds), *Of Marriage and the Market*, London, pp. 16–29 (2nd edn, 1984, pp. 41–54).

Bennholdt-Thomsen, Veronika (1982) *Bauern in Mexiko. Zwischen Subsistenz- und Waren-produktion*, Frankfurt am Main (published in Spanish as *Campesinos: Entre producción de subsistencia y de mercado*, UNAM/CRIM, México 1988)

Bennholdt-Thomsen, Veronika (1984) 'Towards a Theory of the Sexual Division of Labour', in: J. Smith, I. Wallerstein and H-D. Evers (eds), *Households and the World Economy*, Beverly Hills, Sage, pp. 252–71.

Bennholdt-Thomsen, Veronika (1987) 'Hausfrauisierung und Migration', in Bennholdt-Thomsen *et al.*, *Frauen aus der Türkei kommen in die BRD*, Lüdinghausen.

Bennholdt-Thomsen, Veronika (1988a) 'Investment in the Poor: An Analysis of World Bank Policy', in Maria Mies, Veronika Bennholdt-Thomsen and Claudia von Werlhof, *Women – The Last Colony*, Zed Books, London, pp. 51–63.

Bennholdt-Thomsen, Veronika (1988b) 'Why do Housewives Continue to Be Created in the Third World Too?' in Maria Mies, Veronika Bennholdt-Thomsen and Claudia von Werlhof, *Women – The Last Colony*, Zed Books, London, pp.159–67.

Bennholdt-Thomsen, Veronika (1989) 'Die Würde der Frau ist kein Überbauphänomen. Zum Zusammenhang von Geschlecht, Natur und Geld', *Beiträge zur feministischen Theorie und Praxis*, Vol. 12/24.

Bennholdt-Thomsen, Veronika (1990) 'Der Sozialismus ist tot, es lebe der Sozialismus? Gegenseitigkeit statt sozialer Gerechtigkeit', *Kurswechsel* 3, Vienna.

Bennholdt-Thomsen, Veronika (1991a) 'Women's Dignity is the Wealth of Yuchitan (Oaxaca, Mexico)', *Journal of Interdisciplinary Economics*, Vol. 3, No. 2, pp. 327–34.

Bennholdt-Thomsen, Veronika (1991b) 'Gegenseitigkeit statt sozialer Gerechtigkeit. Zur Kritik der kulturellen Ahnungslosigkeit im Patriarchat', in Birgitta Hauser-Schäublin, (ed.), *Ethnologische Frauenforschung*, Berlin.

Bennholdt-Thomsen, Veronika (1992) 'Entwicklung und Fortschritt aus feministischer Sicht', in Werner Hennings, (ed.), *Drei Annäherungen an einen Begriff: Entwicklung aus ökologischer, feministischer und strukturalistischer Sicht*, Unterrichtsmaterialen, Vol. 42, Oberstufenkolleg, Bielefeld.

Bennholdt-Thomsen, Veronika (ed.) (1994) *Juchitán – Stadt der Frauen: Vom Leben im Matriarchat*, Reinbek.

Bennholdt-Thomsen, Veronika (1996a) 'Women Traders as Promoters of a Subsistence Perspective: The Case of Juchitán (Oaxaca), Mexico', in Parvin Ghorayshi (ed.), *Women at Work in the Third World*, Westport, CT and London, Greenwood Press, pp. 167–79.

Bennholdt-Thomsen, Veronika (1996b) 'Wohin führt die Weltwirtschaft für Frauen?', in ITPS, *Rundbrief Subsistenzperspektive* No. 6, *Globalisierung/Regionalisierung*, Bielefeld, April, pp. 22–33.

Bennholdt-Thomsen, Veronika, Mies, Maria and von Werlhof, Claudia (1983/1992) *Frauen, die letzte Kolonie*, Zurich.

BIJA (The seed): 'Farmers Pledge to Stop the Corporatisation of Indian Agriculture', *BIJA* No. 15/16, 1996, pp. 16–18.

BIJA (The seed): 'Intellectual Property Rights, Community Rights and Biodiversity', *BIJA* No. 15/16, 1996, pp. 25 ff.

Binswanger, Hans Christoph (1991) *Geld und Natur: Das wirtschaftliche Wachstum im Spannungsfeld zwischen Ökonomie und Ökologie*, Stuttgart, Edition Weitbrecht.

Binswanger, H.C., Geisberger, W. and Ginsburg, T. (1979) *Wege aus der Wohlstandsfalle: Der NAWU-Report*, Frankfurt, Fischer.

Blaise, Suzanne (1986) *Le Rapt des Origines ou le Meurtre de la Mère* (self-published).

Bloch, Ernst (1961) *Naturrecht und menschliche Würde*, Frankfurt, Suhrkamp.

Bock, Gisela and Duden, Barbara (1976) 'Arbeit aus Liebe, Liebe als Arbeit: Die Entstehung der Hausarbeit im Kapitalismus' in *Frauen und Wissenschaft, Beiträge zur Berliner Sommeruniversität*, Berlin, Courage Verlag.

Boserup, Ester (1970) *Women's Role in Economic Development*, London.

Böttger, Barbara (1987) 'Macht und Liebe, Gleichberechtigung und Subsistenz – kein Ort: Nirgends. Auf der Suche nach einem feministischen Politikverständnis', *Beiträge zur feministischen Theorie und Praxis*, No. 19.

Brodribb, Somer (1992) *Nothing Mat(t)ers: A Feminist Critique of Postmodernism*, Melbourne, Spinifex.

Brownhill, Leigh S., Kaara, Wahu M., and Turner, Terisa E. (1997a) 'Gender Relations and Sustainable Agriculture: Rural Women's Resistance to Structural Adjustment in Kenya',

Canadian Women's Studies, Vol. 17, No. 2.

Brownhill, Leigh S., Kaara, Wahu M. and Turner, Terisa E. (1997b) 'Social Reconstruction in Rural Africa: A Gendered Class Analysis of Women's Resistance to Cash Crop Production in Kenya', unpublished paper, University of Guelph, Canada.

Bruck, Birgitte, Heike Kahlert, Marianne Krüll, Helga Milz, Astrid Osterland and Ingeborg Wegehaupt-Schneider (1992) *Feministische Soziologie: Eine Einführung*, Frankfurt.

Brunner, Otto (1980) 'Vom "ganzen aus" zur Familie', in Heidi Rosenbaum (ed.) *Seminar: Familie und Gesellschaftsstruktur: Materialen zu sozioökonomischen Bedingungen von Familienformen*, Frankfurt a.M, Fischer.

Bublitz Hannelore (1992) 'Feministische Wissenschaft: Patriarchatskritik oder Geschlechterforschung?' in Ingeborg Stahr (ed.) *Wenn Frauen Wissen Wissen schafft: 10 Jahre Frauenstudien und Frauenforschung an der Universität GH Essen*, Essen.

Butler, Judith (1990) 'Gender Trouble', in L. J. Nicholson, *Feminism/Postmodernism*, New York and London, Routledge.

Cavarero, Adriana (1987) 'Liberazione e filosofica della differenza sessuale', in C. Marcuzzo and A. Rossi Doria (eds), *La ricerca delle donne*, Turin, pp. 173–87.

Cavarero, Adriana (1990) 'Die Perspektive der Geschlechterdifferenz', in Ute Gerhard, Mechtild Jansen, Andrea Maihofer, Pia Schmid and Irmgard Schultz (eds), *Differenz und Gleichheit*, Frankfurt a.M., Ulrike Helmer Verlag, pp. 95–111.

CAW (Committee for Asian Women) (eds) (1995) *Silk and Steel: Asian Women Confront Challenges of Industrial Restructuring*, edited by Sister Helene O'Sullivan, Hong Kong.

Chayanov, Alexander V. (1966) *The Theory of Peasant Economy*, edited by D. Thorner, R.E.F. Smith and B. Kerblay, Irwin 1966. (See also Tschajanow.)

Chodorow, Nancy (1978) *The Reproduction of Mothering: Psychoanalysis and the Sociology of Gender*, Berkeley, University of California Press.

Chomsky, Noam (1991), in Komitee für Grundrechte und Demokratie (eds), *Materialien zum Golfkrieg*, Sensbachtal.

Chossudovsky, Michel (1998) '"Financial Warfare" Triggers Global Economic Crisis', *Third World Resurgence*, No. 98, October.

Clarke, Tony and Barlow, Maude (1997) *MAI: The Multilateral Agreement on Investment and the Threat to Canadian Sovereignty*, Toronto, Stoddard.

Clemens, Bärbel (1983) *Frauenforschungs- und Frauenstudieninitiativen in der Bundesrepublik*, Kassel.

Comité d'Information Sahel (1975) *Qui se nourrit de la famine en Afrique?* Paris.

Creutz, Helmut (1993) *Das Geldsyndrom: Wege zu einer krisenfreien Marktwirtschaft*, Aachen.

Cutrufelli, Maria Rosa (1985) *Women of Africa: Roots of Oppression*, London.

Dallacosta, Mariarosa (1973) *Die Macht der Frauen und der Umsturz der Gesellschaft*, Berlin.

Daly, H. and Cobb, J. (1989) *For The Common Good*, London.

Decornoy, Jacques (1995) 'Arbeit oder Kapital – Wer bestimmt die Zukunft?' *Le Monde Diplomatique / Die Tageszeitung/ Wochenzeitung*, May.

Delphy, Christine (1996) '"French Feminism": An Imperialist Invention', in D. Bell and R. Klein, (eds), *Radically Speaking: Feminism Reclaimed*, Melbourne.

Deutscher Bauernverband (ed.) (1995) *Zur wirtschaflichen Lage der Landwirtschaft: Situationsreport 1995*, Bonn.

Deutscher Bauernverband (ed.) (1997) *Trends und Fakten zur wirtschaftlichen Lage der deutschen Landwirtschaft: Situationsreport 1997*, Bonn.

Dickinson, Torry D. (1995) *Common Wealth, Self-Sufficiency and Work in American Communities, 1830–1993*, London.

Duden, Barbara (1993) 'Die Frau ohne Unterleib: Zu Judith Butlers Entkörperung. Ein Zeitdokument', in *Feministische Studien*, Part 2.

Ecologist (ed.) (1992) 'Whose Common Future?', Vol. 22, No. 4, July/August, p. 146.

Economist (1996) 'A Global Poverty Gap', 20 July.

Elson, Diane (1994) 'Uneven Development and the Textiles and Clothing Industry', in L. Sklair (ed.), *Capitalism and Development*, London and New York, Routledge.

Engels, Frederick (1976) *Origin of the Family, Private Property and the State*, in Karl Marx and Frederick Engels, *Selected Works*, Vol. III, Moscow.

Esteva, Gustavo (1992) 'Development' in Sachs, Wolfgang (ed.), *Development Dictionary*, London, Zed Books.

Eurotopia: Zeitschrift für 'Leben in Gemeinschaft', 4/95, *Schwerpunkt: Auf dem Weg zu einer anderen Ökonomie.*

Eurotopia: Zeitschrift für 'Leben in Gemeinschaft', 19/95, *Schwerpunkt: Anders leben, anders wirtschaften.*

Eurotopia: Zeitschrift für 'Leben in Gemeinschaft', 1-2/96, *Schwerpunkt: Love in Action, Politik und Spiritualität.*

Evans, Paul (1995) 'Salford's Urban Oasis', *Guardian Weekly*, 12 November.

Evers, Hans-Dieter and Heiko Schrader (1994) *The Moral Economy of Trade, Ethnicity and Developing Markets*, London and New York.

FAO (1996) *World Food Summit 1996: Technical Papers*, No. 4, Rome.

Faraclas, Nicholas (a) Awareness Training Packets, PNG Trust, University of Papua New Guinea (paper, undated).

Faraclas, Nicholas (b) 'Cargo, Culture and Politics of Cultural Pluralism in PNG: Critical Literacy', University of Papua New Guinea 1992 (unpublished paper).

Faraclas, Nicholas (c) 'From Structural Adjustment to Land Mobilization to Expropriation: Is Melanesia the World Bank/International Monetary Fund's Latest Victim?' University of Papua New Guinea (paper, undated).

Feder, Ernest (1977/78) 'Campesinistas y descampesinistas, tres enfoques divergentes (no incompatibles) sobre la destrucción del campesinado', *Comercio exterior*, Vol. 27, No. 12 and Vol. 28, No.1, Mexico.

Flitner, Michael (1997) 'Biodiversity – The Making of a Global Commons', in Michael Goldman (ed.) *Privatizing Nature: The New Politics of Environment and Development*, London.

Foucault, Michel (1976), *Histoire de la sexualité*, Vol. I: *La Volonté de savoir*, Paris, Gallimard.

Fox Keller, Evelyn (1985) *Reflections on Gender and Science*, New Haven and London, Yale University Press.

Frank, André Gunder (1966) 'The Development of Underdevelopment', *Monthly Review* 18/4, September.

Frank, André Gunder (1971) *Capitalism and Underdevelopment in Latin America*, Harmondsworth.

Fraser, Nancy and Nicholson, Linda (1990) 'Social Criticism without Philosophy: An Encounter between Feminism and Postmodernism', in Linda Nicholson (ed.) *Feminism/Postmodernism*, New York.

Frey-Nakonz, Regula (1984) *Vom Prestige zum Profit: Zwei Fallstudien aus Südbenin zur Integration der Frauen in die Marktwirtschaft*, Saarbrücken.

Füssel, Kuno (1993) 'Es gilt absolut plural zu sein', in Kuno Füssel, D. Sölle and F. Steffensky, *Die Sowohl-als-auch-Falle*, Lucerne.

Füssel, Kuno; Sölle, D. and Steffensky, F. (1993) *Die Sowohl-als-auch-Falle*, Lucerne.

Gambaroff, Marina, *et al.* (1986) *Tschernobyl hat unser Leben verändert: Vom Ausstieg der Frauen*, Reinbek.

Gayle, Rubin (1975) 'The Traffic in Women: Notes on the Political Economy of Sex', in Rayna Rapp Reiter (ed.), *Toward an Anthropology of Women*, New York, Monthly Review Press.

Gilligan, Carol (1982) *In a Different Voice: Psychological Theory and Women's Development*, Cambridge, MA.

Gimbutas, Marija (1991) *The Civilization of the Goddess; The World of Old Europe*, San Francisco.

Goldman, Michael (1995) '"Reinventing the Commons": A Literature Review and Discussion Paper'. Paper presented at the Second Workshop on Reinventing the Commons, Bonn.

Gonzalez, Nancie (1970) 'Towards a Definition of Matrifocality', in Norman E. Whitten and John F. Sweed (eds), *Afro-American Anthropology: Contemporary Perspectives*, New York.

Gorz, André (1983) *Les chemins au Paradis*, Paris, Editions Galilée.

Gorz, André (1985) *Paths to Paradise*, London.

Gorz, André (1989) *Critique of Economic Reason*, London.

Gorz, André and Erich Hörl (1990), '"Archäologie" des philosophischen Fadens: Die ent-Packung der ver-packten Philosophie. Ein Streitgespräch', *Kurswechsel*, Vol. 3.

Groier, Michael (1997) 'AussteigerInnen in ländlichen Regionen: Ergebnisse einer Untersuchung zu soziokulturellen und ökonomischen Aspekten', in AgrarBündnis, (ed.), *Landwirtschaft 97, Der kritische Agrarbericht*, Kassel/Rheda-Wiedenbrück/Bonn, pp. 176–84.

Grossenbacher, Veronika (1996) 'Frauen als landwirtschaftliche Betriebsleiterinnen. Erfahrungen von Frauen aus bäuerlichen Familienbetrieben', in AgrarBündnis e.V. (ed.,) *Landwirtschaft 96: Der kritische Agrarbericht*, Bonn.

Hagemann-White, Carol (1993) 'Die Konstrukteure des Geschlechts auf frischer Tat ertappen? Methodische Konsequenzen einer theoretischen Einsicht', *Feministische Studien* Part 2.

Haraway, Donna (1988) 'Situated Knowledges: The Science Question in Feminism and the Privilege of Partial Perspective', *Feminist Studies*, Vol. 14, No. 3.

Haraway, Donna (1990) 'A Manifesto for Cyborgs: Science, Technology, and Socialist Feminism in the 1980s', in Linda Nicholson (ed.), *Feminism/Postmodernism*, London, Routledge.

Haraway, Donna (1991) *Simians, Cyborgs and Women, The Reinvention of Nature*, London.

Hardin, Garret (1968) 'The Tragedy of the Commons', in *Science*, 162, December.

Hardin, Garret (1973) 'Die Tragödie der Allmende', (German text of his 1968 *Science* article 'The Tragedy of the Commons') in Larry Lohmann (ed.) *Prognosen angloamerikanischer Wissenschaftler*, Munich.

Hardin, Garret (1977) 'The Tragedy of the Commons', in Garret Hardin and John Baden, *Managing the Commons*, San Francisco, W.H. Freeman and Company, pp. 16–30.

Hart, Keith (1973) 'Informal Income Opportunities and Urban Employment in Ghana', *Journal of Modern African Studies*, Vol. 11.

Heider, Frank, Hock, Beate, and Seitz, Hans-Werner (1997) *Selbstverwaltete Betriebe in Hessen I + II*, Giessen.

Henderson, Hazel (1979) *Creating Alternative Futures*, New York.

Henderson, Hazel (1985) *Das Ende der Ökonomie*, München.

Herger, Lisbeth (1989) 'Raus aus der Politik, rein in die Schrebergärten? Kommentar', in *Frauezittig*, No. 31, Zürich.

Hermannstorfer, U. (1992) *Scheinmarktwirtschaft: Die Unverkäuflichkeit von Arbeit, Boden und Kapital*, Stuttgart.

Hobbes, Thomas (1965) *Leviathan: oder Wesen, Form und Gewalt des kirchlichen und bürgerlichen Staates*, Reinbek.

Holland-Cuntz, Barbara (1995) 'Zum Verhältnis von Politik und Politikwissenschaft', in *'Leidenschaft für die unbequeme Sache': Zur Diskussion um die Gründung eines feministischen Instituts im Rahmen der bündnisgrün-nahen Stiftung*, Hamburg.

Holzer, Brigitte (1994) 'Mais, Tauschbeziehungen zwischen Männern und Frauen', in V. Bennholdt-Thomsen (ed.), *Juchitán – Stadt der Frauen: Vom Leben im Matriarchat*, Reinbek.

Holzer, Brigitte (1995) *Subsistenzorientierung als 'widerständige Anpassung' an die Moderne*, in Juchitán, Oaxaca, México, series Ethnien, Religionen, Konflikte, Frankfurt a.M.

Holzer, Brigitte (1997) 'Das Verschwinden der Haushalte. Geschlechtsspezifische und gesellschaftliche Arbeitsteilung in der Wirtschaftstheorie', in Andrea Komlosy et al. (eds), *Ungeregelt und unterbezahlt: Der informelle Sektor in der Weltwirtschaft*, Frankfurt a.M.

Hoppichler, Josef and Josef Krammer (1996) 'Was wird aus Österreichs Bauern?', in Trautl Brandstaller, (ed.), *Österreich 1 1/2*, Vienna.

Illich, Ivan (1982) *Das Recht auf Gemeinheit*, Reinbek.

Imfeld, Al (1975) *Hunger und Hilfe, Provokationen*, Zürich.

Inhetveen, Heide (1986) 'Von der "Hausmutter" zur "Mithelfenden Familienangehörigen": Zur Stellung der Frau in den Agrartheorien', in K. Bedal and H. Heidrich (eds), *Freilichtmuseum und Sozialgeschichte*, Bad Windsheim.

Inhetveen, Heide and Margret Blasche (1983) *Frauen in der kleinbäuerlichen Landwirtschaft*, Opladen.

Kandiyoti, Deniz (1977) 'Sex Roles and Social Change: A Comparative Appraisal of Turkey's Women', *Signs* 3/1.

Keller, Catherine (1986) *From a Broken Web: Separation, Sexism and Self*, Boston.

Kennedy, Margrit (1990) *Geld ohne Zins und Inflation: Ein Tauschmittel des jedem dient*, Munich.

Kindl, Gotthard (1995) *Das Ende der Modernisierung? Polnische Bauern nach dem Zusammenbruch des Realsozialismus*, Frankfurt.

Kirk, Gwyn (1996/97) ' "Rebuilding, Recreating, Respiriting the City from the Ground Up": A Movement in the Making', *Capital, Nature, Socialism*, January.

Klauss, Martin (1997) *Politik für mehr Reichtum, Daten und Anmerkungen zur Entwicklung von Reichtum und Armut in Deutschland*, Freiburg, CfS (ChristInnen für den Sozialismus).

Klein, Renate (1996) 'Dead Bodies Floating in Cyberspace: Postmodernism and the Dismemberment of Women', in D. Bell and R. Klein (eds) *Radically Speaking: Feminism Reclaimed*, Melbourne, Spinifex and London, Zed Books.

Klinger, Cornelia (1988) *'Abschied von der Emanzipationslogik? Die Gründe ihn zu fordern, zu feiern oder zu fürchten'*, in *Kommune 1*, Frankfurt a.M.

Kofra (ed.) (1990) *Frauenforschung und Feminismus*, No. 49, October/November.

Kohr, Leopold (1983) *Die überentwickelten Nationen: Rückbesinnung auf die Region*, Salzburg.

Kolbeck, Thekla (1985) *Landfrauen und Direktvermarktung: Spurensicherung von Frauenarbeit und Frauenalltag*, Gesamthochschule Kassel.

Kollektiv Kommune Buch (ed.) (1996) *Das Kommunebuch: Alltag zwischen Widerstand, Anpassung und gelebter Utopie*, Göttingen.

Kommune Niederkaufungen (ed.) (1996) '10 Jahre Kommune Niederkaufungen', Circular No. 14, November.

Krammer, Josef (1996) 'Österreichs EU-Beitritt: Die verpasste Chance für eine europaweite ökosoziale Agrarpolitik', in AgrarBündnis e.V. (ed.), *Landwirtschaft 96. Der kritische Agrarbericht*, Bonn.

Kristeva, Julia (1984) 'Woman Can Never Be Defined', in, Elaine Marks and Isabelle de Courtivron (eds), *New French Feminisms*, New York.

Kristeva, Julia (1989) *Black Sun: Depression and Melancholia*, New York, Columbia University Press.

Kurz, Robert (1991) *Der Kollaps der Modernisierung: Vom Zusammenbruch des Kasernensozialismus zur Krise der Weltökonomie*, Frankfurt a.M.

Landweer, Hilge (1993) 'Kritik und Verteidigung der Kategorie Geschlecht. Wahrnehmungs- und symboltheoretische Überlegungen zur Sex/Gender Unterscheidung', *Feministische Studien*, Part 2.

Lenz, Ilse (1988) 'Liebe, Brot und Freiheit: Zur neuen Diskussion um Subsistenzproduktion, Technik und Emanzipation in der Frauenbewegung', *Beiträge zur feministischen Theorie und Praxis*, 21/22.

Lerner, Gerda (1986) *The Creation of Patriarchy*, Oxford University Press.

Libreria delle donne di Milano (1988) *Wie weibliche Freiheit entsteht: Eine neue politische Praxis*, Berlin.

Loziczky, Tanja (1997) 'Kooperationsformen zwischen Bauern/Bäuerinnen und VerbraucherInnen: Wege zu einem solidarischen Wirtschaften im ökologischen Landbau anhand von ausgewählten Beispielen', diploma thesis, University for Earth Culture, Institute for Ecological Agriculture, Vienna.

Luxemburg, Rosa (1923) *Die Akkumulation des Kapitals: Ein Beitrag zur ökonomischen Erklärung des Imperialismus*, Berlin.

Lyotard, Jean François (1979) *La Condition postmoderne*, Paris, Editions minuit.

Lyotard, Jean François (1984) *The Postmodern Condition: A Report on Knowledge*. Minneapolis, University of Minneapolis Press.

McNamara, Robert (1973) Address to the Board of Governors, World Bank, Nairobi 24 September.

Mamozai, Martha (1982) *Herrenmenschen, Frauen im deutschen Kolonialismus*, Reinbek.

Märke, Erika (1986) *Ein Weg aus der Abhängigkeit: Die ungewisse Zukunft des informellen Sektors in Entwicklungsländern*, Heidelberg.

Martin, Hans-Peter and Schumann, Harald (1996) *Die Globalisierungsfalle: Der Angriff auf Demokratie und Wohlstand*, Reinbek.

Martin, Hans-Peter and Schumann, Harald (1997) *The Global Trap*, London.

Marx, Karl (1973) 'The Eighteenth Brumaire of Louis Bonaparte', in *Surveys from Exile*, London.

Marx, Karl (1976) *Capital*, Vol. 1, London, NLR/Pelican.

Max-Neef, Manfred *et al.* (1989) 'Human Scale Development: An Option for the Future', in *Development Dialogue*, Cepaur, Dag Hammarskjöld.

Merchant, Carolyn (1980) *The Death of Nature: Women, Ecology and the Scientific Revolution*, Harper and Row, San Francisco.

Meyer-Renschhausen, Elisabeth (1997) 'Der Welternährungsgipfel in Rom und die Gärten der Frauen: Gärten als Anfang und Ende der Landwirtschaft?' in *Tropentag 1996*, Berlin, pp. 197 ff.

Mies, Maria (1978) 'Methodische Postulate zur Frauenforschung – dargestellt am Beispiel der Gewalt gegen Frauen', *Beiträge zur feministischen Theorie und Praxis*, No. 1.

Mies, Maria (1982) *The Lace Makers of Narsapur. Indian Housewives Produce for the World Market*, London.

Mies, Maria (1983) 'Towards a Methodology for Feminist Research', in Gloria Bowls and Renate Duelli-Klein (eds), *Theories of Women's Studies*, London, Routledge & Kegan Paul, pp. 117–39.

Mies, Maria (1983a) 'Subsistenz-produktion, Hausfrauisierung, Kolonisierung', in *Beitrage zur Feministischen Theorie und Praxis*, No. 9/10.

Mies, Maria (1986a) *Indian Women in Subsistence and Agricultural Labour*, Genf.

Mies, Maria (1986b) (1999) *Patriarchy and Accumulation on a World Scale: Women in the International Division of Labour*. London, Zed Books.

Mies, Maria (1992) '"Moral Economy" – a Concept and a Perspective', in R. Rilling, H. Spitzer, O. Green, F. Hucho and G. Pati, (eds), *Challenges: Science and Peace in a Rapidly Changing Environment*, Schriftenreihe Wissenschaft und Frieden, Vol. I, BdWi, Marburg.

Mies, Maria (1994) 'Gegen die Ramboisierung der Männer', in Bündnis 90/Die Grünen NRW (eds) *Zwischen Rambo und Märchenprinz: Ein politischer Diskurs zur Männeremanzipation*. Reader for the First Men's Congress, Düsseldorf.

Mies, Maria (1996a) 'Patente auf Leben: Darf alles gemacht werden, was machbar ist?' in Lisbeth Trallori (ed.), *Die Eroberung des Lebens*, Vienna.

Mies, Maria (1996b) 'Liberating Women, Liberating Knowledge: Reflections on Two Decades of Feminist Action Research', *Atlantis* 21 (1): 10–23.

Mies, Maria (1996c) *Women, Food and Global Change: An Ecofeminist Analysis of the World Food Summit, Rome, 13–17 November 1996*, Institute for the Theory and Practice of Subsistence (ITPS) Bielefeld.

Mies, Maria and Shiva, Vandana (1993) *Ecofeminism*, London, Zed Books (2nd edition 1994).

Mies, Maria and von Werlhof, Claudia (eds) (1988), *Reader zur Tagung 'Die Subsistenzperspektive, ein Weg ins Freie'*, Bad Boll.

Mies, Maria and von Werlhof, Claudia (eds) (1998) *Lizenz zum Plündern. Das Multilaterale Abkommen über Investitionen (MAI). Globalisierung der Konzernherrschaft und was wir dagegen tun können*, Hamburg, Rotbuch/EVA.

Mies, Maria, Bennholdt-Thomsen, Veronika, and von Werlhof, Claudia (1988) *Women: The Last Colony*, London, Zed Books. German edition 1983.

Milborn, Corinna (1997a) 'Die Widerstandsgemeinden in Guatemala (CPR): Versuch der Autarkie in einem agroexportierenden Land', report to the Congress of Austrian Latin-Americanists, Strobl, April.

Milborn, Corinna (1997b) 'Comunidades de Población en Resistencia: Widerstandsdörfer und 500 Jahre indigener Widerstand in Guatemala', diploma thesis, Vienna.

Mitterauer, Michael (1980) 'Der Mythos von der vorindustriellen Grossfamilie', in Heidi Rosenbaum (ed.), *Seminar: Familie und Gesellschaftsstruktur. Materialien zu sozioökonomischen Bedingungen von Familienformen*, Frankfurt a.M.

Mohanty, Bidyut (1996) 'Globalisation and Grass Roots Democracy', in *BIJA* No. 15/16.

Möller, Carola (1991) 'Über das Brot, das Euch in der Küche fehlt, wird nicht in der Küche entschieden', *Beiträge zur feministischen Theorie und Praxis*, No. 29.

Möller, Carola (1997) 'Feministische Ansätze zu einer alternativen Ökonomie', *Kölner Volksblatt*, 5/1997.

Müller, Christa (1994) 'Frauenliebe in einer frauzentrierten Gesellschaft', in V. Bennholdt-Thomsen (ed.), *Juchitán – Stadt der Frauen: Vom Leben im Matriarchat*, Reinbek.

Müller, Christa (1998) *Von der lokalen Ökonomie zum globalisierten Dorf: Bäuerliche Überlebensstrategien zwischen Weltmarktintegration und Regionalisierung*, Campus Verlag, Frankfurt and New York.

Müller, Julius Otto (1988) 'Probleme eigenständiger Agrarkultur im Sahel. Bauern zwischen Erwerbsdruck und Desertifikation', in H. Gödde and D. Voegelin (eds), *Für eine bäuerliche Landwirtschaft*, part of a series published by the Faculty of Town Planning/Landscape Planning, Gesamthochschule, Kassel.

Muraro, Luisa (1993) *Die symbolische Ordnung der Mutter*, Frankfurt and New York.

NACLA (North American Congress on Latin America) (1975) 'US Grain Arsenal', Latin American and Empire Report No. 9, 7 October.

NACLA (North American Congress on Latin America) (1976) *Weizen als Waffe: Die neue Getreidestrategie der amerikanischen Aussenpolitik*, Reinbek bei Hamburg.

Neusüss, Christel (1985) *Die Kopfgeburten der Arbeiterbewegung oder: Die Genossin Luxemburg bringt alles durcheinander*, Hamburg.

Nguiffo, Samuel Alain (1997) 'Tradition versus Modernity: The Defence of the Commons in Cameroon', in Michael Goldman (ed.), *Privatizing Nature: The New Politics of Environment and Development*, London.

Norberg-Hodge, Helena (1991) *Learning From Ladakh*, San Francisco, Sierra Club.

Norberg-Hodge, Helena (1993) *Leben in Ladakh*, Freiburg.

O'Brien, Mary (1989) *Reproducing the World: Essays in Feminist Theory*, Boulder, San Francisco and London, Westview Press.

Paré, Luisa (1979) *Revoluciones verdes para espantar revoluciones rojas*, Mexico City.

Pestemer, Richard (ed.) (1997) *Landwirtschaftliche Selbstversorgung als Überlebensstrategie in der Metropole Tokio. Informationsmaterialien zur Studien- und Vortragsreise von Akemine Tetsuo und Richard Pestemer*, Neunkirchen.

Pfarr, Heide (1996) 'Reservation of Seats for Women in Political Institutions in Germany', in Veena Poonacha (ed.), *Women, Empowerment and Political Participation*, Bombay.

Pinl, Claudia (1993) *Vom kleinen zum grossen Unterschied: 'Geschlechterdifferenz' und konservative Wende*, Hamburg.

Planck, Ulrich (1964) *Der bäuerliche Familienbetrieb zwischen Patriarchat und Partnerschaft*, Stuttgart.

Plumwood, Val (1993) *Feminism and the Mastery of Nature*, London and New York, Routledge.

Polanyi, Karl (1944) *The Great Transformation: The Political and Economic Origins of Our Time*, New York.

Polanyi, Karl (1957) 'The Economy as Instituted Process', in Karl Polanyi *et al.*, *Trade and Market in the Early Empires*, New York.

Ramonet, Ignacio (1995) 'Die neuen Herren der Welt' Formen der Macht am Ende des 20. Jahrhunderts'. *Le Monde Diplomatique/taz/WoZ*, May.

Reformausschuss des Stiftungsverbands Regenbogen e.V. (ed.) (1995) *'Leidenschaft für eine unbequeme Sache': Zur Diskussion um die Gründung eines feministischen Instituts im Rahmen der bündnis-grün-nahen Stiftung*, Hamburg, Redaktion Helga Braun.

Rengam, Sarojeni V. (1997) 'Till Victory: Experiences from Cuba', in PAN AP Safe Food Campaign 1996, *Eat Smart Healthy Local Food*, Penang/Malaysia.

Rich, Adrienne (1977) *Of Woman Born:. Motherhood as Experience and Institution*, Virago, London.

Rifkin, Jeremy (1991) *Biosphere Politics*, New York. Quoted in 'Whose Common Future?' *Ecologist*, Vol. 22, No. 4, July–August 1992.

Rostow, W.W. (1960) *The Stages of Economic Growth: A Non-Communist Manifesto*, Cambridge.

Rott, Renate (1989) 'Strukturen der Frauenerwerbsarbeit im urbanen Bereich am Beispiel Brasiliens: Eine Fallstudie aus dem Nordosten (Fortaleza, CE)', in Elisabeth Grohs (ed.), *Frauen in der Entwicklung Afrikas und Lateinamerikas*, Third World Interdisciplinary Working Group, Vol. 3, University of Mainz.

Rubin, Gayle (1975) 'The Traffic in Women', in *Toward an Anthropology of Women*, New York.

Sager, Krista (1995) quoted in *'Leidenschaft für die unbequeme Sache'. Zur Diskussion um die Gründung eines feministischen Instituts im Rahmen der Bündnisgrünen*, Hamburg.

Sahlins, Marshall (1972) *Stone Age Economics*, Chicago.

Sahlins, Marshall (1974/1984) *Stone-Age Economics*, London.

Sarkar, Saral (1987) 'Die Bewegung und ihre Strategie: Ein Beitrag zum notwendigen Klärungsprozess', in *Kommune* 5, Frankfurt, pp. 39–45.

Sarkar, Saral (1993) *Green-Alternative Politics in West Germany*, Vol. I of *The New Social Movements*, Tokyo, New York and Paris, UNU Press.

Sarkar, Saral (1999) *Ecosocialism or Ecocapitalism?* London, Zed Books.

Schmitt, Mathilde (1997) 'Und welche Rolle spielt das Geschlecht? Landwirtinnen in ihrem Arbeitsalltag', in AgrarBündnis e.V. (ed.), *Landwirtschaft 97: Der kritische Bericht*, Bonn.

Schröder, Tilman (1989) in *Wurzelwerk-Zeitung*, April.

Schultz, Irmgard (1994) *Der erregende Mythos vom Geld: Die neue Verbindung von Zeit, Geld und Geschlecht im Ökologiezeitalter*, Frankfurt a.M.

SEF (Stiftung Entwicklung und Frieden) (ed.) (1993/94) *Globale Trends 93/94, Daten zur Weltentwicklung*, Frankfurt.

Selbstversorgungs-Cooperative Bremen (1987) *Positionspaper von 1977*, Bremen.

Sethuraman, S.V. (1976) 'The Urban Informal Sector: Concept, Measurement and Policy', *International Labour Review*, Vol. 114, No. 1.

Shanin, Teodor (ed.) (1971) *Peasants and Peasant Societies*, Harmondsworth.

Shanin, Teodor (1990) *Defining Peasants: Essays concerning Rural Societies, Expolary Economies, and Learning from Them in the Contemporary World*, Oxford.

Shiva, Vandana (1989) *The Violence of the Green Revolution*, Dehra Dun.

Shiva, Vandana (1993) 'GATT, Agriculture and Third World Women', in Maria Mies and Vandana Shiva, *Ecofeminism*, London, Zed Books.

Shiva, Vandana (1995a) 'Food Security: The Problem', in Seminar No. 433 New Delhi.

Shiva, Vandana (1995b) *Captive Minds, Captive Lives: Ethics, Ecology and Patents on Life*, New Delhi.

Shiva, Vandana (1996a) 'Globalisation of Agriculture and the Growth of Food Security'. Report of the International Conference on Globalisation, Food Security and Sustainable Agriculture. In *BIJA*, No. 15/16, New Delhi.

Shiva, Vandana (1996b) 'The Alternative Corporate Protectionism', *BIJA*, No. 15/16, New Delhi.

Shiva, Vandana, Afsar H. Jafri and Gitanjali Bedi (1997) *Ecological Cost of Economic Globalisation: The Indian Experience* (prepared for the UN General Assembly Special Session on Rio + 5, UNGASS), New Delhi.

Sklair, Leslie (ed.) (1994a) *Capitalism and Development*, London and New York, Routledge.

Sklair, Leslie (1994b) 'Capitalism and Development in Global Perspective', in L. Sklair (ed.), *Capitalism and Development*, London and New York, Routledge, pp. 165–88.

Smith, Joan, Immanuel Wallerstein and Hands-Dieter Evers (1984), *Households and the World-Economy: Explorations in the World-Economy*, Beverly Hills.

Smith, Raymond T. (1987) 'Hierarchy and the Dual Marriage System in West Indian Society', in Jane Fishbourne Collier and Sylvia Junko Yanagisako (eds), *Gender and Kinship: Essays Towards a Unified Analysis*, Stanford.

Spehr, Christoph (1996) *Die Ökofalle: Nachhaltigkeit und Krise*, Vienna.

Spittler, Gerd (1987) 'Tschajanow und die Theorie der Familienwirtschaft', Introduction to Alexander Tschajanow, *Die Lehre von der bäuerlichen Wirtschaft*, Franfurt a.M., 1987 (1923).

Steinbrügge, Lieselotte (1987) *Frauen, das moralische Geschlecht: Theorien und literarische Entwürfe über die Natur der Frauen in der französischen Aufklärung*, Weinheim/Basel.

Steinem, Gloria (1994) *Moving beyond Words*, New York, Simon and Schuster.

Tanner, Nancy (1974) 'Matrifocality in Indonesia and Africa and among Black Americans', in Michelle Rosaldo and Louise Lamphere (eds), *Women, Culture and Society*, Stanford.

Trainer, Ted (1996) *Towards a Sustainable Economy: The Need for Fundamental Change*, Oxford.

Tschajanow, Alexander (1923/1987) *Die Lehre von der bäuerlichen Wirtschaft*, Frankfurt a.M. (See also Chayanov.)

Turner, Terisa E. and Benjamin, Craig S. (1995) 'Not in Our Nature: The Male Deal and Corporate Solutions to the Debt–Nature Crisis', *Review: Journal of the Fernand Braudel Center*, Binghampton, 1995.

Turner, Terisa and Oshare, M. O. (1993) *Gender Relations and Resource Development: Women, Petroleum and Ecology in Nigeria*, Nova Scotia.

Ullrich, Otto (1979) *Weltniveau: In der Sackgasse des Industriesystems*, Berlin.

UNESCO (1996) *Dossier: Internationale Konsultation zum vorläufigen Entwurf einer UNESCO-Erklärung zum Schutz des menschlichen Genoms*. Deutsche UNESCO-Kommission, Bonn.

von Werlhof, Claudia (1978) 'Frauenarbeit: Der blinde Fleck in der Kritik der politischen Ökonomie', *Beiträge zur feministischen Theorie und Praxis*, No. 1.

von Werlhof, Claudia (1985) *Wenn die Bauern wiederkommen: Frauen, Arbeit und Agrobusiness in Venezuela*, Bremen.

von Werlhof, Claudia (1988) 'The Proletarian is Dead: Long Live the Housewife!' in Maria Mies, Veronika Bennholdt-Thomsen and Claudia von Werlhof, *Women: The Last Colony*, London, Zed Books, pp. 168–81.

von Werlhof, Claudia (1988a) 'On the Concept of Nature and Society in Capitalism', in Maria Mies, Veronika Bennholdt-Thomsen and Claudia von Werlhof, *Women: The Last Colony*, London, Zed Books.

von Werlhof, Claudia (1993) *Subsistenz: Abschied vom ökonomischen Kalkül?* Berlin.

von Werlhof, Claudia (1996) *Mutter-Los. Frauen im Patriarchat zwischen Angleichung und Dissidenz*, Munich.

von Werlhof, Claudia (1998) 'MAInopoly: Aus Spiel wird Ernst'. in Maria Mies and Claudia von Werlhof (eds), *Lizenz zum Plündern*, Hamburg, Rotbuch/EVA, pp. 132–76.

von Werlhof, Claudia, Annemarie Schweighofer and Werner Ernst (eds) (1996) *Herren-Los Herrschaft-Erkenntnis Lebensform*, Frankfurt.

Van Allen, Judith (1972) ' "Sitting on a Man": Colonialism and the Lost Political Institutions of Igbo Women', *Canadian Journal of African Studies*, 6/2.

Viezzer, Moema (ed.) (1992) *Con Garra e Qualidade Mulheres em economias sustentaveis: agricultura e extrativismo*. Report of the Women's Workshop, Rio de Janeiro.

Wallerstein, Immanuel (1974) *The Modern World-System*, New York, San Francisco and London.

Wallerstein, Immanuel (1980) *The Modern World-System II*, New York and London.

Wallerstein, Immanuel (1983) *Historical Capitalism*, London. German translation, 1984.

Ware, Helen (1983) 'Female and Male Life-Cycles', in Christine Oppong (ed.), *Female and Male in West Africa*, London.

Waring, Marilyn (1989) *If Women Counted. A New Feminist Economics*, London.

Watkins, Kevin (1997) 'Fast Route to Poverty', *Guardian Weekly*, 16 February.

Wichterich, Christa (1992) *Die Erde bemuttern: Frauen und Ökologie nach dem Erdgipfel in Rio*, Cologne.

Wolf, Eric (1966) *Peasants*, Englewood Cliffs, New Jersey.

Wolf, Heinz Georg (1987) *Die Abschaffung der Bauern: Landwirtschaft in der EG-Unsinn mit Methode*, Frankfurt a.M.

Woodall, Pam (1994) 'The Global Economy', *The Economist*, 1 October.

World Commission on Environment and Development (1987) *Our Common Future*, Oxford and New York, Oxford University Press.

Zi Teng Newsletter (Hong Kong) October 1998, No. 7.

Zohl dé Ishtar (1994) *Daughters of the Pacific*, Melbourne.

Index